55-14290
10-6-67

D0079468

# PHILOSOPHY AND ANALYSIS

The object of philosophy is the logical clarification of thoughts . . . . .

The result of philosophy is not a number of "philosophical propositions" but to make propositions clear.

(*Wittgenstein : Tractatus-Logico-Philosophicus*, 4. 112)

# PHILOSOPHY AND ANALYSIS

*A selection of articles published in ANALYSIS (Oxford)
between 1933–40 and 1947–53.*

EDITED, WITH AN INTRODUCTION

*By*

MARGARET MACDONALD

*Editor of Analysis*

BASIL BLACKWELL   .   OXFORD
1954

FIRST PRINTED 1954
REPRINTED (PHOTOLITHO) 1966

PRINTED IN GREAT BRITAIN IN THE CITY OF OXFORD
BY THE ALDEN PRESS (OXFORD) LTD AND BOUND
BY THE KEMP HALL BINDERY

B21
A53

# LIST OF CONTENTS

103897

JUL 24 '78   103897  Blackwell  4.90  0167   MAY 23   MAY 23 '88

LIBRARY
SAINT MARY'S COLLEGE
NOTRE DAME, INDIANA

# CHAPTER I.   INTRODUCTION.

## By Margaret Macdonald

The first number of a philosophical journal entitled *Analysis* appeared in November 1933. This venture was launched by a group of philosophers from Cambridge, Oxford and London who had been influenced by the philosophical views and methods of Russell, Moore and Wittgenstein. They were supported by others, who shared a similar outlook, in the U.S.A. and elsewhere. Its present publisher, Basil Blackwell of Oxford, undertook to produce the journal.

The objects of the new periodical were given in a statement of policy by its first editor, Mr. (now Professor) Austin Duncan-Jones, which opened the first number.[1]   These were (1) to publish short articles on limited and precisely defined philosophical questions about the elucidation of known facts, instead of long, very general and abstract metaphysical speculations about possible facts or about the world as a whole. (2) To foster the exchange of views and debate in its pages and so be, to some extent, a substitute among like-minded philosophers in different places, for the oral discussions which have always been a valuable stimulus to the development of philosophical ideas. Accordingly, *Analysis* would welcome articles which represented a stage in an author's treatment of some topic and not necessarily his final conclusions. For such articles might provoke others to contradict, confirm or elaborate the original proposals and so help to elucidate and, perhaps, solve the problem. *Analysis*, however, was not founded to support any particular set of conclusions nor to propagate any special gospel. It has been, and is, hospitable to many points of view, so long as they are definite and clearly stated. The policy announced in its first number still fundamentally guides the conduct of the journal. Articles have become a little longer since improved sales made possible in 1949[2] an increase in size from 16 to 24 pages. But they are still concerned with limited and definite issues and are elucidatory rather than speculative though their style and manner have changed somewhat since

---

[1] *Analysis*, Vol. 1, 1933–34, pp. 1 and 2.
[2] I.e. in Vol. 10, 1949–50.

1933. *Analysis*, too, continues to encourage philosophical debate within its pages. Several examples appear in the present volume.

The first volume of *Analysis* for 1933–34 consists of four numbers. Each contains 16 pages and its cover, printed in the now familiar red,[1] announces the title of the journal, the names of the editor and his co-operators who were the late Professor L. Susan Stebbing, Mr. (now Professor) C. A. Mace and Mr. (now Professor) G. Ryle. There was also a list of contents. The price was 1s.[2] After the first volume, the annual number of issues was increased to six, two in each university term, to appear in October, December, January, March, April and June. This programme could, in the early days, sometimes be fulfilled only by producing double numbers.

Naturally, to begin with, the circulation of *Analysis* was small and its finances were insecure. A panel of supporters guaranteed £5 each should the enterprise fail. In 1936 an Analysis Society was formed to support the journal and recruit new subscribers. This had some success. Members paid 10s. 6d. annually which included their subscription of 6s. to *Analysis*. They also met at occasional week-end conferences in London. Some of the papers read at these meetings were published in *Analysis*[3] and others which had appeared in the journal were also sometimes discussed.

As I have already said, *Analysis* from the beginning received support from overseas. This was both by subscriptions and by a supply of articles for the journal. Several early numbers contain articles from America and the continent of Europe. Those from Europe were chiefly from members of the " Vienna Circle " and their associates, who had also been influenced by the work of Russell, Wittgenstein's *Tractatus-Logico-Philosophicus*, and talks with him arising therefrom. Such were Schlick, Carnap and Hempel, who contributed to early volumes of *Analysis*. Most of them[4] rejected traditional philosophy more radically than their English colleagues. They were already being known as

---

[1] Covers of the issues of vol. 7, 1939–40 were printed in black as an economy measure during the 1939–45 war.

[2] The current price (1954) for a single number is 2s. 6d. Annual subscription for six numbers 12s. 6d. (U.S.A. $1.175).

[3] E.g. *Analysis*, vol. 4, pp. 17–32, vol. 5, pp. 65–73, and vol. 6, pp. 1–16.

[4] M. Schlick was perhaps an exception. See his article ' Facts and Propositions ', this collection, pp.

"logical positivists". Many later settled in America there to introduce the now flourishing study of "semantics". They were always more formalist, more uncompromising, dare one say, more "doctrinaire" than the English, who had been influenced by Moore as well as by Russell and Wittgenstein of the *Tractatus*. But they were also immensely stimulating both in written and oral discussion. The link between them and the more conservative English group was A. J. Ayer, then the fiery iconoclast of *Language, Truth and Logic*, published in 1933. Two of his characteristic early contributions are included in this collection.

So, despite difficulties, *Analysis* survived. The guarantors were never called upon for their guarantees and six volumes of the journal were published by 1939. Of course, the quality of the articles varies, but many are excellent and of lasting value. Such, I hope, are those which have been chosen for this lume, though others, equally good, have been unavoidably excluded. Some early numbers contain, besides articles, notes from a lecture or the report of a philosophical discussion. The effect given by the early volumes is that of a comparatively small, fairly homogeneous, band of enthusiasts, known to each other but somewhat isolated as yet in advance of the main army but very confident that the rest will catch up or be replaced by a new model recruited by the new methods.

Then in 1939 came another war and other armies. For a while the editor and publishers carried on *Analysis* and three numbers of volume 7 appeared. However, the dispersal of contributors and subscribers on war service, shortage of paper and newsprint forced *Analysis* out of existence and its last number for seven years appeared in October 1940.

In 1946 an Analysis Committee was formed, and with the co-operation of the former publisher and editor, decided to re-start the journal. The response to it justified this course and *Analysis* has since prospered in a very congenial philosophical atmosphere, at least in English-speaking countries. For the army has caught up, or been recruited by, the advance guard. Where *Analysis* contributors were pioneers, the settlements are now thick. In short, the philosophical methods and attitudes for which *Analysis* stood, almost alone, in the nineteen thirties have become commonplace to a new generation of philosophers. Some credit (or discredit) for this development must be given to the pioneer efforts of *Analysis*. The present editor was appointed in 1948. The Analysis Society has not yet been re-started. One novelty should be recorded. The issue for January 1952 announced the first Analysis " competition ". In an Analysis competition, competitors are invited to try to solve in 600 words a small, definite philosophical problem devised by a setter who also judges the entries. A report on the competition and the three best entries are published in a later issue. Five " problems "[1] have so far been set, with interesting results.

There has long been a demand for early numbers of *Analysis*. This has come both from individuals and libraries. But all the first seven and, indeed, several of the later, volumes are now out of print and difficult to obtain second hand. The publishers, with the approval of the Analysis Committee, therefore decided to publish a selection of some of the more important articles from the journal between 1933–40 and 1947–53. The present editor has selected the articles, in consultation with Professor Max Black of Cornell University who has been associated with *Analysis* since its foundation. This collection will thus help to satisfy the demand from students and may also interest readers of the general, educated public in the work of a pioneer and fertile period of philosophical activity.

Two main principles have governed the choice of articles for this collection. (1) That they should be worth while contributions to the solution of fundamentally important philosophical problems. (2) That they should illustrate by writer, type of problem and its treatment, the special character of *Analysis* throughout its history. The collection includes articles from all but one[2] of the first thirteen volumes. Except for forewords and postscripts to some articles, only the short article by Professor

---

1 As follows : (1) " What sort of ' if ' is the ' if ' in ' I can, *if* I choose ' ? " (set by J. L. Austin, Oxford) ; (2) " What is the difference between saying how you feel and showing by your words how you feel ? " (set by A. Duncan-Jones, Birmingham) ; (3) " Does the logical truth (∃x) (Fx **v**∼Fx) entail that at least one individual exists ? " (set by M. Black, Cornell) ; (4) " If a distraction makes me forget my headache, does it make my head stop aching or does it only stop me feeling it aching ? " (set by G. Ryle, Oxford) ; (5) " Does it make sense to say that death is survived ? " (set by A. J. Ayer, London).

2 Vol. 4, 1936–37. This does not mean that vol. 4 was inferior to the rest but simply that many good articles had to be omitted for lack of space.

Rudolf Carnap on p. 128 has been specially written for the volume. Two further points may be noted. As I have already said, examples have been included of the typical philosophical discussions which *Analysis* was, in part, founded to promote. These occur especially in chapters III, V and VI. I have also explained that most articles in *Analysis* are short. For this reason and because it seemed more convenient and interesting for the reader, several articles on the same subject, or on related subjects, have been grouped together under an appropriate chapter heading. Wherever possible these include articles on the same subject from early and later volumes of *Analysis*. These show how much, or little, the treatment of a subject by writers in *Analysis* has changed during these years.

I have spoken of the special outlook or attitude represented by *Analysis*. There is also the significance of its title. This is generally, and, doubtless rightly, taken to indicate that the contents of the journal are predominantly examples of " philosophical analysis " and of the application of the " method of logical analysis " to philosophical problems. But this, if true, is not enlightening. For there is no general agreement about their exact meaning among those who introduced and who use these terms.[1] Nor shall I attempt to give a precise and exhaustive account. Indeed, I think it very likely that this would be both impossible and unprofitable. I suspect that the words ' analysis ' and ' analytic ', used in a philosophical sense, like the word ' philosophy ' itself, and such words as ' science ' and ' scientific ', ' art ' and ' artistic ' are peculiarly vague. They do not, like a simple, sensory term such as ' red ', cover an indefinite range of similar and differing cases in a single dimension, but a " family " of cases of different dimensions or degrees of consanguinity. Moreover, they have also strong emotive functions. They may all be used effectively to commend or disparage, as well as to describe. Because they are words used of what is of live human interest, their range tends to increase and it would defeat the purpose of language, as well as being foolish, to try to confine them within exact limits by rigid definition. It does not, of course, follow that they may

---

[1] For a valuable discussion of these terms see Max Black, *Philosophical Analysis*, Cornell University Press, 1950. Introduction, pp. 1–14. I am much indebted to this.

be used wildly, or as anyone pleases. They have *correct* or established uses, heads of the family by relation to which the rest are judged. Thus, it is correct to call *The Critique of Pure Reason* a work of philosophy. It would be incorrect so to describe *The Origin of Species*, while one might rightly hesitate about *Sartor Resartus* or some work on Existentialism. What determines correct use, or a correct extension of use? Simply, the actual use by a sufficient number over a long enough period, of serious and responsible users of a language who know the field of study or relevant circumstances. One person, however authoritative, is not enough, unless his use is generally adopted, or is, at least, recognised and quoted as a variant. I do not see from what other source the use of language can arise.

In general philosophical usage, ' analysis ' is opposed to ' synthesis '; ' analytic ' to ' synthetic ' and ' simple ' to ' complex '. If an analytic philosopher is one who tries to elucidate a complex, which is causing a philosophical problem—e.g. the nature or knowledge of the external world—by reducing it to its elements and their mode of combination, there were many analytic philosophers before Russell. Conversely, a synthetic philosopher assumes certain simple elements, axioms, primitive propositions and from them, together with certain rules, deduces the complex to be explained. By this distinction, Hume is generally admitted to be an analytic and Spinoza a synthetic philosopher. English philosophers have usually been both analytic and empiricist. The elements they have reached have been simple sensations and feelings. But it is not necessary that an analytic philosopher should be an empiricist. Descartes' " simple natures " are the result of analysis but are the objects of intellectual intuition, not sense perception. So, likewise, are the monads of Leibniz, and Leibniz is a philosopher very congenial to Russell.[1] Both held that the complex can be understood only as the combination of its simple elements. These need not, however, be empirical. Analysis does not entail empiricism. Nor does empiricism entail analysis. An example of the latter disjunction is Samuel Alexander's, *Space, Time and Deity*.[2] Alexander certainly thought his

[1] C.f. " But I confess it seems to me (as it did to Leibniz) that what is complex must be composed of simples ", B. Russell, " Logical Atomism " *Contemporary British Philosophy*, 1st series, 1924, p. 375. London : Allen and Unwin.
[2] 2 vols. London, 1920.

system empirical, indeed scientific. According to him, philosophy differs from science only in dealing with more general problems about the same subject matter. His method, however, is deductive or synthetic, not analytic. *Space, Time and Deity* is one of the last English metaphysical deductive systems to date. Such facts seem to many to show that these labels of ' analytic ', ' synthetic ', ' empiricist ', ' rationalist ' and others like them, are but futilely applied to the methods and conclusions of philosophers. All philosophers must take account of the same facts ; of particularity and repetition, physical objects and minds, moral and aesthetic values, necessary and contingent truth, etc. What is important is whether they satisfactorily explain these facts, or such of them as they consider ; whether they solve philosophical problems, not whether they use one trick, or wave one banner, rather than another. But though such labels may represent aspects of all or most philosophical investigations and not incompatible alternatives, still their use to emphasize one or other aspect from time to time may be important and fruitful. This is particularly so when one aspect has for too long been over-emphasised and needs compensation. Descartes' appeal for the resolution of a problem into simple ideas which can be clearly and distinctly perceived was important when philosophy had become a welter of confused speculations, even though some of these concerned elements under-estimated by Descartes which later had to be re-emphasized.

But, although the work of earlier philosophers has affinities with that later called " philosophical analysis ", this phrase was introduced as a technical, philosophical term for the work of Moore and Russell. It was later extended to that of Wittgenstein, and is now applied to the work of any philosopher which resembles, or shows the influence of, one of these models. I do not suggest by this a state of mechanical imitation, but only a basis of connection. F. P. Ramsey referred to Russell's theory of descriptions as " the paradigm of philosophy ".[1]   By it Russell seemed to have dispelled a philosophical puzzle about the status of fictitious objects by a closer attention to the meaning of words and sentences. This idea, with which Moore must

1 *Foundations of Mathematics and Other Logical Essays*, London : Kegan Paul, 1931, p. 263, n.

LIBRARY
SAINT MARY'S COLLEGE
NOTRE DAME, INDIANA

also be associated, that philosophical problems might be solved by a better understanding of the meaning of language, was one of those simple, but profound, ideas which modify the thought of a whole philosophical age. Transformed later by the genius of Wittgenstein, it has been continuously fertile. Examples of its effects have always appeared in *Analysis* and now predominate.

The principle of the theory of descriptions is, briefly, that to find out what a sentence means or a proposition asserts one must deduce those other propositions upon which its truth depends. The application of this simple procedure to sentences containing expressions both for real and fictitious objects had the philosophically illuminating effect already mentioned.[1] It provided a new sort of clarification of language and owes nothing to traditional modes of analysis. But Russell connects it with another principle of which it seems logically independent but which is a link with the earlier search for ultimate elements. This is the famous Principle of Acquaintance, expressed in the well-known formula, " Every proposition which we can understand must be composed wholly of constituents with which we are acquainted ".[2] This principle, combined with another favourite device of Russell's, Occam's Razor, led to the contention that all complex objects must be ' reduced ' to combinations of simple elements known by acquaintance ; that all general propositions must be ultimately translatable into particular propositions composed wholly of logically proper names. This result was thought to be achieved by a special form of analysis called " directional analysis " which was frequently discussed up to about 1936. The analysis of facts or propositions or sentences (these writers never seem quite clear whether their investigations are factual or linguistic) must proceed from the more to the less general and terminate in the displaying of absolute simples. Any term in common use which is apparently a name for some kind of object, whether ' the State ', ' the average man ', ' John Smith ' or ' this apple ', signifies a " logical construction " and is itself an " incomplete symbol ". Such symbols, unlike genuine names, refer only in context and

---

[1] I am not concerned to dispute whether or not Russell's theory is wholly correct. I know that it has recently been much criticised. But it was undoubtedly illuminating when first formulated and had the effect I suggest.

[2] See " Knowledge by Acquaintance and Knowledge by Description " in *Mysticism and Logic and Other Essays*, 1918.

indirectly to the simple ultimates which alone really exist and would be named by the proper names of a logically perfect language. The perfect monuments to this doctrine, in which it is elaborated with almost baroque extravagance, are John Wisdom's early articles on " Logical Constructions ".[1] There are one or two specimens of this type of analysis in early numbers of *Analysis* but none is here re-published. It seems to have been a sterile aberration due rather to Russell's mathematical interests and to the ghosts of Leibniz and Hume than to his own original insight into the connection between philosophical problems and linguistic confusions shown by the unadulterated theory of descriptions.[2]

The influence of Moore on the contributors to *Analysis* has always been strong and has lately increased. The statement of policy, already quoted on p. 1 that the contributions to be published " will be concerned, as a rule, with the elucidation ... of facts, the general nature of which is, by common consent, already known " seems to echo Moore's famous " Defence of Common Sense ",[3] that we understand and know for certain the truth of many statements of ordinary life, though we do not know their analysis. We can use them correctly in ordinary life but could not give a satisfactory account of their meaning. This has seemed para-doxical to some critics, though it is surely a common enough experience. But this answer may be insufficient. Moore has, however, always preferred to try to practise, rather than theorise about, analysis. Professor Black has pointed out that one import-ant statement which Moore has made about the relation of an analysis to the proposition analysed seems absurd.[4] For it implies

---

[1] *Mind*, New Series, XL, 1931, pp. 188–216, 460–475 ; XLI, 1932, pp. 441–464 ; XLII, 1933, pp. 43–66, 186–202.

[2] See also Max Black, ' Russell's Philosophy of Language ', in *The Philosophy of Bertrand Russell*, ed. P. Schilpp, pp. 229–255.

[3] *Contemporary British Philosophy*, 2nd series, 1925, pp. 193–223.

[4] *Essays in Philosophical Analysis*, Introduction, p. 9. According to Black, Moore says that to the question " What is the analysis of the proposition expressed by the sentence ' This is a hand ' " there are " three, and only three alternative types of answer possible ". " Suppose that $A_1$ $A_2$ $A_3$ are possible analyses of the proposition P. If one of these is the *correct* analysis of P it must, for Moore, be identically the same proposition as P. So we must have either $P=A_1$, or $P=A_2$, or $P=A_3$ (where " $=$ " means *identically the same as*). Since we know P to be certainly true, we must, therefore, know either $A_1$ or $A_2$ or $A_3$ to be certainly true. How is it, then, that Moore can say that none of the possible analyses of P ' comes anywhere near being certainly true ', without at once using this as a conclusive ground for rejecting all of them ? " (But if all are rejected and they exhaust the alternatives, there is *no* analysis of P, i.e. ' This is a hand '—M.M.)

that there is in fact *no* analysis of the famous statement made by someone looking at his hand, " This is a hand ". Moore has been chiefly concerned with the analysis of statements about physical objects, such as " This is a hand ". He certainly supposes that such analyses would contain statements about sense data and their relations to the surfaces of such objects. No doubt complaints are justified that the notion of " sense datum " has not yet been satisfactorily explained so as to make such analyses intelligible.[1] Nevertheless, Moore's conception of philosophical analysis involves none of the metaphysical apparatus of Russell's " directional analysis ". He has never resorted to mythical " simples " named by " logically proper names ".[2] He has striven to give an ostensive definition of ' sense datum ', by reference to the after image seen with closed eyes after looking at a bright light. Whether or not this paradigm has any relevance to the philosophical clarification of statements about physical objects can, at least, be discussed. But Moore's influence on philosophical method is independent of his peculiar tussles with sense data. Russell has staggered in and out of metaphysics, inventing all sorts of queer objects and theories to provide bogus " scientific " solutions to philosophical problems. The simple theory of descriptions is the exception which shows how right is the position which Moore has consistently held at least since 1910. This may be expressed in two propositions. To be understood, a philosophical statement, or problem, must be explained in ordinary, i.e. non-philosophically technical, language. When so explained, one will find that the problem concerned can be solved, or shown to be insoluble, which is a kind of solution, only by careful examination of the uses of certain words in ordinary contexts. Thus, a philosophical problem about " the Self " or " the Ego " can be understood only when explained by ordinary statements about individual human beings, their names and other designations. From this one will see that a solution depends upon distinguishing, comparing together and relating

[1] *Loc. cit.*, p. 9.

[2] In *Principia Ethica*, ' Good ' and in some very early articles (1898) certain other words are said to be indefinable and to stand for simple, unanalysable notions. But this is a straightforward doctrine connected with the actual use of these terms. Moore never suggests that this presupposes the existence of " atomic " or " basic " facts whose elements can be named only in an " ideal " language.

to the problem, a variety of ordinary uses of such words as ' I ', ' you ', ' he ', ' she ' and personal proper names and descriptions. Having done this, one may decide whether a further use of these words, or another word, should be suggested to meet some new, or neglected, need. More probably, the problem will have dissolved with the study of the words on which it depends. This form of analysis is not the easy task it may sound when described, but is one which seems most promising to many contemporary philosophers.

The influence of Wittgenstein's *Tractatus-Logico-Philosophicus* appears in *Analysis* chiefly through the prominence given to the principle of verifiability, especially by the early logical positivists. This principle which is suggested by some remarks in the *Tractatus* was explicitly formulated and applied by members of the Vienna Group. According to it, a proposition is significant if it is logically possible that it should be verified by one reporting an experience. Theoretically, any experience, though sense experience undoubtedly held a privileged position. If not so verifiable, a proposition is either analytic, tautologous or nonsensical, which includes " metaphysical ". On this view, analysis consists in deducing those propositions about experience which verify the proposition to be analysed. Such analysis was frequently practised and discussed as the solution of philosophical problems, particularly in early numbers of *Analysis*. By 1935, however, Wittgenstein's later doctrines were becoming known, both orally and by the circulation of lectures in typescript. From this time they influence contributions to *Analysis*, especially from Cambridge. This influence has much increased since the war and the publication of works by Wisdom, Ryle and Wittgenstein's own *Philosophical Investigations*.[1] Wittgenstein once described what he did as " one of the heirs of the subject which used to be called philosophy."[2] For he does not so much try to answer philosophical questions or solve philosophical problems as ask in what sense of ' question ' and ' problem ' they are questions and problems and what sort of answer would satisfy those whom they puzzle. His contention is that in no ordinary sense of ' question ' and ' problem ' are philosophical questions and problems genuine. Nor will any sensible answer satisfy a philosopher. Philosophical

[1] Translated by G. E. M. Anscombe. Basil Blackwell, Oxford, 1953.
[2] In a mimeographed set of lectures, the Blue Books.

puzzles are the result of obsessions with certain prominent linguistic forms in ordinary discourse. For example, the noun which names a substance or kind of substance. Both a philosopher and a child may ask, "What is grass? ", "What is water? ", "What is electricity? ", " What is Justice? ", " What is Time? ". Both may be satisfied with expert answers to the first three. Of the last two, the child will be told to wait until he grows up and becomes a philosopher while the philosopher will complain with Polemarchus in Plato's *Republic* and St. Augustine that he understood the words perfectly until he asked these questions. Wittgenstein tries to show that such questions are asked because philosophers are dominated by certain *pictures* ; of every noun correlated with some visible or etherial substance ; of private thoughts and feelings imprisoned in the body like genii in a bottle. One breaks the spell of such pictures by showing how variously most words are actually used and sometimes by inventing " language games " to suggest other possible uses. Such a game might even supply a use of e.g. ' time ' or ' space ' which would satisfy the philosopher's name-substance picture. As one of many other actual and possible uses, however, it would lose its fascination and the philosopher would realise that common language and the technical vocabularies of specialist studies give him all that he needs to express what can be said about any subject. This return to common sense by those who have " lost their way about "[1] is called by Wittgenstein a " cure " brought about by a " therapy " ; a picture which should itself, perhaps, not be over-emphasised. An " illness " whose " cure " supplies so many illuminating " reminders "[2] of the richness of language might be preferred by the intelligent to a state of healthy, but bovine, innocence. There is also a strong similarity between this position and that of Moore. The difference is that, for Moore, the elucidation of the relevant uses of ordinary language *is* the solution of the problem. For Wittgenstein, these ordinary uses are among the illustrations to show that the " problem " is a queer kind of delusion which they will help to dissipate. The distinction is subtle, but in the practice of many of their followers the results are identical.

[1] cf. Philosophical Investigations, Part I, par. 123 'A philosophical problem has the form " I don't know my way about " '.
[2] *Ibid.*, Part I, par. 127.

These few remarks illustrate the use of 'analysis' for the content of most contributions to *Analysis*. Connected with this is the cultivation of small scale rather than large scale philosophizing. According to a theory, due to Russell, philosophers, like scientists, should concentrate on solving separate problems, not on issuing pronouncements about the whole universe. Unlike construction, which cannot be usefully exhibited in progress, analyses can be given of single problems or parts of problems without involving others. Analytic philosophers now realise, however, that this is true only up to a point, since philosophical problems do tend to cluster in groups, not march in single file. Another feature, typical of *Analysis* and analytic philosophy of this period, is a concentration on some problems to the almost complete ignoring of others. There are no discussions in *Analysis* on either political philosophy or aesthetics. A few appear on ethics, of which one example is included in this collection. The majority, however, are on questions in logic and epistemology ; problems of e.g. meaning, knowing, truth and probability. Such are those of chapters II to IV, VII and VIII. Chapter II contains two interesting early articles ; one by Professor C. A. Mace on the relation between language used to assert propositions and that used to convey feelings. To this the author has added a valuable foreword. The other, by Professor A. J. Ayer, denies an alleged similarity between poetry and metaphysics and is a good example of his early style. In chapter IV one early contributor, C. Lewy and two later writers, Professors Alonzo Church and Rudolf Carnap may be compared on the subject of assertion. Chapter V illustrates an *Analysis* joint discussion on an important border-line subject between philosophy and psychology. This discussion has already been welcomed by experts in both subjects. This chapter also contains an interesting early article on ethics by Professor Gilbert Ryle. Chapter VI, which contains articles on the relation of time to propositions and their assertion is separated, for its special interest, from other, more general, discussions of meaning. Chapter VIII includes an acute, but also charming, discussion on truth and correspondence by the late Professor Moritz Schlick of Vienna, an early comment on it by Professor Ayer, and three later discourses on truth. The last chapter illustrates an interest of *Analysis* supporters and many of their contemporaries before 1939. This was as near political controversy as the journal ever reached. Dialectical materialism was much discussed and seemed to need examination by analytic philosophers. A week-end meeting of the Analysis Society was held on the subject in January 1939 at which speakers from both sides took part and the papers here published were among those discussed. They are still often consulted by students. So it seems desirable to republish them. That on " Things and Processes " is included on the advice of Professor Max Black.

I have not thought it necessary to mention every article. They may now all be left to the reader's perusal. I regret that too little space has excluded many other good articles. Especially I regret that it was not possible to include Dr. F. Waismann's valuable series entitled "Analytic-Synthetic " of which six have so far been published.[1] But the articles are long and the series not yet complete. Nor was Dr. Waismann able to combine points from them into a single article of suitable length. So they are, unfortunately, absent.

Finally, I must thank the authors who have permitted their articles to be re-published and those who have written additional notes to bring them up-to-date. Where there are no such notes, it must not be thought that a writer necessarily continues to hold views he may have expressed many years ago. Nor that he does not. The articles are presented simply as contributions to philosophy. I also thank Professor Max Black for advice and encouragement in preparing the volume.

*Bedford College, London.*                                    *July*, 1954.

[1] *Analysis* (i) Vol. 10, pp. 25–40 ; (ii) (iii) and (iv) Vol. 11, pp. 25–38, pp. 49–61, pp. 115–124 ; (v) and (vi) Vol. 13, pp. 1–44, 73–89.

# CHAPTER II. POETRY, METAPHYSICS AND LANGUAGE

## REPRESENTATION AND EXPRESSION
### *By* C. A. MACE

#### FOREWORD

[AN author re-reading his philosophical juvenalia is apt to say " I wonder what I meant when I wrote that ". But another curious thing can happen. He finds that he agrees with his younger self, but now means by the words he uses something very different from what he meant before. This latter is what has happened in the case of my paper on " *Representation and Expression* ". I would even now try to defend most of what I wrote in that paper, but what I should be defending would differ from what I think I thought I was defending in 1934.

In 1934, I was just going into " Behaviourism " (of a kind). In 1954 I am coming out on the other side. I was taking into Behaviourism much that I had learnt from Brentano (or from Brentano as he had been ingested by Stout). And I am now taking it all out again. But, oh, how different it all *feels* !

It was also in 1934 that John Wisdom published his *Mind and Matter*. In this book he attributes to Stout and to myself the doctrine, which he himself doubted, that " every mental fact, not only does but must contain a material fact ". Neither I nor (possibly) he would be happy to-day with that way of stating the issue, but the thesis which I defended and Wisdom doubted is assumed in this paper ; and I could still defend it subject to the reservation noted in the text.

In 1934 I had not been trained to translate statements from the " material mode of speech " to the " formal mode ", and maybe I did think then that I was stating some important truth about the nature of the universe. Now, I am more inclined to agree that part of what I was saying is something that follows from a system of verbal habits prevailing in 1934 but which may not follow from the verbal habits of 1954—or, for that matter from the verbal habits of earlier centuries. In those days there was a consistent and attractive use of the word ' mental ' such that the things to which this word was most obviously to be applied were things that seemed to " contain " a non-mental fact. At that time I was not much worried by the considerations which worried Wisdom in the suggestion that we should conform to that convention. Nor am I much worried by these considerations now. I am all the less worried, and perhaps he is less worried too, because of another important change in our ways of talking. This change might be described as one from the " metaphysical " to the " natural " or common mode of speech. When Brentano and Stout talked about " mental attitudes " and " modes of reference of the mind to its objects " they " explained " what they meant by linking this up with the scholastic conception of " intentional inexistence ". This concept, however, was one that might well be veiled from vulgar understanding. Now, however, we should explain what we mean in a different way. We should say that a " mental attitude ", like other attitudes, is a " state of readiness ", a disposition to do or say certain things in certain situations. We should deprecate the finding of any mystery in " objective reference ". We should say : " Of course, you can't think without thinking about something : you can't be angry without being angry with something or somebody. You can't talk without talking *to* somebody (possibly yourself) and without talking *about* something. You can't behave without behaving in relation, or with reference, to somebody, something or some situation."

No doubt, what was said in " *Representation and Expression* " could be, and needs to be, said in the common mode but it still might be worth saying. People still find a puzzle in the Cartesian *cogito* argument. How, they ask, does this argument differ from any other argument the cogency of which rests upon the fact that its denial would be self-contradictory? A part of the answer is that the *apparent* self-contradiction in saying " I never think " arises from the inconsistency between (in the language of 1934) what is " represented " and what is " expressed ". It is not self-contradictory thoughtfully to say " I never think ". It is not self-contradictory to say (in English) " There are no words in the English language ". There is just a peculiar incoherence between what is said and the saying of it. If someone says " I never say anything ", we can take this statement as the nearest to hand negative instance to refute him. And that of course is a neat point to make. But we have not convicted the speaker of self-contradiction in the ordinary sense—of *saying two incompatible things* in the same breath. He has said something, but did not *say* that he said it.

If " *Representation and Expression* " were re-written the later paragraphs, about " emotive congruence ", etc., would need to be drastically overhauled. There is, I think, a point here, but the point is not clear. Nor can·the matter be put right until philosophers think about the verbal expressions of emotion with something of the subtlety and rigour which they have applied to the verbal expressions of belief.]   (C.A.M., 1954)

## REPRESENTATION AND EXPRESSION

MUCH good use has been found in recent years for I. A. Richards' distinction between the ' scientific ' and the ' emotive ' use of language.   The articulate sentence cast into statement form may be put, it is said, to two contrasted uses.  It may *represent* a fact or proposition, or it may *express* an emotion or otherwise purely subjective state of mind.  Disaster follows when we confuse the scientific with the emotive function.  It is the purpose of this communication to suggest that the useful points in this distinction are retained, and certain others gained, by a measure of reformulation.  I propose to·replace this single distinction by two others ; (1) a more general distinction between the ' representative ' and the ' expressive ' functions of a sentence, (2) a more specific distinction between direct and indirect representation.

To speak of the second use of language as " emotive " unduly restricts the function to which representation may most conveniently be opposed.  A more fundamental distinction is that between the representation of a fact or proposition and the expression of a state of mind.   Undue emphasis upon emotive states has encouraged the tacit assumption that scientific statements are purely representative, and devoid of expressive function. This however is clearly not the case.  A scientific statement is an expression of belief or supposition.  The peculiarity of scientific discourse is not that it is purely representative, but that it expresses only a few of the possible attitudes of mind, these generally being of a pale and diaphanous kind.

Conversely, when the expressive function of a statement is the more important the objective reference is apt to become obscure; but it is almost impossible to find an example of an articulate utterance from which the representative or referential function has wholly disappeared. Conventional ejaculations approximate to what we should here require. To assert that " the country is going to the dogs " does not provide determinate information concerning national events. It expresses primarily what the speaker feels about these events. But the statement does concern events, the characters of which are very broadly sketched.

The expressive function of a sentence is defined by reference to the relations between that sentence and a precedent state of mind; its representative and referential functions in terms of its relations to a fact or proposition to which that state of mind stands in one or other of a certain class of relations. My thesis is that facts and propositions attain to representation only in sentences which also express a state of mind; and that all assertions that express states of mind also exhibit reference to a fact or a proposition. If this position can be maintained it would be an error to regard the two functions of language as alternative. They are essentially conjunctive. They become alternative only through gross degeneration. If an utterance fails to shew its objective reference it may be purely emotive in effect. If it fails to communicate an attitude of mind it may perhaps be said to be " objective ", and hardly " scientific ".

Space does not allow me to defend or even to elucidate all that so obviously calls for elucidation and defence. I shall content myself with some preliminary observations on certain special cases.

Let us suppose that there could be, and is, a fact which consists simply in a certain determinate quality, $Q_1$, (say a quite specific shade of red) uniformly occupying a determinate place, $P_1$, for a determinate time, $T_1$. There is, in other words, a fact composed of the elements $Q_1$, $P_1$, $T_1$, united in the way in which a quality, a place and a time are united when that quality uniformly occupies that place for that time. Call this fact, for short, $F_1$.

Clearly, $F_1$ cannot attain to representation, so to speak, by its own inherent powers. It does so only by reason of its relations to an organism which can apprehend it and can speak. The organism's apprehension of $F_1$ is another fact. Call it $F_2$. Then $F_2$, being in the psycho-physical context that it is, may be *expressed*. The organism may utter a set of words equivalent in import to " $Q_1$ occupies $P_1$ for $T_1$." This set of words may be said to *represent* $F_1$ and to *express* $F_2$.

When $F_2$ consists in an awareness of $Q_1$ as occupying $P_1$ for $T_1$ then all the elements of $F_1$ are elements of $F_2$. S (the "subject" apprehending $F_1$) is " acquainted with " $Q_1$, $P_1$ and $T_1$. To assert that in a certain mode of apprehension of a fact S must be acquainted with all the elements of that fact is but another way of asserting that all the elements of that fact are elements of the fact of awareness.

But $F_2$ not less certainly contains elements which are not elements of $F_1$. For one thing if S apprehends $Q_1$ as occupying $P_1$ and $T_1$ S must do so at or for a certain time. To avoid the inconvenience of dealing with facts in which precisely the same time occurs twice we may suppose that $F_2$ consists in S apprehending Q as occupying $P_1$ for $T_1$ *at* $T_2$. In accordance with a venerable tradition we may refer to $T_1$ as the time *in* predication and to $T_2$ as the time *of* predication.

It remains to deal with S, and the simplest way of dealing with him is to define him as the place *of* predication—which is contrasted with the place *in* predication as the time of predication is contrasted with the time in predication. $F_2$ may now be stated in the form : *At $T_2$ $Q_1$ appears from $P_2$ to occupy $P_1$ for $T_1$.* The essentially topical nature of S is suggested by considerations of the following kind. When we analyse " This is red " in the way suggested by the formula " Red here now " the word 'here' retains its "spatial" significance. Red is at a place which stands in a certain determinate relation to something else which is " there ". If we succeed in withdrawing attention from everything else in the presented field we naturally state the fact in the form " Red *there* now ", where 'there' signifies that the place " confronts " me. It is *there* as contrasted with *here*—where I am. The place in predication is conveyed by reference to the place of predication. Of course it would be a libel to describe the percipient *merely* as a place. He is not an " empty place " but a place occupied by another quality—say $Q_2$. Hence, when in the fact represented there is one quality, one place and one time in the fact expressed there are two qualities two places and two times.[1]

One other point with regard to $F_1$ and $F_2$ requires to be noted. In the case of most—and I *think* all—of the " modes of apprehension " it is not possible to analyse $F_2$ so as to exhibit it as containing $F_1$ as a part. Facts of the type of $F_2$ require to be analysed in terms of some multiple relation which unites all the elements of what is represented together with the elements of what is expressed.

The relations of $F_1$ and $F_2$ to the sentence by which one is represented and the other expressed are disconcertingly complex. Facts of the type $F_1$ cannot be expressed at all. Facts of the type $F_2$ can be either represented or expressed. But whilst one and the same sentence expresses one fact and represents another no sentence can both represent and express the same fact. When I say " $Q_1$ is there now $_2$ " I am representing $F_2$ and expressing $F_1$. When I say " I am aware of $Q_1$ as there now " I am representing $F_2$ but expressing a fact $F_3$ which stands to $F_2$ as $F_2$ stood to $F_1$ in the former case. No ordinary sentence, it would seem, is constructed on principles which enable us with ease to distinguish the elements of what is represented from the elements of what is merely expressed. The individual words, as well as the sentence as a whole, serve the dual purpose. The words ' is ' ' was ' etc. are notoriously busy—representing the time in predication and expressing the time of predication, representing the nexus of elements and expressing the act of assertion. Only an extremely artificial system of symbolism enables us to differentiate representation from expression.

So much for the thesis that all representation in ordinary language involves expression. The converse thesis, that no ordinary language is purely expressive, would require more detailed argument than is possible here. Briefly, its defence would proceed along the following lines.

The conception of a purely emotive use of language would seem to be based upon the doctrine that there are purely subjec-

---

[1] In the peculiar and special case in which I apprehend that I am here now (if I do apprehend this) a certain Q, a certain P and a certain T are the elements of the facts represented. They are also the sole elements of the facts expressed, but in this fact each of them occurs twice.

tive states, a view for which there is a good historical explanation but which has otherwise little to recommend it. The more plausible alternative is one that is generally stated in the form that all mental states involve " objective reference " ; but the point may be put in another way. Physical and mental facts are not co-ordinate either in a dualistic or in a neutral monistic sense. Given any possible physical fact there is a corresponding set of possible mental facts. The mental facts contain all the elements of the corresponding physical fact and other elements as well. I am inclined to think that some of the elements of the mental facts are peculiar to mental facts, but it is just conceivable that there is a " behaviouristic " or " physicalistic " alternative to the view. In either case a mental fact would always exhibit the feature of reference.

The most important point, however, in the doctrine of emotive language is that a sentence *cast into statement form* may be merely expressive of emotion. Against this view there are more specific objections. All that seems to me to be quite certain about the statements of poets, politicians and philosophers (the cases usually cited) is (1) that the statements are expressive of emotion and (2) that they do not assert what they seem to assert when interpreted in a literal way. It is however gratuitous to conclude that these statements are merely expressive of emotion, when the alternative is open that the specious assertion of one thing may be employed as a technical device for asserting something else.

The relevant distinction in cases of this kind is not the very general distinction between representation and expression, but a distinction between two very different ways of representing that some thing or other is the case. What helps us most to understand what is being said in the more indirect method of assertion is a principle which may perhaps be described as the principle of emotive congruence : *If a proposition p evokes in its apprehension the same subjective element as a proposition q then the assertion of p will serve as a substitute* (particularly in the context of a poem) *for the communication of q.*

Of course the poet does not rely upon this principle alone. What makes things so very complicated is that poetic language involves a subtle blending of the principles of direct reference and the principle of reference by emotive congruence. In the same sentence one word will be employed in a direct referential way, whereas the reference of other words will be indirect.

The case which comes nearer home (to philosophers) is that of metaphysical verbiage. It is suggested that many of the utterances of philosophers are strictly meaningless nonsense ; and that the biological function of these utterances is simply to express and to relieve the philosophers' emotions. A less extreme doctrine, perhaps, is enshrined in the deservedly-much-quoted epigram of A. J. Ayer—to the effect that many of the utterances of philosophers should have been published in the *London Mercury*[1] rather than in *Mind*. The doubt I feel in this connection is whether this epigram itself deserves the publicity of the *Mercury* or the publicity of *Mind*. Since it points to a profound philosophical truth I must refer it to *Mind*. But the truth is so well— and so " feelingly "—stated that, by the implied criterion it belongs to the *Mercury*, too. This I am inclined to think is the case, in a slightly different way, with metaphysical verbiage as well. Much of it is admittedly nonsense of a kind, but is it not —like poetic utterance—the kind of nonsense the function of which is to communicate sense? The sentences in question, if properly translated, are at least significant. It suggests, I am inclined to think, a certain lack of ordinary psychological insight to suppose that anyone *ever* talks literal nonsense. When inspired poets and misguided philosophers are appearing merely to gibber it is not merely charity, but in accordance with the probabilities, to suppose that what has happened is simply that they are using words in some unusual way. The point of interest in such a situation is not so much the question whether what they are asserting happens to be true, but how we might conceivably discover what they want to say. At present, analytical philosophers are busy trying to ascertain the significance of sentences in which words are employed in the ordinary way. But the further question is bound sooner or later to arise : may not emotive language have a logic of its own?

[1] *The London Mercury.* A literary journal edited by J. C. Squire, London, 1919–1939.

# THE GENESIS OF METAPHYSICS

## By A. J. AYER

IN his interesting article on " Representation and Expression ", published in *Analysis*[1], Mr. Mace puts forward the view that the metaphysician is not, any more than the poet, merely making agreeable or disagreeable noises ; but that he is definitely saying something, and only appears to be talking nonsense because he is using words in an unusual way. While agreeing with Mr. Mace that in the great majority of cases where the use of language is primarily emotive, it is also being used scientifically, I deny that it is so in all cases. In the first place there are writers, who, like Miss Stein, produce sentences that are apparently not intended to have literal meaning but only rhythm and balance, as for example " Rose is a rose is a rose is a rose " : and secondly there are writers who produce sentences that are intended to have literal meaning but fail to achieve it. It is to this second class that most if not all metaphysicians belong.

To Mr. Mace, and I daresay to most other people, it seems incredible that a man should be able to write plain nonsense without seeing that it is nonsense. To think this is to overlook the way in which metaphysical verbiage mostly comes to be produced. The comparison of metaphysics to lyric poetry is unfortunate in this respect : for it leads one to suppose that the metaphysician plans to write metaphysics in the way that the poet plans to write poetry. But in fact very few of the many philosophers who have made metaphysical statements or asked metaphysical questions, have done so in an endeavour to expound a mystic vision. The vast majority have simply let themselves be caught in linguistic traps : and it takes more to make a mystic than the commission of logical mistakes.

The best example I can give of the way in which metaphysics normally comes to be written is a passage from Heidegger's " Was ist Metaphysik " which Carnap quotes in his article " Ueberwindung der Metaphysik durch logische Analyse der Sprache " (Erkenntnis 2. 4.). " Only Being," says Heidegger, " ought to be explored and besides that—nothing : Being alone and further —nothing : Being solely and beyond that—nothing. How about

---

[1] This collection pp. 15–22.

this nothing? Is there the nothing only because there is the not—
that is Negation? Or is it the other way about? Is there Negation
and the not only because there is the nothing? We assert : the
nothing is more fundamental than the not and Negation. Where
are we to look for the nothing. How are we to find the nothing?
We know the nothing. Anxiety (Die Angst) reveals the nothing.
That for which and about which we made ourselves anxious was
" really " nothing. In fact the nothing itself, as such, was there.
How does this nothing? The Nothing nothings itself. (Das
Nichts selbst nichtet)."

This passage is important not merely because it shows the
psychologist what down right nonsense a philosopher, accounted
eminent, will in all innocence produce, but even more because
it exemplifies so very clearly the kind of error which lies at the
root of almost all metaphysics. For what sustains this rubbish
is the single false assumption that the sentences " there is snow
on the ground " and " there is nothing on the ground " express
propositions of the same logical form. It is this that leads the
author to enquire into the state of the nothing, just as he might
ask about the state of the snow, and finally to the introduction of
the nonsense verb to nothing by analogy with the verb to snow.
The fallacy is one which readers of Lewis Carroll will enjoy to
recognise. "I am sure nobody walks much faster than I do." "He
can't do that," said the king, " or else he'd have been here first."

Crude as the fallacy may seem, it typifies the kind of error
from which much of our traditional philosophy originates.
Thus the whole stock of senseless questions about Being derives
from the assumption, unquestioned before Kant, that " Socrates
exists " is a proposition of the same logical form as " Socrates
thinks ". Then again the senseless use in philosophy of the
term substance clearly depends on the false assumption that to
the grammatical distinction of subject and predicate there must
always be a logical distinction which corresponds. Nor, finally,
would we have been troubled with subsistent entities, if philosophers had been able to see through the superficial similarity of
" Mr. Pickwick is imaginary " and " Nelson is hurt ". These
examples are few and briefly stated. Many more are available. But
I have said enough to show how it is psychologically possible for
metaphysicians to make statements which are literally meaningless.

From this it appears that the fashionable conception of the

metaphysician as a literary artist in philosopher's clothing is not altogether accurate. For the literary artist, whose primary aim is to express or arouse emotion, in nearly all cases writes sentences which have a definite literal meaning, whatever they may be intended to suggest ; whereas the metaphysician produces plain nonsense in the attempt to give straightforward information. The view becomes more plausible when it is limited to those metaphysicians who are really mystics, and not merely victims of the deceptiveness of language. But even their utterances appear to have no literal meaning : and in general I would apply to them Dr. Johnson's remark about Jacob Boehme " If Jacob saw the unutterable, Jacob should not have attempted to utter it ".

Mr. Mace believes that " the sentences " of the metaphysician " if properly translated, are at least significant ". This is plainly untrue with regard to those sentences which are simply the embodiment of logical mistakes. Is it true of the mystic's sentences either? I see no ground for supposing that for every sentence written—say—by Spinoza an equivalent sentence can be found in ordinary speech. Certainly I cannot find them. The most, I think, one has any right to suppose is that sentences can be found to do duty for whole chapters or books. Thus the message of an absolutist metaphysic might perhaps be tritely expressed in a few such sentences as " if you take a broad enough view you will see that what appears to be evil in this world is always a factor in some greater good ". This sentence expresses what is at any rate a significant proposition, however little reason there may be for thinking it true.

I see now that the epigram of mine which Mr. Mace quoted did not correctly represent my views. In saying that the writings of metaphysicians ought to have been published in the *London Mercury*, I implied that I thought them at least significant which I do not. It would have been better if I had said *transition*.[1] But in any case the point I wished to stress was that they were not philosophical writings. And with this Mr. Mace agrees. What I fail to understand is his doubt about the status of the epigram itself. Surely it is a plain " scientific " statement about the policy of two periodicals, and the nature of the sentences which certain people write. He should be the first to admit that it does not cease to be such because it is feelingly expressed.

[1] *transition*. An "advanced" literary periodical edited by Eugene Jolas and Elliot Paul. Paris, 1927–1938.

# CHAPTER III.   SOME PROBLEMS OF MEANING.

## DEMONSTRATIVES AND PROPER NAMES
### By A. M.. MacIver

IN this article I am going to try to clear up some confusions regarding demonstrative pronouns and proper names, by reference to the actual use of language for purposes of communication.

Language is used both *symbolically* and *suggestively*. More exactly : every sentence *symbolises* at least some part of its meaning, but in the case of many sentences the remainder of the meaning is only *suggested*. (I speak here of " part of " the meaning of a sentence in such a sense that what is meant by *Something is mortal* would be " part of " what is meant by *Socrates is mortal*.) I say that a sentence " symbolises " a meaning, if that meaning can be understood (by anyone who knows the language in which the sentence is) merely from the composition and structure of the sentence : I say that a sentence " suggests " a meaning, if anyone who is to understand the meaning from the sentence has to take into account factors other than its composition and structure (e.g. the context in which it is uttered). In other words, language is used " suggestively ", if the hearer has, to some extent, to *guess* the meaning.

The " composition and structure " that I am here talking about is *grammatical* composition and structure (or, as a philologist would say, more exactly, *lexical and grammatical*)—the fact that the sentence consists of such-and-such words (and not others) grammatically related to one another in such-and-such ways (and not others). And I may say that I take it for granted that it is only the " type-sentence " (as Ramsey and others call it) which primarily *has* such composition and structure. If we say that a " token-sentence " (so called) has grammatical structure and composition (that it is divided into words, one of which is the grammatical subject, one the main verb, etc., etc.), this is only in a derivative sense : it is only a shorthand way of saying that the " type-sentence " of which it is an instance has this structure and composition. The spoken " token-sentence " may be divided by phoneticians, and the written " token-sentence " by graphologists, into parts within parts *ad infinitum* ; but none of these parts can be called " words ", except in the sense that they represent the words into which the " type-sentence " is divided, of which the " token-sentence " is an instance, (the word being a " part " of the " type-sentence " in the sense of being something which two such sentences, otherwise different, may have in common). This seems to me a fundamental point in the Theory of Language, though it is seldom explicitly recognised. It follows at once from the admission that language, in so far as it is symbolic, is *conventional* : for the convention must connect with the meaning something which can be repeated, which therefore cannot be the particular utterance (" token-sentence "), but must be the " type " of which that utterance is only one instance.

Ordinary language is, to a very large extent, *suggestive*. Anyone who reflects upon an ordinary conversation must observe how much of his meaning the speaker leaves to be guessed by the exercise of the hearer's common sense (i.e. his judgment of what the speaker is *likely* to mean). Speaking in the suburbs of Leeds someone says : *I shall be going to town soon,* and leaves it to his hearer to guess (assuming that he will guess correctly) whether he means that he will be going to the centre of Leeds within the next hour or so, or that he will be going up to London within the next week or so. The *symbolic* use of language is certainly the most interesting ; for by this means alone we are able to communicate a wholly novel meaning (one which nobody could be expected to guess). But the purely symbolic use is almost confined to the sciences and philosophy ; and I doubt whether even here it is more than an ideal limit, to which the scientist or philosopher strives to approximate (by the use of precisely defined terms, approximation of grammatical to logical form, etc. etc.).

But every sentence (even that which leaves most to suggestion) *symbolises something* : there is something which can be understood merely from the composition and structure of the sentence by anyone who knows the language, or it would not be a sentence at all, but only an ejaculation. For example, the sentence *I shall be going to town soon* would be understood by anyone who knew English, even if he knew nothing whatever about the context (if he met the sentence, say, quoted as an example in an English grammar), to mean at least that someone was supposing that he would be going sometime to some town (and not, say, that there were lions in some zoo).

There are, however, certain linguistic forms which are only used when what is strictly symbolised by the sentence is only a small part of what the speaker wishes to convey, a very important remainder being left to be guessed from the context. (The use of such a form, therefore, constitutes an invitation to make such a guess). Included among these forms is, I think, the use of demonstrative pronouns and proper names. I believe that the whole confused theory of " logically proper names " is due to the false belief that a complete particular perceptible fact can be *symbolised* in language, when in fact only *part* of it (i.e. a corresponding *general* fact) can be symbolised and the remainder can only be *suggested*.

For example, if, pointing to a conspicuous black-and-white bird with an upturned bill, I say to someone who has never seen such a bird before : *That is an avocet*, all that this sentence strictly symbolises (all that could be understood from it by someone who was unaware of the context of utterance) is that something is an avocet (or in other words, that an avocet exists) ; but I use the demonstrative pronoun *that*, because what I am really concerned to convey to my hearer is not this very indefinite (or general) proposition, but the much more definite one that the bird actually before us is an avocet, which can only be understood from the sentence by someone who recognises and takes into account the context of utterance.

It would be a mistake to say that, in this case, my full meaning is *symbolised*, not indeed by the sentence alone, but by a larger symbol, of which the sentence is one part and my pointing at this particular bird another part. My pointing is simply a device (and my use of the word *that* in conjunction with it a further device) to ensure that my hearer will be attending to this particular bird when he hears the sentence uttered, and thus will be likely to *guess* correctly what I am referring to. If he were already attending to the bird, the pointing could be left out, and so could the use of the word *that*. For example, if we were both engaged in watching a flock of birds, only one of which was black-and-white, I could say simply : *The black-and-white bird is an avocet*, and be tolerably sure that he would guess my reference correctly. I could even say, with the same effect: *There's an avocet feeding a little apart from all the other birds* (where the word *there* is not demonstrative, but used exactly as in *There's milestones on the Dover road*, as is shown by the emphasis), if there was only one bird feeding apart from the others. What is strictly symbolised by *There is an avocet feeding apart from the other birds* is just what might also be symbolised by *There is a flock of birds, one of which is feeding apart from the others and is an avocet*, which is evidently a wholly general proposition: but my hearer judges that I would not be likely to utter it unless it had some relevance to the scene before us, and so he is enabled to identify the avocet.

Among demonstrative pronouns, in this sense, we must include personal pronouns, such as *I* and *you*, and demonstrative adverbs, such as *here* and *there, now and then*. For example, the sentence *I am in Leeds* would be properly used by me to convey to a hearer (say, at the other end of the telephone) the proposition that A. M. MacIver was in Leeds at a particular time (namely the time at which I utter the sentence); but the sentence does not *symbolise* this proposition, for there is nothing in its structure or composition to indicate that it is about A. M. MacIver at all. The most that is symbolised is the proposition that somebody is not only in Leeds but also saying that he is; but *who* this is, is left to be guessed by the hearer from evidence outside the symbol itself.

(Tenses of verbs are also demonstratives in the same sense, the use of a tense being equivalent to the use of a demonstrative adverb or adverbial phrase, such as *now* or *before now*.)

I have said that a sentence containing a demonstrative is understood by reference to the *context* of utterance. But there are two *sorts* of contexts, which I will call "*extra-linguistic*" and "*intra-linguistic*" contexts. The extra-linguistic context of an utterance is the external circumstances in which the utterance occurs: in all the examples that I have so far given, the context referred to has been extra-linguistic (the fact that there is only one black-and-white bird in sight, the fact that it is A. M. MacIver who is speaking, etc., etc.). The intra-linguistic context, on the other hand, is the series of sentences uttered in conjunction with that under consideration, or only not uttered because they "go without saying."

The use of a demonstrative in a sentence may suggest a

meaning by reference either to an extra-linguistic, or to an intra-linguistic context. For example, if I say : *He was at Harrow and Balliol*, with a slight stress on the word *he* and a glance towards a particular man, I shall be understood, from this extra-linguistic reference, to be talking about that man. If, however, the sentence *He was at Harrow and Balliol* occurs in a narrative part of a novel, the full meaning of the sentence as it there occurs will be understood by a reference back to other sentences which have gone before it in the narrative (or perhaps a reference forward to some which come after), which constitute an intra-linguistic context : there is no reference outside the whole series of the sentences which make up the novel.

But suggestion by reference to an intra-linguistic context (unlike suggestion by reference to an extra-linguistic context) can always be eliminated by restatement. Whatever is represented by a series of sentences could always be represented by a single longer sentence. The choice between the two is purely a matter of literary style. The approved literary style of some languages, such as Latin and German, often uses a single long sentence to express what, in the approved style in English, would be expressed in a series of shorter sentences : but the series of short sentences is *possible* in Latin or German, and the single long sentence is *possible* in English ; it is only not " good style ". But, if we take a sentence whose full meaning is suggested by reference to an intra-linguistic context and restate the whole series of sentences which form that context, together with the sentence itself, in one long sentence, then the suggestion by intra-linguistic reference will disappear : what was formerly only suggested will now be symbolised. Take for example the series of sentences : *Lord Aubrey de Vere walked down Piccadilly. He carried a walking-stick in his hand.* Consider the second sentence. Only part of its meaning is symbolised, for, from its composition and structure, we can only gather that *somebody* carried a walking-stick in his hand on *some* occasion ; to understand *who* it was and *when*, we must refer to the sentence that went before. But, if we restate these two sentences in one longer sentence, we get *Lord Aubrey de Vere walked down Piccadilly carrying a walking-stick in one hand*, in which this suggestion by intra-linguistic reference has disappeared.

The use of a *proper name* is just like that of a demonstrative, except that it is *only* used to suggest an *intra-linguistic* reference. The simplest case is that of the proper name in fiction. To take W. E. Johnson's example, the fairy-tale begins : *Once upon a time there was a boy whose name was Jack. One day Jack set out to go to market*—and so proceeds, with a continual use of the name *Jack*. But it would be possible (though inconvenient) to eliminate the proper name, and to begin : *Once upon a time there was a boy, who set out one day to go to market* and tell the whole story of Jack and the Beanstalk in one long sentence, composed of an immense series of relative clauses, without ever using the name *Jack* at all. The practice would, indeed, soon become intolerably clumsy in English, especially if more than one character was introduced into the story, owing to the uncertainty of reference of the relative pronouns ; but it could be carried a good deal further, using participial constructions as well as relative clauses, in a language (such as Latin or Greek) in which participles decline in case, number and gender, making some of the references more certain ; and, in principle, it could be carried to any extent. The proper name is, in fact, nothing but a stylistic substitute for a relative pronoun. (It follows that the proper name has only linguistic, not logical, importance.)

In this case the story begins with the existential sentence *Once upon a time there was a boy*, which involves no extra-linguistic reference at all. If it had been history and not fiction, the logical beginning would have been a *demonstrative* sentence ; for example : *You see that boy over there? Well, his name is Jack*—the story continuing, as before, with the name *Jack* used as a substitute for a relative pronoun, referring back to this original sentence. Or the reference might be indirect ; for example : *You see that house there? Well, there is a boy who lives in it, whose name is Jack*—the story proceeding, again, as before. (Or—showing clearly the nature of the demonstrative—the beginning might have been : *You see a house among some trees at the top of a hill? Well. . . .* etc.) Here there *is* extra-linguistic reference, which cannot be eliminated ; but it is due, not to the proper name (whose reference is only intra-linguistic), but only to the demonstrative to which the proper name refers back. The whole story of Jack is only a more complicated case of the principle exemplified in *That is an avocet* (being equivalent to *That is a boy who . . .* or *That is a house in which there lives a boy who . . .*) The story, so far as *symbolic* representation goes, might be the story of *any* boy ; nobody who merely knew English could tell whose story it was ; but the hearer is given cause to *guess* that it is the story of the boy whom he sees, or who lives in the house which he sees.

The demonstrative sentence to which I refer when I use a proper name need not be actually uttered by me, if it is something that " goes without saying ". If I want to say something about Mr. Baldwin to a contemporary educated Englishman, I need not begin : *You see this bit of ground that we are now standing on. Well, it is part of a much larger piece of ground called England, which is all under one government ; and the present executive head of that government is a man called Stanley Baldwin.* I can take all that for granted, and begin straight off : *I see that Baldwin has been making a speech.* In the same way, the modern novelist does not begin in the style of the fairy-tale : *Once upon a time there was . . .* He trusts his reader to supply that, and starts straight off : " *Damn,*" *said the Duchess.* But still this is only understood because the reader *does* supply *Once upon a time there was a Duchess*, as something that the novelist would have asserted if he had thought it necessary to take the trouble. And in the same way, the sentence *I see that Baldwin has been making a speech* is only understood, if there is some demonstrative sentence, which the hearer recognises that the speaker might have uttered if it had been necessary (such as *That is Baldwin*, pointing to the man, or *This is England*, indicating the place), which would suggest (though not, of course, symbolise) something within the hearer's own experience to provide a reference, direct or indirect, for what he was going to say.

## RUSSELL'S THEORY OF DESCRIPTIONS

### By P. T. GEACH

A RECENT article in *Analysis*[1] discussed certain *prima facie* diffi-culties of Russell's theory of definite descriptions. I shall here maintain : (I) that even as applied to his own sort of examples from ordinary language, his analysis of sentences containing

[1] Sören Halldén, " Certain Problems connected with the Definition of Identity and Definite Descriptions given in *Principia Mathematica* ", *Analysis*, Vol. 9, 1948–49, pp. 29–33.

definite descriptions is very defective ; (II) that as a convention for a symbolic language his theory involves intolerable complications.

(I) On Russell's view " the King of France is bald " is a false assertion. This view seems to me to commit the fallacy of ' many questions '. To see how this is so, let us take a typical example of the fallacy : the demand for " a plain answer—yes or no ! " to the question " Have you been happier since your wife died ? " Three questions as here involved :

1.  Have you ever had a wife?
2.  Is she dead?
3.  Have you been happier since then?

The act of asking question 2 presupposes an affirmative answer to question 1 ; if the true answer to 1 is negative, question 2 *does not arise*. The act of asking question 3 presupposes an affirmative answer to question 2 ; if question 2 does not arise, or if the true answer to it is negative, question 3 *does not arise*. When a question does not arise, the only proper way of answering it is to say so and explain the reason; the " plain " affirmative or negative answer, though grammatically and logically possible, is *out of place*. This does not go against the laws of contradiction and excluded middle ; what these laws tell us is that *if* the question arose " yes " and " no " *would be* exclusive alternatives.

Similarly, the question " Is the present King of France bald? " involves two other questions :

4.  Is anybody at the moment a King of France?
5.  Are there at the moment different people each of whom is a King of France?

And it does not arise unless the answer to 4 is affirmative and the answer to 5 negative. (The mere use of the word ' King ' does not require a negative answer to 5 ; there used to be two Kings of Sparta at a time). If either of those answers is false, the affirmative answer " yes, he is bald " is not false but simply out of place.[1] This view agrees, I think, with common sense ; a

---

[1] *Cf.* Frege, *Ueber Sinn und Bedeutung*, pp. 39–41 (pp. 69–70 in *Philosophical Writings of Gottleb Frege*, Blackwell, 1952).

plain man, if pressed for an answer, would be very likely to reply : " Don't be silly ; there isn't a King of France."

The mere use of the definite description " the King of France " does not *always* presuppose an affirmative answer to question 4 and a negative answer to question 5. For, as Russell rightly holds, these two answers together are logically equivalent to " the present King of France exists " ; so, if they were *always* presupposed when we say " the King of France ", we could not ask the question whether there is somebody who " is the King of France " without presupposing that in fact there *is* somebody ; which is absurd. Russell's analysis of ordinary *existential* assertions containing definite descriptions, like " the King of France exists ", is quite adequate. And again, his analysis works out all right when " the King of France " is a logical *predicate* ; " George VI is not the King of France " is logically equivalent to " either George VI is not *a* King of France, or there are several people each of whom is *a* King of France ", and it does not assert or presuppose that there is a present King of France. (In the existential assertion itself, it is " the King of France ", *not* " exists ", that is the logical predicate ; for the assertion is logically equivalent to " somebody is the King of France ".) But Russell's theory breaks down for sentences in which " the King of France " is a logical *subject*, such as " the King of France is bald " and " an assassin has stabbed the King of France ". Such sentences presuppose an affirmative answer to the question " does the present King of France exist? " ; since that answer is false, use of " the King of France " as a logical subject is out of place.

It is important to distinguish my view that the existence of the present King of France is *presupposed* by the assertion " the King of France is bald " from Russell's view that his existence is *implied* by this assertion. If $p$ implies $q$, and $q$ is false, $p$ is of course false. But to say $p$ presupposes $q$ is to say that $p$ is an answer to a question that does not arise unless $q$ is true. If $q$ is false, or if $q$ in turn is an answer to a question that does not arise, the assertion of $p$ is not false but simply out of place.

(II) The incorrectness of Russell's theory as an account of ordinary language in no way goes against it as a proposed convention of symbolism. In symbolic language we try to avoid the situations in which a formula is " out of place " because it is an

answer to a question that does not arise ; we do this by altering
the meaning of the question. Take the case of zero. In ordinary
language, the question " May I give you some more tea? "
presupposes that you have already had some ; otherwise it is
out of place—as Alice said : " I've had nothing yet, so I can't
take more ". The Mad Hatter's retort was : " You mean you
can't take *less* ; it's very easy to take *more* than nothing ". The
Hatter, like mathematicians, treats " nothing " or " o " as an
answer to the question ' how much ? " on the same level as any
other answer ; this does not quite fit ordinary usage, but symbolically it is most convenient.

There are, however, decisive technical reasons against
Russell's theory. Russell does not define the definite description
' ($\imath x$) (F$x$) ' as such, but only its use in a context ' G . . . '
($\imath x$) (F$x$) ' is defined to mean ' (E$y$) : G$y$. ($x$). F$x \equiv x = y$ '. Now
in applying this definition we have to decide what is the context
represented by ' G . . . '. For instance, if we apply the definition
to a formula containing ' ($\imath x$) (F$x$) ' in one of its clauses, we have
to decide whether ' G($\imath x$) (F$x$) ' is to be taken as short for this
clause or for the whole sentence ; and the results of expounding
the formula will be different in the two cases. To avoid different
*definientia* for the same *definiendum*, Russell lays down rules in
*Principia Mathematica* (*14) as to the " scope " of a definite description—i.e. rules to determine how much of a formula is to be
taken as the ' G($\imath x$) (F$x$) ' of the definition. Unfortunately, these
rules are insufficient. Take the expression ' ($\imath x$) (F$x$) R ($\imath x$) (F$x$) '.
This contains no part that is a sentence or sentential function in
which ' ($\imath x$) (F$x$) ' occurs ; hence Russell's conventions of "scope"
are inapplicable. But there are several different ways of expounding it according to the above definition.

(i) One might take ' G ' in the *definiendum* to represent ' . . .
R . . . ' (both blanks to be filled the same way), so that ' G$y$ ' in
the *definiens* is ' $y$R$y$ '. This, the simplest, course is adopted by
Russell himself (*14.28).

(ii) One might take ' G ' to represent ' . . . R ($\imath x$) (F$x$) ', so
that ' G$y$ ' in the *definiens* is ' $y$R ($\imath x$) (F$x$) '. The definite description ' ($ix$) (F$x$) ' will then occur in the *definiens* with the scope
' $y$R ($\imath x$) (F$x$) ', and must be eliminated by a second application of
the definition. To avoid confusion of variables, we must introduce

a new variable, '$\chi$' say, into the *definiens* of 'G $(\imath x)$ (Fx)', in place of '$y$'; since the context 'G . . .' is '$y$R . . .', 'G$\chi$' in this definiens will be '$y$R$\chi$'.

(iii) We get similar results if we take 'G . . .' to represent '$(\imath x)$ (Fx) R . . .', so that 'G$y$' in the *definiens* is '$(\imath x)$ (Fx) R$y$'. To eliminate this occurrence of '$(\imath x)$ (Fx)' with the scope '$(\imath x)$ (Fx) R$y$', we replace the variable '$y$' in the *definiens* of 'G$(\imath x)$ (Fx)' by '$\chi$', as before, and then take 'G . . .' to be '. . . R$y$', so that 'G$\chi$' in this *definiens* is '$\chi$R$y$'.

Now it is easy to prove that the results of these three ways of expounding '$(\imath x)$ (Fx) R $(\imath x)$ (Fx)' are logically equivalent. But they are not the same expression; and '$(\imath x)$ (Fx) R $(\imath x)$ (Fx)' cannot legitimately be used as an abbreviation for all three indifferently, until their logical equivalence *has* been proved; just as we cannot legitimately write '$a + b + c$' for '$(a + b) + c$' and '$a + (b + c)$' before establishing the associative law for addition.

I am sure a little ingenuity would enable one to find other cases, unnoticed by Russell and Whitehead, in which the same *definiendum.* containing a definite description, has more than one *definiens*; even, it may be, cases where the *definientia* are *not* logically equivalent.[1] Now complications like these cannot be allowed in good symbolism; so Russell's "contextual definition" of definite descriptions will not work as a symbolic device. (Various alternative conventions have been proposed, *e.g.* Frege's and Quine's; but it is not my concern to discuss these here).

An added defect of Russell's theory is that he defines the meaning of '$(\imath x)$ (Fx)' in the existential assertion 'E! $(\imath x)$ (Fx)' by a special definition *14.02" and not in terms of the general definition of 'G $(\imath x)$ (Fx)'. His pretext is that it would be impossible to find a function to define 'E!$y$', in the *definiens* '$(Ey){:}E!y.(x)Fx \equiv x=y$' that we should get by applying the general definition. But this is not true; it is very easy to find a suitable function—e.g. '$(E\chi)y=\chi$' (cf. *14.204). Moreover, without finding such a function, one could still bring 'E ! $(\imath x)$ (Fx)' under the general definition, by defining it to mean 'F$(\imath x)$ (Fx)' (*cf.* *14.22).

---

[1] Such a proof that the conventions of "scope" are inconsistent has been put forward by Chwistek, *Cf.* Black, *The Nature of Mathematics*, p. 83.

# HETEROLOGY AND HIERARCHY

### By NATHANIEL LAWRENCE

## I

IN *An Inquiry into Meaning and Truth*, Bertrand Russell states that " The arguments for the necessity of a hierarchy of languages are overwhelming, and I shall henceforth assume their validity."[1] A score of pages later, however, he cannot resist the opportunity to demonstrate by exhibiting an ' antinomy ', that " the hierarchy . . . is essential ".[2] The antinomy is one associated with the word ' heterological '.

The object of the present paper is to examine this alleged antinomy to discover whether or not it supports the necessity for a hierarchy of languages. The general question of whether there is *any* need for a hierarchy of languages is one which could stand considerable critical appraisal. At present there is a runaway enthusiasm among philosophical students of language for an affirmative answer to this question.[3] But the general problem is not here examined. I merely consider the smaller problem : Does the paradox connected with the term ' heterological ' require capitulation to a theory of language hierarchy?

## II

I shall first consider Russell's statement of the paradox, expanding the latter part of it for the sake of clarity.

"A predicate is ' heterological ' when it cannot be predicated of itself ; thus ' long ' is heterological because it is not a long word, but ' short ' is homological. [' German ', ' learned ', ' beautiful ' are heterological ; ' English ', ' erudite ', ' ugly ' are homological].[4] We now ask : Is ' heterological ' heterological? Either answer leads to a contradiction. To avoid such antinomies, the hierarchy of languages is essential."[5]

---

[1] W. W. Norton, New York, 1940, p. 75.
[2] *Op. cit.*, p. 97.
[3] By no coincidence at all, there is, among this same group of people, a careless enthusiasm for the proposition that Plato regarded the ' forms ' as disparate entities residing in ' heaven '. E.g., Russell, *op. cit.*, p. 27.
[4] The sentence in square brackets is Russell's footnote to the passage.
[5] *Op. cit.*, pp. 96–97.

The ' contradiction ' to which Russell refers needs examination. Clearly what Russell means is that should we answer either ' yes ' or ' no ' to the question, " Is ' heterological ' heterological? " we obtain results which issue in self-contradictory conclusions. Let us consider the two cases.

(1) If I say, " Yes, ' heterological ' is heterological ", then I am saying that it is incapable of self-predication ; but the first part of my argument consists in doing just that. From the assertion in which I predicate a term of itself, I draw the conclusion that such predication is impossible. So far, so good. Let us, for the time being, assume that this part of the antinomy holds.

(2) If I say, " No, ' heterological ' is not heterological ", then I am saying that it *is* capable of self-predication ; however, the first part of my assertion is one in which I specifically *deny* the predicate of heterologicality to ' heterological '. So once again I have apparently made an assertion from which a conclusion is drawn that contradicts the assertion.

Before I examine the ' antinomy ' further I shall first consider two features of the property of being heterological with which Russell does not deal. These two points will serve to sharpen the evident need for a careful examination of the meaning of heterologicality.

(i) If it is a paradox that is desired we do not need to go so far as to ask whether or not ' heterological ' is self-predicable. There are paradoxes aplenty without involving ourselves in a regress of languages. For instance, ' heterological ' and ' homological ' must be contradictories or the paradox we have examined falls through. Now we ask, " Is ' long ' heterological? " The answer is that it is. ' Long ' is a short word. Then if anything is homological (non-heterological) it must be non-long. But ' polysyllabic ' is homological and is therefore non-long. However, this is false, since the average number of letters in English discourse is five.[1]*

[1] Space estimation of manuscripts to be set up in type relies upon this assumption for instance.

* Note for re-publication : This paragraph, as may be evident, contains an intentionally sophistic argument, ignoring the distinction between use and mention, in the case of the term ' long '. In condensing the article for publication I accidentally omitted a concluding sentence indicating that the carelessness which gives rise to the fallacy of heterology, is not of radically different order from that in the given sophism about ' long ' and ' non-long '. (N.L.)

(ii) What of the examples Russell gives us? ' Ugly ' is judged homological because it does not strike Russell's eye or ear well. ' Erudite ' is homological because of the relatively small number of people who can define it accurately. But suppose I think ' ugly ' is beautiful? It has a nice balance of vertical strokes above and below the scanning line. The closed loop of the *g* is metamorphosed into the generously welcoming open loop of the *y*, and so forth. The whole word has a sense of strength, grace, balance, and friendliness. As for the sound of the word, it is reminiscent of that tenderest of scenes, a child nursing. And so, tongue in cheek or not, I might defend any word. Again, with no change in meaning, the word ' erudite ' could become as unerudite as the word ' integrate ', which was at one time in the vocabulary of only a few. If Churchill's next speech includes the phrase, " erudite authors of labour policy " the illiteracy with regard to the meaning of this word will vanish overnight, with the assistance of the Press.

The first of these two points shows that the concept of heterologicality encounters difficulties before it is ever, so to speak, turned on itself. The second point shows that despite the ideal of a language in which words have, in some sense, a stable status, certain aspects of words will always be fluctuating and open to subjective variability. This second point thus serves to warn us that when we deal with the concept ' heterological ' we are dealing with a characteristic of words which may depend as much upon taste and circumstance as upon logic. I may not turn aside here to the several opportunities for analysis which the presence of these subjectively and otherwise variable factors offers. The two points together should show that when one is asked, "Is ' heterological ' heterological? " no answer need be given until the notion of heterologicality is further analyzed. It may be that then the question can be shown to be meaningless, for in the definition of a heterological word as being one which is not predicable of itself there is an epidemic ambiguity which is present throughout the definition. There is ambiguity in what is meant by ' word ', by ' heterological ', by ' predicable ', and by ' self '. At bottom these are all the same ambiguity. I shall approach this ambiguity at its most accessible and familiar portal, the variety of meanings of the term ' word '.

## III

The main line of the following analysis is not to be understood as in any sense novel. Russell himself, of course, spends considerable effort in analyzing what is meant by ' word '[1] and in so doing develops the analytic machinery which, with very little adapting, could have been employed to resolve the paradox of ' heterology ' without introducing the notion of a language hierarchy and the difficulties which are attendant on this notion.

The word ' word ' is, of course, ambiguous. I take some examples, beginning with those which Russell himself chooses to exhibit the puzzle.

The word ' long ' is heterological because it is a short word. Here the word ' long ' apparently refers to the physical properties displayed by a physical object, spoken or written. But it is important to notice that there are at least two meanings of 'word' buried in this one example. (i) 'Word' means "unique physical object, numerically different from all similar instances ". (ii) ' Word ' also means " that of which this physical instance is an occurrence ". Let us call these $W_1$ and $W_3$ respectively. Each $W_3$ may be either spoken or written. Thus $W_3$ is what is representable by an indefinitely large variety of type faces, etc., on the one hand, and accents, etc., on the other. Each of these indefinitely large groups is distinct from $W_1$ and $W_3$. We rarely call them words ; rather we say they are ways of speaking or kinds of writing or printing, etc. But since they mediate between $W_3$ and $W_1$, let us call them $W_{2s}$ and $W_{2p}$ respectively. Each member of $W_{2s}$ and $W_{2p}$ can itself have an indefinitely large number of $W_1$'s as well as an indefinitely large number of companions in the same group. Thus any $W_1$ is an instance of some $W_2$, which is itself one of many $W_2$'s which are channels of expression for $W_3$. $W_3$ is what we are talking about when we say, " I'm going to find out what that word I heard means ". In these circumstances, we don't care which $W_1$ we get or what $W_2$ it is an instance of although, for psychological reasons, we are likely to prefer some $W_{2p}$ that is legible and a $W_1$ that is also legible.

These psychological reasons are in themselves oblique to the purpose of our present inquiry, but they uncover a pertinent

[1] *Op. cit.*, ch. 1.

point. We may have a ' legible ' $W_2$ or a ' legible ' $W_1$. Thus we may have a perfectly legible type face of adequate size but its individual instance may be ' illegible ', being inadequate in ink, on poor paper, or simply too old. Keeping this distinction in mind, what do we mean by saying that a word is ' long '? It should be clear at once that we are not talking about $W_1$, although $W_1$ may give us tangible support for our decision. Thus the word ' war ' is longer in most headlines than the word ' inhuman ' is in the account. Again, a little girl of two and a half years, whom I know, repays her parents' prohibitions of her impulses, with interest, by saying, ' No-o-o-o-o-o '. What is required of the judgment that a word is long is that it be referred to other ' words ' of the same $W_2$ group, that is, the same mode of expression of $W_3$. This can be done by selecting other $W_1$'s representing the same $W_2$ group, but there is no need to do so. It is true that I may need a visual or auditory image of other $W_1$'s in order to make any judgment about the length of the word which I am examining, but the function of such an image is analogous to the service which a diagram in a geometry book provides for the student of geometry. It suggests by example. Furthermore, consider the sentence, " Schultz ate a banana ". In $W_{2p}$ the subject of the sentence is longer than the object; in $W_{2s}$ it is shorter. The length of a word depends upon the $W_2$ group to which it belongs. That is, when we speak of a word's length we are talking about its $W_2$ properties. Are there any instances where the concept of ' heterological ' could be applied to $W_1$'s? There are; the words ' black ' and ' loud ' serve as illustrations for $W_{2p}$ and $W_{2s}$ respectively.[1] And this in turn makes it clear that $W_1$ should also be divided into $W_{1p}$ and $W_{1s}$, with $p$ and $s$ being derivative properties of any $W_1$ gained from the $W_2$ group of which it is an instance.

Let us now consider the homologicality of the word ' erudite '. $W_1$ is obviously out of the picture, except as the immediate mechanical agency of communication. $W_2$ is equally out of the picture, for it does not matter whether the group in which ' erudite ' is found is an $s$ group or a $p$ group, or whether it be

---

[1] That is, ' black ' is either heterological or not, depending on whether or not black ink is used, etc.; ' loud ' is heterological or not, depending on the vocal force of its instance.

in a Lancashire burr or in a Limehouse chatter, in brevier extended
or pica condensed. It is still an erudite word. On the other
hand, it is not as a meaning that 'erudite' is erudite; since to
the extent that it, as a meaning, can be reduced to familiar
synonym or simplified explanation, it is available to those who
are bookish or not, learned or otherwise. Thus, when we say
that the meaning of 'erudite' is itself erudite we are saying
somewhat elliptically that to state what 'erudite' means by the
use of that juxtaposition of letters is to state the meaning eruditely.
It could be stated by other patterns of letters in a way that could
be generally understood.[1] When we deal with such words as
'erudite', 'declinable', etc., we are dealing at the $W_3$ level.
Here we are dealing with 'word' in the sense that 'erudite' is
an English 'word', the sense in which the English language is
composed of a certain number of 'words', say a hundred
thousand. Thus 'erudite', 'erudit', and 'kenntnisreich'
would fall into classifications $W_{3e}$, $W_{3f}$, and $W_{3g}$, symbols for
English, French, and German 'words' respectively, and would
all be homological. A corresponding listing of 'learned', 'savant',
and 'gelehrt' would fall into the same categories respectively, but
each would be heterological. Nevertheless, all six 'words'
would have the same meanings.[2]

We may safely assume at least one more level of what is
meant by a word, then; this is the controversial level of its
meaning, what it seeks to convey, describe, indicate, name, etc.
Translation is based on the assumption that community of
meaning underlies diversity of languages. This assumption
flourishes with such words as 'Buch' and founders with such
words as 'Begriff', but such facts should make us all the more
aware of the distinction between $W_3$ and what we shall call $W_4$.

There is no place in this study for a detailed examination of
'meaning', and no need of one. The distinguishing of $W_1$,
$W_2$, $W_3$, and $W_4$ which has been undertaken in these remarks
will survive, I think, any of the varieties of analysis to which $W_4$

---

[1] It is, it would seem, dubious whether any meaning is itself erudite, strictly
speaking. This problem in reduction of meaning and analysis of definition is one
of the many which the present investigation must ignore.
[2] A well-informed analysis of the meanings would undoubtedly show subtle
shades of meaning. The difficulty about ideal identity of meanings, that is, exact
synonymity, should not damage the significance of the illustration.

has been submitted, whether it be the simple division of $W_4$ into denotative and connotative, or one of the more complicated modern analyses.[1] It is equally possible that a more thorough-going study will reveal other W's ; the division into four types is not presumed to be exhaustive, and any such additions, based on subtler distinctions, would reinforce rather than vitiate the conclusions which we are now in a position to draw.

## IV

We have seen that ' heterological ' is a term applied to words which are not predicable of themselves. We have further seen evidence that the expression ' themselves ' in this definition is either elliptical or ambiguous, however, since the ' self ' is not a self at all. The ' word ' which is ' predicated ' is always $W_4$. *But that of which it is predicated is not.* Thus when we ask, " Is ' ugly' ugly? " we are asking, " Is the meaning of the word ' ugly ' appropriate to some (customary) symbolic representation of that meaning? " In general when we ask, " Is ' X ' X? " we are asking, " Is the meaning of ' X ' appropriate to some level of symbolization of that meaning which is identified by the same name? "[2]

A glance at our examples shows us that this is the presumption upon which the judgment of the heterologicality of a word rests. ' Long ' is heterological because its $W_4$ is inappropriate (under standardized conditions) to its $W_2$. ' Erudite ' is not heterological, because its $W_4$ is appropriate to its $W_3$. An example of a type not given by Russell will complete the analysis as far as we have taken it. ' Red ' is heterological in the present instance of writing, *i.e.* its $W_4$ is not appropriate to its $W_1$. Were this journal printed in red ink, ' red ' would not be heterological. It is important to recall that this analysis may very well be incomplete. More levels of W's may be required in order to cover adequately the wide variety of meanings possible for ' word '. The present analysis has been undertaken with only certain very limited objectives.

[1] *E.g.*, that of C. I. Lewis in *An Analysis of Knowledge and Valuation*. Open Court, 1950, ch. 3.
[2] Actually not all sentences in which the form " Is ' X ' X ? " appears can be regarded as ones in which the second ' X ' (without quotation marks) refers to the meaning of X : *e.g.*, " In French is ' defiance' defiance? " But such exceptions do not obscure the analysis of heterologicality.

Now let us ask ourselves what has occurred in the case of the question, "Is 'heterological' heterological?" Plainly, the second use of the term 'heterological' in the sentence is designed to point to its $W_4$, its meaning. What about the first appearance of 'heterological'? To which kind of W does it direct our attention? Not merely to itself, *i.e.* its $W_1$, obviously, nor to its $W_2$. What about $W_3$? That is, what about regarding the first word as a 'word' in the sense that any language has a vocabulary of a certain number of 'words'? Let us alter $W_3$ and see. Suppose we tentatively add to the Esperanto vocabulary by adding to it the word 'suononpredicato' as an exact translation of 'heterological'. Now, suppose I ask, "Is 'suononpredicato' heterological"? The paradox appears as before. It should be apparent that any synonym offered for 'heterological' and substituted for that term in its first use in the paradox fails to reduce the paradox. The paradox does not depend upon a consideration of the first appearance of 'heterological' as a physical object. Nor does it depend upon 'heterological' as being an example of a mode of writing or speech. And we have just seen that it does not depend upon 'heterological' as being a word in a language. Rather it depends upon heterological *as having a certain meaning*; that is, it depends upon the *first* use of 'heterological' as *also* referring to its $W_4$. It is 'heterological' as a meaning, not 'heterological' as an object, a class of expressions, or a constituent element in a language that gets us in trouble. These are all present also but they create no confusion. Our analysis of the meaning of 'heterological' has shown, however, that the concepts of heterologicality and homologicality depend upon a predication of the meaning of a term of something which is *not* its meaning. That such is the case is clearly indicated by the examples given.

The proper answer, then, to the question, "Is 'heterological' heterological?" is that it is non-heterological. But this does not mean therefore that it is homological. One might just as well decide that because a rock is non-ambidextrous it must favour one arm or another. 'Heterological' is both non-heterological and non-homological. 'Heterological' and 'homological' are contradictories only within a universe of discourse which is confined to words whose $W_4$'s are predicated of W's of some other levels. What is required of a solution of ' the paradox of heterology ' is simply that ' heterological ' be used in an unambiguous and consistent fashion. If this is done, the definition of ' heterological ' which is implicit in the use of the given examples to illustrate the meaning of ' heterological ' prohibits us from attributing either heterologicality or homologicality to it. This prohibition is a warning not to commit a fallacy. Viewed in one light the fallacy is that of equivocation ; viewed in another it is the fallacy of false dichotomy. Other names could perhaps be suitably employed, but that is not important. The fallacy is a familiar one, capable of being exposed by ordinary methods of analysis. There is required no hierarchy of languages, nor even a hierarchy of words (which would by no means necessitate a hierarchy of languages). The claim that the paradox of heterologicality requires the introduction of special techniques and instruments of analysis is unjustified.

## HETEROLOGICALITY

### By GILBERT RYLE

MR. LAWRENCE ably criticises Russell's use of an alleged paradox (that of ' heterological ' being homological, if heterological, and *vice versa*) as a proof of the thesis of language-hierarchies. I agree with his conclusions, but I do not think he brings out the main reason why it is an improper question even to ask whether ' heterological ' is heterological or homological. '

Some people introduce themselves on meeting strangers. Others do not do this. They might be distinguished as ' self-nominators ' and ' non-self-nominators '. If Dr. John Jones, on meeting a stranger begins by saying, ' Dr. John Jones ' he acts as a self-nominator. So, too, if he says ' Captain Tom Smith ', save that now he gives a pseudonym. If he says ' it's a fine day ', ' I'm a doctor ' or ' I'm a self-nominator (or a non-self-nominator) ', then he has given a true or false description of the weather, his profession or his practice of announcing or withholding his name ; and in the last case his action belies or bears out his remark. But he has not given his surname, Christian name, nickname or pseudonym. " . . . a self-nominator ' and ' . . . a non-self-nominator " are the tail ends of character descriptions. Such descriptions require that the person described has a name to give, though this is only referred to, not given. Epithets are not names, even when they carry references to names.

A perverse parent might name his child ' Non-self-nominator', as there was once a club named ' The Innominate Club '. The son might then correctly give his name as ' Master Non-self-nominator Brown '. But he would no more have belied his announcement than a big man does by introducing himself as 'Alderman Little '. Names are not epithets, even though the same vocables constitute an epithet in some language or other.

To say ' I am a self-nominator (or non-self-nominator) ' not only is not to give one's name ; it is not even to describe one's name, as I might describe my name by saying that it rhymes with ' smile '. Unfortunately the term of art ' description ' is often used to cover idioms which, in ordinary life, would not be called ' descriptions ' at all. No policeman would accept as a description the phrase ' my name ' (in " I never volunteer any name "). What I refer to with such expressions can, in principle, be specified or particularised. But ways of referring to things are not ways of answering consequential requests for information about those things. Very often we employ referring expressions, which also have a descriptive force, e.g. ' she ' and ' yonder lame horse ', and a hearer may get the reference while contesting the attribution of femininity or lameness.

For it to be true that I do or do not give my name, there must be a ' namely-rider ' of the pattern " . . . . namely, ' John Jones ' ". Nor could it be true that a person had a profession or a disease without there being a namely-rider, of the pattern " . . . namely, the Law " or " . . . namely, asthma ". The namely-riders need not be known to the persons who make or understand the statements that have them. I know that there is a day of the week on which I shall die, but I do not know what it is. The day of my death could not be *just* the day of my death, but no particular day of the week.

Like anything else, linguistic expressions can be described or misdescribed by appropriate epithets. An epitaph, a peroration, a sonnet, a phrase, or a word may be English, mispronounced, vernacular, full of sibilants or obscene. The vocabulary of philologists is necessarily full of epithets appropriate to linguistic expressions, as the vocabulary of botanists is of those appropriate to plants. The methods of finding out what epithets can be truly applied to particular expressions are (crude or refined) philological methods. The properties of expressions established by these methods are philological properties. Thus ' dissyllabic ', ' of Latin origin ', " rhymes with ' fever ' ", ' solecism ' and ' guttural ' are philological epithets, standing for philological properties.

Most epithets, like astronomical, pharmaceutical and botanical epithets, are not appropriate to linguistic expressions. Cottages, but not phrases, may be thatched or unthatched, tiled or untiled. Reptiles do or do not hibernate ; adverbs neither do nor do not. When an epithet is not a philological epithet, the question whether or not it applies to a given expression is an improper question.

Philological epithets do not constitute a proper genus. There are widely different interests that amateur or professional philologists may take in expressions, and widely different questions that they can raise about them. Phonetic epithets are not congeners of stylistic, orthographic, grammatical or etymological epithets.

It is no accident that a philological epithet may stand for a property of expressions and itself be one of the expressions that has that property. ' English ', like ' cow ', is an English word; ' polysyllable ', like ' Saturday ', is a polysyllable. Conversely, a philological epithet may stand for a property the possession of which can be truly denied of that epithet. ' French ' is not a French word ; ' monosyllable ' is not a monosyllable ; ' obsolete ' is not obsolete. The question whether the property for which a philological epithet stands does or does not belong to that epithet itself is a proper question, e.g. whether ' dactyl ' is or is not a dactyl and whether ' mispelt ' is or is not misspelt.

One may then construct two artificial parcels, one of those philological epithets which have the philological properties for which they stand ; the other of those which lack the properties for which they stand. The first might be called ' self-epithets ' ; the second ' non-self-epithets '. ' Deutsch ' is a self-epithet, ' obscene ' a non-self-epithet. ' Written,' here, is a non-self-epithet ; in manuscript it was a self-epithet.

Now the question is supposed to arise "Are ' self-epithet ' and ' non-self-epithet ' themselves self-epithets or non-self-epithets? In particular, is ' non-self-epithet ' a non-self-epithet or a self-epithet? "

But before starting to wriggle between the horns of this dilemma, we must consider whether the question itself is a proper question, i.e. whether ' self-epithet ' and ' non-self-epithet ' belong to the class of philological epithets at all. As we have seen, most epithets do not belong to this class, so we cannot assume that these two (invented) classificatory expressions do so either. Certainly at first sight they look as if they do belong to it, since we can ask whether ' monosyllabic ' is a self-epithet or not, and decide that it is a non-self-epithet. The predicate end of the sentence " ' monosyllabic ' is a non-self-epithet " does look like a philological epithet of ' monosyllabic '. It's a predicate of a quoted expression, isn't it?

But, if we recollect that ' self-nominator ' and ' non-self-nominator ' were not names but epithets carrying references to unmentioned names, we may suspect that ' self-epithet ' and ' non-self-epithet ' are not philological epithets, but expressions carrying references to unmentioned philological epithets. And this suspicion can be confirmed.

How do we decide (*a*) whether words (including ' English ' and ' polysyllabic ') are English or polysyllabic, etc., and (*b*) whether words, like ' English ' and ' polysyllabic ', are or are not self-epithets? We decide questions of the former sort by (elementary or advanced) philological methods. We consult dictionaries, count syllables, use stop watches, and listen to linguaphone records. But we do not decide whether words are self-epithets or not by examining them by further philological methods. There is no visible, audible, grammatical, etymological or orthographical feature shared by ' French ', ' monosyllabic ', ' obscene ' and ' misspelt '. On the contrary, we call them ' non-self-epithets ' because we find by various philological methods that ' French ' is not a French word, ' obscene ' is not an obscene word, ' misspelt ' is not misspelt ; and we have decided to list as ' non-self-epithets ' all those philological epithets which lack the philological properties for which they stand. We find by philological methods that these and other quite different philological epithets stand severally for, perhaps, not even generically kindred philological properties, and that the epithets lack the properties for which they stand; we then collect them together as ' non-self-epithets ' not in virtue of any common philological properties that they all stand for but in virtue of their being alike in lacking the philological properties for which they severally stand. So ' non-self-epithet ' and ' self-epithet ' do not stand for any philological properties of expressions. Their use is to assert or deny the possession of ordinary philological properties by the epithets which stand for them. Their use *presupposes* the ordinary use of philological epithets in the description of expressions of all sorts (including philological epithets); it is not, therefore, a part of that ordinary use. ' Orthographic ' is a self-epithet only *because* ' orthographic ' both has and stands for a certain philological property, namely that of being correctly spelled. Unless there · was an opening for this namely-rider, there would be no job for the expression ' self-epithet ', just as there would be no job for the expression ' self-nominator ' if there were no opening for such a namely-rider as " . . . namely, ' John Jones ' ". As ' self-nominator ' carries a reference to a name which it is not and does not mention, so ' self-epithet ' carries a reference to an ordinary philological property which it does not itself stand for.

At first sight, however, the statement that ' English ' is a self-epithet does seem not merely to refer to but to mention the philological property of being in the English tongue. For we English speakers are all so familiar with the· use of the word ' English ', that we are tempted to suppose that to be told that ' English ' is a self-epithet is to be told that ' English ' is an English word. But this is not so. A person who knew no German but had been told the use of ' self-epithet ' and ' non-self-epithet ' could understand and believe the statement that the German adjective ' lateinisch ' is a non-self-epithet. He would be believing that ' lateinisch ' stands for some specific philological property or other (he would not know which) and that ' lateinisch ' lacks that property. He knows that it is now proper to ask the rider-question " Namely, which philological property? " since if this question had no answer, then ' lateinisch ' could not be either a self-epithet or a non-self-epithet. For ' lateinisch ' to be a non-self-epithet, it must be false that ' lateinisch ' is *lateinisch*, whatever being *lateinisch* is. ' Lateinisch ' could no more be *just* a non-self-epithet, without there being a specific, but as yet unmentioned, philological property which it lacked, than a person could be *just* christened, without being christened ' John ' or ' James ' or . . .

' Self-epithet ' and ' non-self-epithet ' do not stand for any of the specific philological properties which could be mentioned in the namely-riders for which they leave openings, any more than "christened ' . . . . ' " is a Christian name. Logicians' category-words are not among the words listed under those category-words. ' Fiction ' is not the name of one of the novels catalogued under the librarian's heading of ' Fiction '. ' Self-epithet ' and ' non-self-epithet ' are not philologists' epithets, but logicians' ways of dividing philologists' epithets into two artificial parcels, which, naturally, are not among the contents of those parcels.

In this connection I adopt and adapt an important argument of Mr. Lawrence.[1] ' English ' is a self-epithet, because ' English ' is an English word. But ' self-epithet ' does not *mean* . . . ' is an English word ' else " ' Deutsch ' is a self-epithet " would be false, instead of being true. Or, if " ' English ' is a self-epithet " could be paraphrased by " ' English ' is an English word ", then since German words are not English and ' Deutsch ' is a German word, " ' Deutsch ' is a non-self-epithet " would have to be true, when in fact it is false. Of itself, ' self-epithet ' tells us nothing about the tongues to which ' English ' and ' Deutsch ' belong, any more than about the tongue to which ' polysyllabic ' belongs, which is also a self-epithet. ' Either English or German or Lithuanian or a self-epithet " would be an absurd disjunction. So would any disjunction be absurd in which ordinary philological epithets were coupled by ' or ' with ' self-epithet ' or ' non-self-epithet '. ' Self-epithet ' and ' non-self-epithet ' convey no philological information about words. They are specially fabricated instruments for talking *en bloc* about the possession or non-possession by philological epithets of whatever may be the philological properties for which they stand. Such instruments are not among the philological epithets that they help logicians to discuss.

[1] cf. p. 38.

To put all this in the official terminology of 'heterological' and 'homological'. We can say "'obsolete' is heterological", because 'obsolete' has not gone out of fashion and 'obsolete' *means* 'gone out of fashion'. We can say "'polysyllabic' is homological", because 'polysyllabic' *is* a word of many syllables and *means* 'of many syllables'.

Now the words 'heterological' and 'homological' have and lack a number of ordinary philological properties. They are adjectives, polysyllabic, English (perhaps), cacophonous, aspirated and neologistic; they are *not* prepositions, slang, or of Latin origin. But what we are asked to decide is whether 'heterological' and 'homological' are themselves heterological or homological, i.e. whether among the philological properties which 'heterological' and 'homological' have and lack, they have or lack the philological properties of homologicality and heterologicality. But to ask this is to suppose that 'heterological' and 'homological' *do* stand for philological properties, i.e. that there could be words which were *just* heterological or *just* homological and not heterological or homological *because* lacking or possessing such and such ordinary philological properties. And this supposition is false. For to say that a word is heterological or homological is to refer to, without mentioning, some philological property (*not* heterologicality or homologicality) for which that word stands and which does or does not belong to that word. In using 'heterological' and 'homological' we are not mentioning word-properties, but referring to unmentioned word-properties. And references to unmentioned word-properties are not mentions of those or of extra word-properties, any more than references to unspecified diseases are themselves the specifications of those or of extra diseases. If unpacked, the assertion that 'heterological' is heterological would run :—"'Heterological' lacks the property for which it stands, namely that of lacking the property for which it stands, namely that of lacking the property ..." No property is ever mentioned, so the seeming reference to such a property is spurious.

This seeming paradox arises from treating certain umbrella-words, coined for the purpose of collecting epithets into two families as if they were themselves members of those families. To ask whether 'heterological' and 'homological' are heterological or homological is rather like asking whether Man is a tall man or a short man. We do not need stature-hierarchies to save us from deciding whether Man is a tall or a short man ; or language-hierarchies to save us from deciding whether ‘ hetero-logical ’ is heterological or homological. It is not even, save *per accidens*, a matter of minding our inverted commas but a matter of minding our grammar. Minding our inverted commas, in the required ways, *is* minding our grammar.

The same inattention to grammar is the source of such para-doxes as ‘ the Liar ’, ‘ the Class of Classes . . . ’ and ‘ Impredica-bility ’. When we ordinarily say “ That statement is false ”, what we say promises a namely-rider, e.g. “ . . . namely that to-day is Tuesday ”. When we say “ The current statement is false ” we are pretending *either* that no namely-rider is to be asked for *or* that the namely-rider is “ .. . . namely that the present statement is false ”. If no namely-rider is to be asked for, then “ The current statement ” does not refer to any statement. It is like saying “ He is asthmatic ” while disallowing the question “ Who? ” If, alterna-tively, it is pretended that there is indeed the namely-rider, “ . . . namely, that the current statement is false ”, the promise is met by an echo of that promise. If unpacked, our pretended assertion would run “ The current statement {namely, that the current statement [namely that the current statement (namely that the current statement . . . ”. The brackets are never closed ; no verb is ever reached ; no statement of which we can even ask whether it is true or false is ever adduced.

Certainly there exist genuine hierarchies. My Omnibus ‘ Short Stories of O. Henry ’ is not a short story by O. Henry ; nor is my batch of (five or six) Omnibus books a sixth or seventh Omnibus book. But “ I possess a batch of Omnibus books ” has the namely-rider “ . . . namely, ‘ The Short Stories of O. Henry ’, ‘ The Short Stories of W. W. Jacobs ’, etc., etc. ” ; just as “ I possess the Omnibus ‘ Short Stories of O. Henry ’ ” has the namely-rider “ . . . namely, “ The Third Ingredient ”, etc., etc.” Obviously, we could go on to talk of the set of batches of Omnibus books in the possession of Oxford professors, and so on in-definitely. But at no stage can the mention of a set, or batch, or Omnibus *be* the mention of what it carries a reference to, but is not a mention of, namely what would be mentioned in their promised namely-riders, if these were actually provided.

In ordinary life, we commonly have different words with which we make our different references, such as ' Centre Forward ', ' team ', ' Division ', ' League '. This prevents there being any linguistic temptation to talk as if a team might sprain its left ankle, or as if the League might win or lose the Cup. If we stick to one such word the whole way up the ladder (like ' class ' and ' number ') we are so tempted. Having failed to prevent such confusions arising, we have to seek remedies for them after they have arisen.

There are genuine hierarchies, so there exist (efficient and inefficient) ways of talking about them. But our (quite efficient) way of talking about footballers, teams, Divisions and Leagues is not itself to be described as a hierarchy of languages or ways of talking. Talking about the Berkshire League is not talking about talking about talking about the individuals who play, e.g. for a given village. Certainly the talk about the League is on a high rung of generality ; a whole échelon of namely-riders goes unstated. But no inverted commas are improvidently omitted. The relation of referring expressions to their namely-riders is not to be elucidated in terms of the relation of comments on expressions to the expressions on which they are comments. On the contrary, the relation of a comment to the expression on which it is a comment is (when it refers to this without citing it) just another case of the relation of a referring expression to the content of its namely-rider.

Many of the Paradoxes have to do with such things as statements about statements and epithets of epithets. So quotation-marks have to be employed. But the mishandling which generates the apparent antinomies consists not in mishandling quotation-marks but in treating referring expressions as fillings of their own namely-riders.

A team neither does nor does not sprain its left ankle. It is not one of its eleven possessors of left ankles, though a mention of the team carries a reference to these possessors of ankles. ' Heterological ' neither has nor lacks any philological property for which it stands. It is not one of the philological epithets to which it and its opposite number are special ways of referring.

# ON LIKENESS OF MEANING

## By Nelson Goodman

### FOREWORD

[Every so often someone steers me into a quiet corner and asks whether I am really in earnest about my paper " On Likeness of Meaning ". There is perhaps some ground for the feeling that I am rather less in earnest about it than are some of my opponents. The problems it deals with do not seem to me to have quite the paramount importance that is commonly attached to them these days. And while I am increasingly convinced that any reasonably adequate explication of the misbegotten notion of synonymy is likely to yield the conclusion that no two terms in a natural language are exactly synonymous, I care very little whether that particular conclusion stands or falls.

Nevertheless my paper is a serious and I hope not wholly unsuccessful attempt to deal with what I consider an interesting question. If we resolve to confine ourselves to terms and the things they refer to, renouncing concepts, intensions, senses, meanings, criteria in mind, and the like, how are we to do justice to the ostensible difference in meaning between two words, such as " centaur " and " unicorn ", that have the same extension?

Since my second paper was published, my attention has been called to two further points that may need clarifying.

First, if all we seek is some difference between " centaur " and " unicorn ", why not point simply to their shape or their spelling? The answer is that degrees of difference in shape or spelling do not correspond even approximately with what we ordinarily regard as degrees of difference in meaning. Comparison of the extensions of the various parallel compounds into which the two terms enter is much more pertinent. And when simple extensional agreement of two terms is not a strong enough relation for a given purpose, what is usually wanted in addition is extensional agreement of certain parallel compounds. The set of compounds for which this demand is made—and what in practice constitutes sufficient synonymy—varies from discourse to discourse.

The second objection is that precisely by entertaining expressions like " picture of a centaur ", where replacement of " centaur " by an extensionally identical term like "unicorn" will change the extension of the whole, I have already transgressed the boundaries of extensional language and thus forfeited my goal. But I did not at all want to propose keeping within the confines of extensionality so construed. Rather, I have tried to suggest how the recognition of certain contexts that are indeed non-extensional by this criterion nevertheless enables us to explain the difference in meaning between such words as "centaur" and "unicorn" without involving us in any of the more distressing aspects of intensionalism.    (1954 N.G.)]

### ON LIKENESS OF MEANING[1]

UNDER what circumstances do two names or predicates in an ordinary language have the same meaning? Many and widely varied answers have been given to this question, but they have one feature in common : they are all unsatisfactory.

One of the earliest answers is to the effect that two predicates have the same meaning if they stand for the same real Essence or Platonic Idea ; but this does not seem to help very much unless we know, as I am afraid we do not, how to find out whether two terms stand for the same Platonic Idea.

A more practical proposal is that two terms have the same meaning if they stand for the same mental idea or image ; or in other words, that two predicates differ in meaning only if we have a mental picture of something that satisfies one but not the other of the two. Thus even though in fact all and only pelicans have gallon-sized bills, we can easily imagine a sparrow or a kangaroo with a gallon-sized bill ; and thus the predicates "is a pelican" and "has a gallon-sized bill", even though satisfied by exactly the same actual individuals, do not have the same meaning. There are two familiar difficulties with this theory. In the first place, it is not very clear just what we can and what we cannot imagine. Can we imagine a man ten miles high or not? Can we imagine a tone we have never heard? To decide these cases is only to be confronted by new and harder ones. But the

---

[1] Read before the Fullerton Club, at Bryn Mawr College, Pennsylvania on May 14, 1949. I am deeply indebted to Drs. Morton G. White and W. V. Quine, with whom I have frequently and profitably discussed the problem dealt with in this paper.

second and more serious difficulty is that of predicates that pretty clearly have no corresponding image, such as " clever " or " supersonic ". Of course there is imagery associated with these terms ; but that is hardly to the point. There is imagery associated with nonsense syllables.

The image theory thus sometimes give way to the concept theory :—the theory that two predicates differ in meaning if and only if we can conceive of something that satisfies one but not the other. This enables us to transcend the narrow boundaries of imagination, but unfortunately it hardly seems to provide us with any criterion at all. Presumably we can conceive a five-dimensional body since we can define it although we cannot imagine it. But similarly we can define a square circle very easily (as a rectangle with four equal sides and such that every point of it is equidistant from a centre) or a five-sided triangle. If it be objected that because such definitions are not self-consistent they do not represent genuine concepts, I must point out that the claim of inconsistency here can be supported only by appeal to just such meaning-relationships as we are trying to explain. We cannot use them in trying to define them. If the objection is put rather in the form that although we can define a square circle there is no possible thing that can satisfy the definition, then it is clear that we are not judging possibility by conceivability but rather judging conceivability by possibility. Our criterion of sameness of meaning has thus changed : we are saying that two predicates have the same meaning if and only if there is nothing possible that satisfies one but not the other.

The possibility theory is somewhat ambiguous. Does it say that two terms differ in meaning only if it is possible that there is something that satisfies one but not the other? If that is all, then any two terms we know to have the same extension have the same meaning. If I know that Mr. Jones is in New York, I no longer regard it as possible that he is not in New York ; and similarly if I know that two predicates are satisfied by exactly the same individuals, the possibility is excluded that they are not satisfied by the same individuals. But this formulation seldom satisfies proponents of the possibility theory, who will cite cases of terms that, even though acknowledged to have the same extension, have different meanings. The thesis, they say, is rather that two predicates differ in meaning if there "might have been" something that satisfied one but not the other; or in other words, if there is a possible but non-actual entity that does satisfy one but not the other predicate. The notion of possible entities that are not and cannot be actual is a hard one for many of us to understand or accept. And even if we do accept it, how are we to decide when there is and when there is not such a possible that satisfies one but not the other of two terms? We have already seen that we get nowhere by appealing to conceivability as a test of possibility. Can we, then, determine whether two predicates " $P$ " and " $Q$ " apply to the same possibles by asking whether the predicate " is a P or a Q but not both " is self-consistent? This is hardly helpful; for so long as " $P$ " and " $Q$ " are different predicates the compound predicate is logically self-consistent, and we have no ready means for determining whether it is otherwise self-consistent. Indeed the latter question amounts to the very question whether " $P$ " and " $Q$ " have the same meaning. And since we began by asking how to determine when two predicates have the same meaning, we are back where we started.

All these difficulties suggest that we might try the very different and radical theory that two predicates have the same meaning if and only if they apply to exactly the same things—or in other words, have the same extension. This thesis has been attacked more often than it has been advanced; but some of the familiar arguments against it seem to me worthless. An example is the absurd argument that the extension of a term is different at different times and that therefore by this thesis two terms may be synonymous at one time and not at another. The extension of a predicate consists, of course, of everything past, present, and future to which the term applies; neither the making or the eating of cakes changes the extension of the term " cake ".

Certain other similar arguments apply not against the thesis that two terms have the same meaning if they have the same extension, but against the different thesis—that does not concern us here—that the extension of a term is its meaning. For example, against the latter thesis, one may argue as follows :—before we can investigate whether a given predicate " $P$ " applies to a given thing $a$ we must know what " $P$ " means, and if the meaning of

"P" is its extension we must know the extension of "P"—
and therefore must know whether it applies to a—before we can
set about finding out whether "P" applies to a. But this
argument does not apply against the weaker thesis that two predicates have the same meaning if they have the same extension; for
obviously we may decide by induction, conjecture, or other
means that two predicates have the same extension without
knowing exactly all the things they apply to.

And yet, while many of the apparent objections seem to me
unsound, I think we cannot maintain the unqualified thesis that
two predicates have the same meaning if they have the same
extension. There are certain clear cases where two words that
have the same extension do not have the same meaning. "Centaur" and "unicorn", for example, since neither applies to
anything, have the same (null) extension; yet surely they differ
in meaning. I do not mean to suggest that identity of extension
with difference of meaning occurs only where the extension is
null, but such cases are enough and are the most striking.

Now the precise way in which the proposed thesis failed
must be particularly noted. Obviously if two terms have the
same meaning they have the same extension; the trouble is
that two terms may have the same extension and yet not have the
same meaning. Extensional identity is a necessary but not a
sufficient condition for sameness of meaning. In other words,
difference of extension does not draw distinctions as fine as those
drawn by difference of meaning.

Does this mean, then, that we must return to the dismal
search through Never-Never land for some ghostly entities
called "meanings" that are distinct from and lie between words
and their extensions? I don't think so. Despite the obvious
inadequacy of the thesis we have been considering, I think that
difference in meaning between any two terms can be fully
accounted for without introducing anything beyond terms and
their extensions. For while it is clear that difference in meaning
of two terms "P" and "Q" is not always accompanied by
difference in extension, I think it is always accompanied by
difference in the extension of certain terms other than "P" and
"Q". Let me explain:

Since there are no centaurs or unicorns, all unicorns are

centaurs and all centaurs are unicorns. Furthermore, all uncles of centaurs are uncles of unicorns ; and all feet of unicorns are feet of centaurs. How far can we generalize on this? Leaving aside absurd or ungrammatical variations, we must exclude the analogues in terms of " thoughts ", or " concepts " or even " meaning " itself ; for there is no guarantee that thoughts of centaurs are thoughts of unicorns. This is usually attributed to the mental reference or the vagueness of such terms. We have in logic the theorem that if all $\alpha$'s are $\beta$'s, then all the things that bear the relation P to an $\alpha$ are things that bear the relation P to a $\beta$ (see *Principia Mathematica*, 37.2) ; and it might naturally be supposed that this guarantees the truth of sentences like those we have been considering about centaurs and unicorns, provided the phrases involved apply only to physical objects if to anything. But actually this is not the case ; for *pictures*—i.e. paintings, drawings, prints, statues—are physical objects, yet not all pictures of centaurs are pictures of unicorns, nor are all pictures of unicorns pictures of centaurs. At first sight this seems to violate the cited theorem of logic. Actually, what it shows is that "picture of " is not always a relation-term like " foot of " or " uncle of ". If $x$ is a foot of centaur, then $x$ bears the relation " foot of " to some $y$ that is a centaur. Thus if there is any foot of a centaur or any uncle of a centaur then there is a centaur. But in contrast, if there is—as indeed there is —something that is a picture of a centaur, we cannot infer that there is some centaur—as there certainly is not. A phrase like " picture of a centaur " is a single predicate, and the fact that it applies to one or many things plainly does not enable us to conclude that there are objects that these things are pictures of. To avoid the temptation to make such unjustified inferences, perhaps we had better speak during the rest of our discussion not of " pictures of " centaurs or unicorns but rather of centaur-pictures " and " unicorn-pictures," etc.

A centaur-picture differs from a unicorn-picture not by virtue of its resemblance to a centaur and lack of resemblance to a unicorn ; for there are neither unicorns nor centaurs. " Centaur-picture " and " unicorn-picture " merely apply to different objects just as " chair " and " desk " apply to different objects, and we need no more ask why in the one case than in the other. The simple fact is that although " centaur " and "unicorn" apply to nothing and so have the same extension, the term "centaur-picture" applies to many things and the term "unicorn-picture" applies to many others.

Now the important point here is this : Although two words have the same extension, certain predicates composed by making identical additions to these two words may have different extensions. It is then perhaps the case that for every two words that differ in meaning either their extensions or the extensions of some corresponding compounds of them are different. If so, difference in meaning among extensionally identical predicates can be explained as difference in the extensions of certain other predicates. Or, if we call the extension of a predicate by itself its *primary* extension, and the extension of any of its compounds a *secondary* extension, the thesis is formulated as follows : two terms have the same meaning if and only if they have the same primary and secondary extensions. Let us, in order to avoid entanglement with such terms as " thought of . . . ", " concept of . . . ", " attribute of . . . ", and " meaning of . . . ", exclude from consideration all predicates that apply to anything but physical things, classes of these, classes of classes of these, etc. If the thesis is tenable, we have answered our question by stating, without reference to anything other than terms and the things to which they apply, the circumstances under which two terms have the same meaning.

This explanation takes care of well-known cases discussed in the literature. For instance, Frege has used the terms " (is the) Morningstar " and " (is the) Eveningstar " as examples of two predicates that have the same extension—since they apply to the same one thing—but obviously differ in meaning. This difference in meaning is readily explained according to our present thesis, since the two terms differ in their secondary extensions. There are, for example, Morningstar-pictures that are not Eveningstar-pictures —and also, indeed, Eveningstar-pictures that are not Morningstar-pictures.

But is our thesis satisfactory in general? Perhaps the first question that arises is whether it takes care of cases where we have two terms " $P$ " and " $Q$ " such that there are no $P$-pictures or $Q$-pictures—say where " $P$ " and " $Q$ " are predicates applying to odors or electric charges. These present no difficulty ; for the secondary extensions of a predicate " $Q$ " consist not merely

of the extension of " $Q$-picture " but also of the extensions of
" $Q$-diagram ", " $Q$-symbol " and any number of other such
compound terms. Indeed *actual word-inscriptions* are as genuine
physical objects as anything else ; and so if there is such an
actual physical inscription that is a $P$-description and is not a
$Q$-description, or vice-versa, then " $P$ " and " $Q$ " differ in their
secondary extensions and thus in meaning.

This makes it look more and more as if every difference in
meaning will be reflected by a difference in primary or secondary
extension. Indeed, I think we can now show this to be true.
For, given any two predicates whatsoever, say " $P$ " and " $Q$ ",
do we not have in an inscription of the phrase " a $P$ that is not
a $Q$ " something that is a $P$-description and not a $Q$-description?
Clearly the predicate " centaur-description " applies while the
predicate " unicorn-description " does not apply to an inscription
of " a centaur that is not a unicorn ". Likewise, the predicate
" acrid-odor-description " applies while the predicate " pungent-
odor-description " does not apply to an inscription of " a pungent
odor that is not an acrid odor " ; and thus the two predicates
" pungent-odor " and " acrid-odor "—whatever may be the
relationship of their primary extensions—differ in secondary
extension and thus in meaning. Again " triangle " and " trilateral " differ in meaning because " triangle that is not trilateral " is a triangle-description but not a trilateral-description.
We do not, however, get the absurd result that " triangle " differs
in meaning from " triangle " ; for of course it is not the case that
" triangle that is not a triangle " is and is not a triangle-description.

But now see how far we have come. If difference of meaning
is explained in the way I have proposed, then *no two different words
have the same meaning.* We have assuredly answered the complaint
that in terms of extensions alone we cannot draw fine enough
distinctions. Here we get distinctions that are as fine as anyone
could ask. But now we risk the opposite complaint : for can
we accept the conclusion that a word has the same meaning as
no word other than itself?

Before we decide that we cannot tolerate this conclusion, let
me note that in the course of developing our criterion we have
incidentally shown that there are no two predicates such that they
can be replaced by the other in every sentence without changing

the truth-value, *even if we exclude the so-called intensional contexts in which such words as* " necessary ", " possible ", " attribute of ", or " thought of " occur. Thus if we maintain that two different words have the same meaning, their lack of interreplaceability in some context other than these can immediately be offered as evidence that the words do not have the same meaning. It seems apparent, therefore, that the demands we commonly make upon a criterion of sameness of meaning can be satisfied only if we recognize that no two different predicates ever have the same meaning.

Theoretically, then, we shall do better never to say that two predicates have the same meaning but rather that they have a greater or lesser degree, or one or another kind, of *likeness* of meaning. In ordinary speech when we say that two terms have the same meaning, we usually indicate only that their kind and degree of likeness of meaning is sufficient for the purposes of the immediate discourse. This is quite harmless. But we must remember that the requirements vary greatly from discourse to discourse ; often it is enough if two terms have the same primary extension ; in other cases, identity in certain secondary extensions or others is also required. If we overlook this variation and seek a fixed criterion of sameness of meaning that will at once conform to these differing usages and satisfy our theoretical demands, we are doomed to perpetual confusion.

Just a few further words to suggest a bearing this paper has on another question. It is sometimes said that a sentence like "All *A's* are *B's* " is *analytic* if the meaning of *B* is contained in that of *A*. Our investigation has shown not only that two different predicates like "*A* " and " *B* " never have quite the same meaning ; but further that, so to speak, neither is meaning-included in the other ; for there is an *A*-description that is not a *B*-description, *and* a *B*-description that is not an *A*-description. Thus, at least according to the suggested interpretation of " analytic ", no non-repetitive statement will be analytic. The most we can say is that it is more, or less, nearly analytic. This will be enough to convince many of us that likewise a non-repetitive statement is never absolutely necessary, but only more or less nearly so.

# ON SOME DIFFERENCES ABOUT MEANING

## By NELSON GOODMAN

IN the light of many discussions of my paper " On Likeness of Meaning " I want to clarify and amplify some of its main points, then (in Section II) answer briefly certain specific comments, and finally (in Section III) suggest a minor but perhaps welcome amendment.[1]

## I

The hopeless confusion of attempts to define synonymy in terms of images, concepts, possibilities, etc. leads us to seek a definition solely in terms of actual, even of physical, objects. Yet we must face the fact that some clearly non-synonymous names or predicates apply to exactly the same objects ; the most striking but not the only examples are those where, as in the case of " centaur " and " unicorn ", neither term applies to anything.

One main point of my earlier paper is that difference in meaning even between such terms can be explained without reference to anything but physical objects. Pictures, for example, are physical objects and yet some (indeed most) pictures of centaurs are not pictures of unicorns. In other words, while " centaur " and " unicorn " apply to exactly the same objects, " picture of a centaur " and " picture of a unicorn " do not by any means apply to exactly the same objects. This suggests that we should take into account not only what is denoted by a given term itself but also what is denoted by compounds containing that term (otherwise than in quotation marks). My proposal is that two terms are synonymous if and only if

(a) they apply to exactly the same objects, and

(b) each compound term constructed by combining certain words with either of the terms in question applies to exactly the same objects as the compound term constructed by combining

---

[1] Concerning two articles published since the first appearance of the present paper, one by Lester Meckler in *Analysis*, vol. 14 (1954), pp. 68–78, and one by David Shwayder in *Philosophical Studies*, vol. 5, (1954), pp. 1–5. I can say only that these writers have, in different ways, seriously misunderstood me.

the same words in the same way with the other of the terms in question. .

This criterion recommends itself by accounting, without reference to anything but physical objects, for differences in meaning between coextensive terms. But if we can picture these differences that are not exemplified in actuality, just where does the power of pictorial differentiation end? The limits of realistic or representational depiction may seem rather narrow ; but as a matter of fact there is no purely representational depiction. Conventionalization to some degree is always present, and increases rather gradually from the realistic painting through the sketch, the semi-abstract picture and the ideographic sign to the word in ordinary language. The string of inscriptions that we call a description is in effect merely a highly conventionalized picture. But description, or word-picturing, is so delicate and potent an instrument that there is virtually no limit on the distinctions it can make. The difference between a man twenty feet tall and a man twenty and one one-hundredth feet tall is hard to paint but easy to state. Indeed, we can even find triangle descriptions that are not trilateral descriptions. A couple of rather clear examples are :

(i) " plane figure of three angles and four sides "
(ii) " triangle that is not a trilateral."

That these apply to nothing doesn't matter ; centaur descriptions likewise apply to nothing. And, even if we allow ourselves to speak of possibility for the moment, it doesn't matter that these descriptions apply to nothing possible. All that matters is that despite the non-existence and even impossibility of triangles that are not trilaterals we have actually before us in (i) and (ii) *descriptions* of such triangles. " Triangle description ", then, applies to some strings of inscriptions that " trilateral description " does not. Thus " triangle " and " trilateral " differ in at least one of their corresponding secondary extensions, and accordingly differ in meaning by our criterion. By similar argument, every two terms[1] will differ in meaning.

Now of course I cannot define descriptions precisely any

---

[1] That is, every two names or predicates in a natural language like English. Restricted artificial languages can easily be so constructed that some terms will have the same meaning as others by this criterion.

more than I can define pictures precisely. Exact and inclusive definition of pictures of centaurs would be no less difficult than exact and inclusive definition of descriptions of triangles. But the most that is required here is that there be an appreciable number of clear cases, and that anomalous and paradoxical cases can be dealt with by reasonable rules. In the next section, I shall discuss some questions that have been raised concerning the applications of " triangle description " ; but there are other compound terms, having more easily specifiable ranges of application, that may equally well be used in carrying through the argument of the preceding paragraph. For example, " literal English triangle word " may be taken as applying just to those inscriptions which are tokens of " triangle ",[1] and " literal English trilateral word " as applying just to tokens of " trilateral ". Since these corresponding compounds have different extensions, the terms " triangle " and " trilateral "—and, by similar argument, every two terms—differ in meaning.

Now I am well aware that various plausible grounds for ruling out these examples need to be considered (see Section II) ; but proving that every two terms differ in meaning is no part of my primary goal. The paramount problem is to deal with comparisons of meaning without reference to intensions, attitudes, or modalities. The proposed criterion in terms of primary and secondary extensions meets this requirement and yet successfully explains evident differences in meaning even between coextensive terms like " centaur " and " unicorn ". In view of these virtues, I am willing to accept the apparent consequence that no two terms are synonymous. Anyone who shows that this conclusion does not follow at all, or that it can be precluded by suitable provisos, will simply render my criterion more generally acceptable. But I hold that the criterion is not, anyhow, disqualified by the result that no two terms are absolutely synonymous ; for this result seems to me unfamiliar rather than intolerable. The extreme difficulty of finding in practice any two terms that surely have exactly the same meaning opens the way to aceptance of the view that there are no absolute synonyms but only terms that have a greater or lesser degree, or one or another kind, of likeness of meaning.

[1] Whereas " literal English ' triangle ' term " applies to tokens of " ' triangle ' "

## II

Mr. Rudner is correct in saying[1] that I should want any final statement of my views to be formulated in terms of a strict nominalism that regards words as actual inscriptions or events, some of which are said to be *replicas*[2] of one another rather than ' tokens ' of a common type. But I now think that Mr. Rudner is wrong and Mrs. Robbins[3] right about the consequences of such a restatement. What follows is not that every two word-events differ in meaning but only that every two word-events that are not replicas of each other differ in meaning.

The " wild results " that Mr. Rollins cites[4] are therefore not forthcoming. His chief objection, however, is that a definition of synonymy that makes every two terms differ in meaning departs too far from ordinary usage. *Prima facie* this is reasonable enough ; but the departure from ordinary usage is less drastic and better motivated than at first appears. Suppose we have a pile of logs, some of them being for all practical purposes of the same length as others. Will Mr. Rollins reject a process of measurement that gives the result that no two of these logs are of exactly the same length? A certain conformity to ordinary usage is indeed demanded of any definition ; but even where the usage is much clearer and more constant than in the case of meaning, what is commonly spoken of as sameness may turn out, according to a perfectly good definition, to be only approximate sameness.[5] And resistance to the conclusion that no two terms are exactly alike in meaning ought to be softened considerably by the recognition that some terms like " triangle " and " trilateral " are, through being interreplaceable in most compounds, very much alike in meaning.

Thus I think the second of Mr. Price's[6] objections can be answered by saying that dictionary definitions are useful because

[1] "A Note on Likeness of Meaning," *Analysis*, vol. 10 (1950), pp. 115–118.

[2] See my *Structure of Appearance* (published in England by the Oxford University Press, 1951), p. 290.

[3] " On Synonymy of Word-events," *Analysis*, vol. 12 (1952), pp. 98–100.

[4] " The Philosophical Denial of Sameness of Meaning," *Analysis*, vol. 11 (1950), pp. 38–45.

[5] Mr. Wienpahl, I take it, in " More about the Denial of Sameness of Meaning " —*Analysis*, vol. 12 (1951), p. 19–23—is making this same general point that clarification as well as conformity is required of a definition.

[6] "A Note on Likeness of Meaning," *Analysis*, vol. 11 (1950), pp. 18–19.

they join expressions that are much alike in meaning—although the degree of likeness varies considerably. Mr. Price's first objection I cannot follow. He says that " glub " and " gloob " differ in meaning by my criterion because " glub that is not a gloob " will be a glub description but not a gloob description. But I am dealing with names or predicates in a language. When nonsense syllables are incorporated like words in a phrase, the phrase itself is nonsense. Or in other words, if " glub " is not in the language then neither is " glub description ".

Mr. Thomson says[1] that two words are synonymous because they have the senses they have. This is much like saying that a city is north of another because of the locations they have ; and it seems to me misleading and irrelevant. It obscures the fact that cities in quite other places are such that one is north of the other ; and it appears to deny that we can define the predicate " is north of " in an appropriate and useful way without reference to the location of any particular city. Mr. Thomson seems to be objecting to all definition of general terms rather than pointing to any special difficulty about synonymy. Nor can I accept Mr. Thomson's argument that if I am willing to use " centaur picture " without being able to define it precisely, I should be equally willing to use " Platonic Idea of a centaur ". The difference is that I do know some things to which the term " centaur picture' ' clearly applies and I don't know anything to which the term " Platonic Idea of a centaur " applies. I should be glad to have a full explication of " picture " in order to settle borderline cases ; but I need an explanation of " Platonic Idea " before I can apply it at all.

Many questions have been raised about what constitutes a description.[2] No complete definition is needed. If the animal before us is clearly a polar bear, the question whether there are polar bears on our island is settled even though we neither know how to define " polar bear " nor are sure whether it applies to certain other animals. To show that two secondary extensions

[1] " Some Remarks on Synonymy," *Analysis*, vol. 12 (1952), pp. 73–76.

[2] For example, by Mr. Church in the *Journal of Symbolic Logic*, vol. XV (1950), pp. 150–151. The various suggestions that Mr. Smullyan despatches so easily in " φ-Symbols "—*Analysis*, vol. II (1951), pp. 69–72—are too far afield to have called for consideration in the first place. As my example of centaur pictures and unicorn pictures was designed to show, we cannot define " P-picture " or " P-description " solely in terms of what " P " applies to.

differ we need only a case in point. Now if we remember that we can perfectly well describe what is not actual or even possible, then "isosceles triangle", "triangle with angles totalling 110 degrees", and "triangle that is not a trilateral" are all triangle descriptions according to ordinary usage. In other cases, like that of "triangle that is not a triangle", direct appeal to ordinary usage may yield no firm decision. Then we must formulate rules that fit ordinary usage where it is clear and that can be projected to decide these doubtful cases. There is no one correct way of doing this, but a reasonable rule covering the present question runs as follows : Any phrase of the form "—that is . . . " is both a—description and a . . . . description ; and a not-a-soandso description is not a soandso description unless required to be by the first clause of this rule. Thus "triangle that is not a triangle" is both a triangle description and a not-a-triangle description, while "trilateral that is not a triangle" is a trilateral description and is not a triangle description. As explained in Section I, we may avoid all these complications about descriptions by choosing certain other compounds as our examples.

Mr. Clarke argues[1] that a compound such as "triangle description" ought to be ruled out on the ground that it implicitly mentions the word "triangle" in much the same way that "John is so-called . . ." implicitly mentions the word "John". A phrase implicitly mentions a term, in his view, if the expansion of the phrase explicitly mentions it. He would, of course, regard my example of "literal English triangle word" as even more obviously open to this criticism. Turning Mr. Clarke's own argument against him, one might well contend that the expansion of "the expansion of" explicitly refers to synonymy and that his argument thus begs the whole question. But unlike Mr. Clarke, I am unwilling to rest any argument on the notion of *the expansion of* a phrase. Let us grant—overlooking the point about implicit reference to synonymy—that any given phrase can, so to speak, ' be rewritten ' in various longer ways. Still, in the absence of any formal systematization, any of these longer phrases qualifies as well as any other as *an* expansion of the phrase in question. Now does Mr. Clarke exclude compounds having some expansion

[1] "Reflections on Likeness of Meaning," *Philosophical Studies*, vol. III (1952), pp. 9–13.

that mentions the term in question? Then he excludes all compounds ; for even " white boat " can be rewritten " white thing to which ' boat ' applies ". Or does he exclude, rather, compounds of which every expansion applies to expressions containing the term in question? Then, since an expansion must obviously apply to just what the original compound applies to, he could have dispensed with all talk of expansions and simply ruled out compounds that apply to such expressions. Even so, the exclusion is ineffectual ; for if it bars " triangle description " and " literal English triangle word ", it does not bar " non-English triangle description " or " literal German triangle word ", which serve the same purpose. Stronger prohibitions that readily suggest themselves likewise prove to be inadequate.

### III

The reader may still feel that the compounds cited in deriving the conclusion that every two terms differ in meaning are somehow exceptional and trivial, and that a feasible way of ruling them out must eventually be found. This feeling I can understand ; when a single form of compound has a different extension for every term, the fact that it has different extensions for two given terms is of no striking or special interest. Let us, then, simply exclude every compound for which the corresponding compounds of every two terms have differing extensions. We do not, indeed, thereby insure ourselves against the result that no two terms are synonymous, since for each two terms we may well be able to find corresponding compounds having different extensions. But we honour the feeling or principle that the interesting differences between two terms are just those which are not shared by every two terms. The net change effected is not great, amounting merely to this : instead of saying that every two terms differ in meaning but that some may not differ in interesting ways, we say that two terms differ in meaning only if they differ in certain interesting or peculiar ways. While it may be true that every two terms differ in meaning in some interesting way, this way of putting the matter may nevertheless, alleviate some discomfort.

## NEGATIVE TERMS

### By Morris Lazerowitz

It is not uncommon for philosophers to take scornful attitudes
to each other's views and to dismiss them as ridiculous and an
outrage to our intelligence. Indeed, one is tempted to think
that an important *technique of refutation* in philosophy is scorn
and ridicule, a technique, that is to say, of intellectual intimida-
tion. But it need hardly be remarked, or perhaps it *does* need
pointing out, that such an emotive procedure leads to no insight
into the theories dismissed. For it has to be realized that of all
the disciplines which make use of proofs and refutations, philosophy stands alone in having no solidly established results.

In the present paper I wish mainly to consider a view which
has been dismissed by many philosophers as scandalous nonsense
and as being based on the grossest of mistakes. My purpose is
to examine this view soberly and dispassionately and try to see
what it comes to and also to discover whether it is based on the
gross mistake some people think it is based on. The view I
propose to examine has been expressed in sentences like the
following : "Anxiety reveals the nothing "; "We know the
nothing " ; "The nothing exists ".

What is to be made of these sentences ; how are we to interpret them? And what sort of mistake, if any, is a person making
who utters them with the assured air of stating propositions
about the truth of which there can be no doubt? The sentences
are strikingly unusual because, for one thing, they use the word
" nothing " in a grammatically strange way. In ordinary speech
" nothing " is not prefaced with the definite article ; it is not
grammatical English to speak of "the nothing ". And for
another thing, the word "nothing", quite apart from the
strangeness of its being combined with the definite article in the
sentences, is being used in a queer way that eludes our understanding. It is hard for us to see what anyone, for example, the
sophist Gorgias, wishes to convey with the words "Nothing
exists ".[1] Some philosophers have voiced the complaint that
the sentence "The nothing exists " does not have a translation

[1] See John Burnet, *Greek Philosophy, Pt. I, Thales to Plato*, p. 120.

into the common vernacular and have, on the basis of this fact, proceeded to the position that the sentence is literally without sense. Thus, the sentence, if it does have sense, presents us with two difficulties which stand in the way of our interpreting it : (1) the use of " nothing " with the definite article, " the nothing " ; and (2) its use with " exists ", " Nothing exists ". And before trying to interpret its use in " The nothing exists " it will be helpful to divide our problem and first attempt to arrive at an understanding of what a philosopher is saying who declares that " Nothing exists ".

Imagine someone saying in earnest : "At this moment, for instance, I see nothing on the small table next to the armchair in my study, and I also see nobody in my armchair. I *see* nothing and nobody, so of course they exist. Unquestionably others too have also seen nothing and nobody in various places, so other people also know perfectly well that nothing and nobody exist. Many people, of course, deny that nothing and nobody exist, but it is not easy to understand the psychology of such sceptics." Said in all seriousness by a person, these words produce a mystifying effect. For he uses language which is like the language of someone who is talking about extremely refined and subtle objects, ghost-like entities which those of us with less refined perception or those of us who lack the necessary rapport with the occult are not privileged to see.

His words suggest the occult ; but, despite his talk, reason cannot permit its being supposed that he is seeing or claiming to see a very refined and subtle object. A person who truly says that he sees nothing on the table and nobody in the armchair does not see an object on the table nor does he see anybody in the chair. When two people inspect the same table and one declares that he sees nothing on it while the other declares that he does not see anything on it, it is not the case that one sees something which the other somehow fails to see : what is seen is the same for both. Only as a Lewis Carroll joke should we say to the second person, " Rub your eyes and look harder ". Nor can it be supposed that the first person is suffering from some sort of hallucination, is stating the existence of something which he imagines he sees. His words do not, nor are they intended to, express an empirical belief about the existence of something he thinks he sees, a belief which could elicit from us the comment, " He thinks he sees nothing, but he isn't really seeing it ". His mistake, if he is making one, is not a perceptual mistake with regard to a state of affairs. Apart from his words, his behaviour, it is to be noted, is in no way different from that of the person who says he does not see anything on the table. It is not like that of a person who is suffering from a hallucination. In the present context, the assertion, that nothing exists quite plainly cannot be construed as an utterance which is intended to state an empirical fact about the existence of something. It cannot be construed as affirming the existence of a kind of thing nor can it be construed as denying the existence of everything—as denying, *e.g.*, that the table on which there is nothing exists. Philosophers are using the sentence to do a different kind of work.

More natural, perhaps, than the idea that the statement makes an empirical claim about a state of affairs is the idea that it is an instance of the improper use of language or that it misdescribes the use of an ordinary word : more specifically, that the statement either uses the word " nothing " in an improper, senseless way or is a misdescription of the use of the word. The latter idea is more natural, though by no means the more important one to examine. The notion that metaphysical propositions are empirical is too easily dismissed now-a-days, with the result that what is dismissed without sufficient insight remains to trouble and make ambiguous the reasoning of philosophers who dismiss it. However that may be, the usual charge levelled against what we may call the Metaphysician of the Reality of Nothing is that he has committed the gross blunder of thinking that because " nothing " is a substantive word it is the name of an object.

It is quite possible, to be sure, for a person to believe that the word " nothing " is the name of a thing. Imagine a newcomer to the English language being taught nouns like " house ", " moon ", " Jones ", and how to use them in simple sentences. Along with these words, which are classified for him as substantives under parts of speech, he is told that " nothing " is a noun but is not taught its use. It could easily happen in such a case that he would think that " nothing ", like the other substantives he had been taught, is the name, either general or proper, of a thing. We can imagine, further, the sort of trick that the two rascally tailors in the fairy tale played on the gullible king. His teachers not only classify " nothing " as a substantive, they also utter such sentences as " Nothing is next to the chair ", " I see that nothing is now on the table ", and behave as if they were talking about something. They carry their prank so far as to act amazedly and become somewhat condescending when he conveys to them that he does not see anything. Finally, to cover his embarrassment over his supposed optical inferiority, he starts talking and behaving like his teachers. Such a person would have a false notion about the actual use of " nothing ".

The case of the metaphysician who gives the impression of believing that " nothing " is the name of a thing is entirely different. He does not lack *complete* information about the use of the word nor has he had a verbal prank played on him. He was taught not only its grammatical classification but also its actual use and knows it perfectly well. And if, in spite of this, he nevertheless does in fact believe that it is the name of a thing, then he is indeed *grossly* mistaken. But this precisely is the trouble with the idea that he has a mistaken belief about the ordinary use of the word : the mistake is *too gross* for him to have made it. If it is hard for us to conceive of anyone who has been properly trained in the use of words like " chair " and " coat " and uses them correctly every day as well as responds appropriately to their use by others *believing* that the words are *not* names of articles of furniture and clothing, it should, if we stop to think of it, be equally hard to think of anyone who has been properly trained in the correct use of " nothing " actually believing that it is the name of an object. It should be hard to think this of anyone, despite his *philosophical talk*, which, it has to be admitted, lends superficial plausibility to the charge. To be sure, it is psychologically possible to have a belief which conflicts with what we know perfectly well; when the *need* to believe is great enough, we believe, in spite of what we know. But it would be foolish to suppose that a metaphysician's need to believe that " nothing " is the name of an entity is so great as to blind him completely to the crudity of his blunder, and so great, moreover, as to prevent his seeing his blunder when it is pointed out to him. For it is completely safe to bet that if it were patiently explained to him

that the word is not used in ordinary language as a name he would
be quite unmoved. For some mysterious reason, he does not
accept ordinary usage as in any way showing the incorrectness or
impropriety of his *philosophical* sentences, though he does accept
common usage as a corrective to any linguistic mistakes he may
make in *non-philosophical* conversations. It is this mystifyingly
stubborn refusal to accept correction that needs to be explained
and remains unexplained on the view that he has made a linguistic
blunder.

It may be said that a philosophical belief is entirely different
from an ordinary, everyday belief. Philosophical beliefs are one
thing and ordinary beliefs and doubts are quite a different thing,
it may be-contended, and we must not expect from the former
what we expect from the latter. A philosopher once gave me an
argument which he said was a conclusive refutation of a current
view about the nature of ethical statements. I asked him whether
the most important advocate of this view, a philosopher with
whom he had discussed the view on a number of occasions,
would accept his refutation and give up his view, and was told
in a voice which reprimanded me for being so naive, " No, of
course not ". But our not expecting from a philosophical belief
and argument what we expect from an ordinary belief is in need
of explanation, and it is not explained one bit by saying that
philosophical propositions are believed *philosophically*. To call
a belief " philosophical " is only to give a name to something we
do not understand. What we want to understand is the supposedly
mistaken belief that " nothing " is the name of an object ; and
it is of no help to say that the person who believes it cannot see
his mistake because his belief is philosophical and quite different
from the belief a well-known philosopher humorously confessed
he had until recently, that " longitude " was pronounced with a
hard " g ". It is no help whatever to distinguish between a
stranger to the English language who has a wrong ordinary
belief about the use of a word and the metaphysician, by saying
that the latter's wrong belief is philosophical.

It seems clear, if we think soberly and with detachment on
the subject, that it is unplausible to suppose a philosopher
believes that " nothing " is commonly used as the name of an
entity, while at the same time not denying that he knows its

actual use. The impulse to *refute* plays a considerable part in the barrier we erect against our seeing this and against our understanding the nature of the theories we " refute ". But over-easy Sir Lanceloting is little more than Don Quixote charging a windmill ; it slays no metaphysical ogres.

Philosophers who place no weight on the consideration that it is unplausible to suppose that a metaphysician can continue to believe, in the face of criticism, that " nothing " is the name of an object give two main reasons for not thinking the hypothesis unplausible. For one thing, it is maintained that it is quite possible to know how to *use* a word correctly and nevertheless misdescribe its use. And for another thing, it is maintained that the force of an argument for a philosophical view can be so persuasive as to convince a philosopher of the truth of his view, despite his knowing on other grounds that it is false, that he can be *swept away* by his argument into holding his view. Let us examine these reasons separately.

The point that knowing how to use a term correctly is different from knowing how to *explain* its use, so that it is possible for a person to misdescribe its use while being able to use it perfectly well, is not to be disputed. This point reminds us of the distinction G. E. Moore has made between knowing the meaning of a word and knowing the analysis of its meaning. Just as a person may be able to walk unerringly from Victoria Station to Picadilly Circus but misdescribe the route to others, or even be at a loss altogether to describe it, so it is possible for us to be able to use a word properly but, nevertheless, give a wrong explanation of its use. In order to be able to use words like " nothing " and " yesterday " it is not necessary to be able to describe or explain *in other words* their use. But anyone who is able to use a word correctly is able to *show* how it is used ; for all that is required to show how a word is used is to *use* it.

And not only this. A person who knows the use of a word but misdescribes it will *give up* his description if his attention is called to an instance of actual usage with which his description does not square. If, for example, someone who knows how to use " chair " tells us that it *means* any object which is used by people to sit on, and is really trying to explain in other words what the word means, then, if it is pointed out to him that people sometimes sit on tables, tree stumps, and even floors, and that tables, tree strumps, and floors are not chairs, he will admit that his explanation is wrong and give it up. He will admit it is wrong, just as a person who misdescribes the way to Piccadilly Circus will admit his directions are wrong if we take him with us and, following his directions, end up in Chelsea. But the case is different with the metaphysician : facing him with evidence of actual usage does not make him give up his apparently false description. The distinction between use of a word and description of its use explains how it is possible to have mistaken ideas about words we know how to use perfectly well, but it does not explain why, in the case of a philosophical misdescription of a word, bringing instances of actual usage to bear against the misdescription does not result in its being given up. It does not explain the remarkable difference between a metaphysical mistake and an ordinary linguistic error. It throws no light on the question as to why a metaphysician who believes that " nothing " is the name of a thing fails to give up his belief when it is pointed out to him that, unlike saying that a book is on the table, saying that nothing is on the table is the same as saying there is not anything on the table.

It can be seen that the second reason, namely, that a metaphysician is able to hold his view despite what he knows because he is convinced by the argument which backs it also fails to clear up this mystery. There is no question but that, quite in general, we are frequently led to hold false views by fallacious arguments which seem sound to us. But is it as plain as anything can be that no reasoning, regardless of how sound it may seem, can stand up against known fact, and that no argument, however impeccable it may seem, can prevent us from rejecting a proposition which we know to be false. And it is just as plain, with regard to an ordinary case of someone having been misled by an argument into accepting a false proposition, that if he is presented with undeniable fact which goes against the proposition, he will accept the fact and reject the proposition and its proof. He would not insist in the face of fact that the argument *is* sound and that therefore the proposition it backs *is* true. But precisely the opposite happens time and again in metaphysics. Calling a metaphysician's attention to actual usage, to instances of the way he uses an expression and to the way he responds to its use by other people in everyday discourse, does not discourage him about the validity of his argument and the truth of his view. Instead of discarding his argument as certainly containing a fallacy, even though he cannot discover the fallacy, he resists the idea that the facts conclusively show that the argument must be fallacious. It is this resistance against admitting that the facts invalidate the argument and show his proposition to be false that is not accounted for by those who maintain that he holds his view because he is taken in by its demonstration. An argument can sometimes beguile us into accepting a proposition which we should otherwise reject as false, but to imagine that it can continue to do its magic work in the face of presented and undeniable fact is to indulge in unrealistic thinking. Indeed, it seems more plausible to think that metaphysicians become ingenious on behalf of the views they are determined to hold than to think that they become convinced of the views by arguments.

The mystery increases when we consider the purported reason on which the view that nothing exists is based ; for taken as an *argument*, it is so transparently false that we do not understand how anyone could be taken in by it, nor why the mistake is not recognized immediately on its being pointed out. The supposed argument for the view, *i.e.*, the reasoning which leads to holding the view, is that " nothing " must be the name of an object because it is a substantive word. But this argument is so transparently fallacious that we are puzzled to think that anyone could be taken in by it. We can hardly imagine anyone seriously arguing that " chair " and " coat " are not names of things because " nothing " is a noun which is not the name of anything. And we should find it equally hard to imagine anyone seriously arguing that because " coat " and " chair " are names of things, the substantive " nothing " must also be a name. And supposing the miracle of someone actually being taken in by it, we are at a complete loss to understand what could have happened to prevent his seeing the mistake once it is pointed out to him that not all substantives are names, and that from the fact that " nothing " is a substantive it does not follow that it is a name.

It seems plain that if we go on the assumption that the metaphysician is either misdescribing the use of " nothing " or has been led into talking nonsense because of a misconception of its use we can give no reasonable account of his resistance to correction. There can be no hope of understanding why he does not *feel* corrected. There is, however, another possible hypothesis left to consider. This is not that the metaphysician has made a blunder and for some unaccountable reason resists correction but that he has not made any sort of mistake. This hypothesis does not come naturally to us ; it is entirely foreign to our way of looking at metaphysics. But it will not seem as strange and unplausible as it does at first if in conjunction with the fact that the metaphysician knows the ordinary use of " nothing " we take seriously his resistance to correction of *his* idea of the use of the word. It is, after all, possible that he knows better than we do what *he* is doing with the word and does not accept correction because he is not using or describing the word mistakenly. This is a hypothesis which a genuine desire to understand what has happened should lead us to investigate.

Now, if unlike " Existence exists ", the sentence " Nothing exists " neither uses " nothing " in a senseless way nor misdescribes its actual use in ordinary language, what does the sentence come to, what is its interpretation? What is being done with the word " Nothing "?

Suppose a physicist at a party where couples are waltzing were to say, " Those people are working only moderately hard ". We would be rather shocked to hear him speak in this way and protest that they were not *working*, that they were *waltzing* and entertaining themselves. And if he went on to say that he could see they were waltzing but that nonetheless they were working, that waltzing is a form of work, we might naturally think he had a wrong notion of the use of " work " and was applying it improperly to the dancing couples. We should then feel inclined to correct his language. But if he went on to explain that he was quite familiar with the ordinary, vulgar use of " work " but in the present situation was using it in its technical physical sense of *expenditure of energy*, then we should no longer feel shocked or think he was using the word in an improper, mistaken way. We should no longer be tempted to correct him, though we might well think that he was using an ordinary term in a special technical sense in a situation where people would be misled.

In the same way, a metaphysician who uses the word "nothing" in a way which surprises and baffles us is using it in a special, philosophical way, which a little ingenuity suffices to penetrate. If, like the physicist, the metaphysician were in a position to explain how he is using " nothing ", what he is doing with the word, we should be pacified and no longer try to correct him, though our interest in his utterance might vanish with our puzzlement. Unfortunately, he cannot explain what he is doing with the word in the statement " Nothing exists " ; he can only use it in a way which fascinates and satisfies him. There is nothing cryptic in this remark once it is realized that we use language in unconscious ways as well as in conscious ways. And what we have to try to do is to understand the unconscious thing he is doing with the word. There is a strong and understandable temptation to think that a metaphysician who uses a familiar word in a way we do not understand and, furthermore, can give no explanation of his usage, is talking nonsense, is using the word senselessly. But it has to be realized that it is psychologically possible to use language in unusual ways and, without being able to explain our use, still make sense, though not obviously so. Like the artist who paints his pictures without being able to explain their underlying meanings, the metaphysical artist creates with words but cannot explain his creations. The hidden things he does we have to discover for ourselves.

Consider the following sentences taken from "Alice Through the Looking Glass " :

" ' I see nobody on the road ', said Alice.

' I only wish I had such eyes ', the King remarked in a fretful tone. ' To be able to see Nobody. And at that distance too! Why it's as much as I can do to see real people in this light! '

. . . . . . . . . . . . . .

' Who did you pass on the road '? the King went on, holding out his hand to the Messenger for some hay.

' Nobody ', said the Messenger.

' Quite right ', said the King, ' this lady saw him too. So of course Nobody walks slower than you '.

' I do my best ', the Messenger said in a sullen tone. ' I'm sure nobody walks much faster than I do '!

' He can't do that ', said the King, ' or else he'd have been here first! ' "

This is delightful linguistic whimsy which we can enjoy and understand. A humorous *game* is being played with the word " nobody ", and what makes it possible to play this game with a semblance of verbal realism is the fact that the word grammatically lends itself to the verbal game. The word " nobody " is quite plainly being used, in pretence, *as if* it were the name of a person, an unrealish and more subtle and difficult person to see than an ordinary, substantial, everyday person like John Smith. What makes this engaging, make-believe use of " nobody " possible is that it is a grammatical substantive. The word " nobody " is, of course, *only a grammatical substantive* ; it is not, to invent an expression, a *semantic substantive*, that is to say, a substantive which, like " Massachusetts " or " moon ", is a general or proper name of an object. But the fact that " nobody " functions grammatically like a semantic noun creates the whimsical possibility of pretending that it also *is* a semantic noun. Lewis Carroll has not written literally nonsensical sentences, sentences which are empty verbal jingles devoid of any sense. We can quite well understand what he is doing, with the word " nobody ", the language game he plays with it, and we can enter into his game with enjoyment of the comical utterances the word lends itself to.

We now have a clue to the metaphysical use of " nothing ", a clue which if taken together with Plato's profound observation that the genius of comedy is the same with that of tragedy can lead to considerable insight. Like Carroll, the Metaphysician of the Reality of Nothing knows the linguistic facts, grammatical and semantic, about the use of " nothing " and " nobody ", and we may well conjecture that he too is playing a verbal game. But he plays his game with " nothing " with a different attitude. He takes it seriously, without his tongue in his cheek.

For some reason, which may go quite deep psychologically,[1] the metaphysician is seriously dissatisfied with the fact that the word " nothing " has the grammatical function of a substantive but does not, so to speak, get enough linguistic credit for its grammatical work. He is discontented with its being *merely* a grammatical noun and sees the possibility of assimilating it into the class of semantic nouns, without making it the name of anything. What he does to correct the unsatisfactory linguistic

[1] The assertion that *anxiety* reveals the nothing suggests this,

state of affairs is to make more pronounced the similarity between the functioning of " nothing " and that of words like " moon " and " ghost ". He gratifies his wish to have " nothing " as a thing-denoting substantive, instead of as a noun which does not name, by *creating* a bit of language in which " nothing " is used *as if* it were a name. The sentence " Nothing is on the table " is like the sentence " The inkwell is on the table," but not like enough for him ; for " Nothing is on the table " has, in ordinary English, the translation " There is not anything on the table ". And what he does to make the sentences more alike, make the function of " nothing " more like that of " inkwell ", is to preface " nothing " with the definite article. Instead of saying, " Nothing is on the table ", he says, " The nothing is on the table ", and so prevents the translation of " nothing " into " not anything ". The metaphysical statement " The nothing exists " informs us that " nothing " is being treated as a semantic substantive in the private grammar book of the metaphysician. The word has not actually been changed into a thing-denoting substantive. It has become a name with *zero naming function*, a name by grammatical courtesy only. The statements " The nothing exists " and " we know the nothing " simply realize the metaphysician's wish, not in fact to use " nothing " as the name of a thing, but to use it in such a way in sentences as to make it *look* as if " nothing " is the name of a thing. And he realizes his wish by *exaggerating* a grammatical similarity at the expense of a semantic difference.

It is easy to see now what has been done with the adverbial particle " not " in the queer sentence " The nothing nots ". " Not " has been changed into a grammatical verb and formally classified with verbs denoting an action. But like " nothing " which names no thing, " nots " names no action. The sentence " The nothing nots " produces the eerie illusion of stating the existence of a mysterious something which does a mysterious act, and perhaps the grammatically curious things done with " nothing " and " not " have been done with the purpose of producing this illusion. In any case, it is possible to make sense of what has been done with language. In the ordinary sentence " The rabbit runs ", " rabbit " is the general name of an animal and " runs " is a verb which denotes an action. In the metaphysical sentence " The nothing nots " the words " nothing " and " nots " are only linguistically make-believe name and verb. But just as we can understand ordinary make-believe, so we can also understand the more subtle linguistic make-believe of a metaphysician.

The present reconstruction of what has happened makes intelligible the metaphysician's resistance to the usual criticisms directed against this view. He is not talking nonsense, and so remains unmoved by the charge that he is. Nor is he misdescribing the ordinary uses of " nothing " and " not ". For his use of these terms is a *changed* use. It is a new grammatical use which we can understand and either accept or reject, depending on whether it appeals to us or repels us.

The explanation we have arrived at throws light on the further and more sophisticated metaphysical theory that " the real is the positive ",[1] the theory, in other words that there are no negative facts, *e.g.*, that " there is not a fact ' sun-not-shining ' which is affirmed by the true statement ' The Sun is not shining ' ".[2] Consider the following :

" Let us take a very simple negation, such as ' this is not white '. You say this, we will suppose, in the course of a discussion with the laundry. The phrase ' this is white ' is in your mind, this is before your eyes, and ' this is grey ' is a sentence describing what you see, and yet, on the basis of what you see, you are sure that it is true, in other words, that ' this is white ' is false ".[3]

And also the following :

" Suppose you are told ' there is butter in the larder, but no cheese '. Although they seem equally based on sensible experience, the two statements ' there is butter ' and ' there is not cheese ' are really on a very different level. There is a definite occurrence which was seeing butter, and which might have put the word ' butter ' in your mind even if you had not been thinking of butter. But there was no occurrence which could be described as ' not seeing cheese ' or as ' seeing the absence of cheese '. You *judged* this, you did not see it ; you saw what each thing was, not what it was not."[4]

[1] H. W. B. Joseph, *An Introduction to Logic*, pp. 171–72.
[2] B. Russell, *Human Knowledge*, p. 500.
[3] B. Russell, *Inquiry Into Meaning and Truth*, p. 99.
[4] Ibid, pp. 89, 90.

To many readers, and in particular to philosophical defenders of ordinary language, these quotations will seem to contain downright mistakes about ordinary language. If we interpret the statement that " ' this is not white ' is not a sentence describing what you see " as making a factual linguistic claim about " this is not white " (and a whole host of similar negative sentences), it is obviously false. For interpreted as making such a claim, the statement declares that the words " I see that this is not white " are devoid of intelligibility. Just as " I hear the sweetness of honey " makes no literal, descriptive sense in English because the phrase " the sweetness of honey " does not describe anything which we could with sense be said to hear, so, according to the interpreted claim, " I see that this book cover is not white " makes no descriptive sense because " This book cover is not white " does not describe anything which we could with intelligibility be said to see. But, of course, " I see that this is not white " is a perfectly intelligible sentence in ordinary English and frequently expresses what is true. And this could hardly be unknown to a metaphysician who seems, on the surface, to deny it; and it certainly could not be denied by him once his attention is called to it.

Or, again, take the words " There was no occurrence which could be described as ' not seeing cheese ' or as ' seeing the absence of cheese ' ". These words appear to express the claim that the ordinary phrase " seeing the absence of cheese " describes no conceivable occurrence; and if this is in fact the claim that is being made, then it amounts to stating that " seeing the absence of cheese " is an empty phrase, syntactically correct, but otherwise devoid of sense. For if the phrase had a meaning, it would describe an occurrence, actual or theoretically imaginable; and if it describes nothing, it is meaningless. If this is the claim made by a philosopher who says that " There was no occurrence which could be described as ' seeing the absence of cheese ' ", then there can be no real question as to whether he is mistaken. For it is an easy matter to think of any number of occurrences which would properly and correctly be described by phrases of the form " sees the absence of x ", " sees no x ", " sees that there is no x ", " notices the absence of x ", etc. If, for example, you go to a party hoping to see your friend Jones there, you could, after having looked at all the guests present and not seen him, truthfully and certainly with literal sense say to your host, " I see that Jones is not here ". A school teacher on frequent occasions can be described as " seeing the absence of one of his students ". And it is sometimes true and properly describes an occurrence to say, " To his annoyance he saw that the dictionary was not in its accustomed place on the table ". Without going into tedious repetition, it cannot with any sort of plausibility be thought that a philosopher who *seems* to be claiming that such expressions are senseless is actually claiming this.

Consider, further, the word " judge ". In ever so many cases of a person not seeing a thing, for example, in the case of your failing to find a collar button for which you are looking in a cluttered drawer, it would be a proper way to describe the situation to say, ' 'I have looked long enough ; I judge that it isn't there ". The sentence " Jones did not see his coat in the cloakroom and inferred it was not there " describes what happened, even if it were true that Jones' coat was concealed by other coats and his inference was false. In other cases, however, it would be linguistic tomfoolery to use " judge " and " infer ". Suppose you wanted your dictionary, went to the small stand on which you usually kept it and found it was not there. In such a case it would be incorrect English, a misuse of " judge ", to say, while looking at the bare stand, " I *judge* that the dictionary is not on the stand ". This would be as much an absurdity of language as it would be for you to say at a time when you are in your study, " I judge that there is no elephant in my study ". And it would also be improper English, in the circumstance of your looking at the bare stand, to say, " I do *not see* that the dictionary is not on the stand ", while it would be a proper way of describing the situation to say, " I *see* that the dictionary is not on the stand ".

But we miss entirely the point of what the metaphysician is doing if we think he is making mistakes about ordinary language. The fact that the putative mistakes which dupe a metaphysician are so very obvious and glaring to *others* should warn us that there is much more than appears on the surface.

A philosopher who tells us that " the statements ' there is butter ' and ' there is no cheese ' are really on a very different level " is in an obscure way calling attention to an actual linguistic difference between the statements. And it is not difficult to discover what the difference in " level " is. When we truly assert that we see butter, there is *something* which we are seeing. But when we truly assert that we see no cheese, or that we notice the absence of cheese, there is not a thing that we are seeing. The nouns " butter " and " cheese " are names of articles of diet, but the terms " no butter " and " absence of cheese " are not names of anything. The words " white " and " grey " are adjectives which name colors, but the terms " not white " and " not grey " are not names of colors. The difference in " level " between " there is butter " and " there is no cheese " and between " this is grey " and " this is not white " lies in the difference between the fuctioning of " butter " and " no cheese " and in the difference between the functioning of " grey " and " not white ".

Consider what has been said about the conjunction " or " : " But how about ' or '? You cannot show a child examples of it in the sensible world. You can say : ' Will you have pudding or pie? ' but if the child says yes, you cannot find a nutriment which is ' pudding or pie ' ".[1] Children are, of course, successfully taught the use of " or ", but they are not taught it by being shown " examples of it in the sensible world ". The use of " or " is not taught in the way " cow " and " pudding " are taught. We teach a child the word " cow " by applying it to some things and withholding its application to other things : we point to cows, each time pronouncing the word " cow ", and correct the child when it calls the wrong things " cow ". But we don't teach it " or " in this way, *i.e.*, by showing it examples in the " sensible world ". The reason why we cannot find examples of " or " in the sensible world is not that there is some sort of practical difficulty which stands in the way of our finding them, or that, like centaurs, none happen to exist; we cannot find examples because no value of " x or y " is the name of a thing. Unlike " pie " and " pudding " and " man " and " mouse " " pudding or pie " is not the name of a nutriment and " man or mouse " is not the name of an animal. The impossibility of finding an article of diet answering to " pudding or pie " is an impossibility which is created by a linguistic fact of usage. And a

[1] B. Russell, *Inquiry Into Meaning and Truth*, p. 89.

philosopher who remarks that you *cannot* find a nutriment which
is *pudding or pie* or an animal which is *man or mouse* is in an unclear
form of speech pointing out that it *makes no sense* to speak of
finding any objects answering to these terms because they are
not names of a nutriment or of an animal. What he is concerned
to do is to point out the semantic difference between the names
" pudding " and " pie " and the expression " pudding or pie ".

Similarly, a philosopher who states that " there is butter " and
" there is no cheese " are on a different level is referring to the
semantic difference between the terms " butter " and " no
cheese ", " grey " and " not white ", the difference, namely,
that " butter " is the name of an article of diet and " no butter "
is not, and that " white " is the name of a color and " not
white " is not. By permitting such sentences as " I see no cheese
in the larder " and " It is plain to see that this shirt is not white ",
ordinary language tends to conceal the semantic difference
between negative and positive terms and, furthermore, creates
the temptation, to which some metaphysicians succumb, to
assimilate negative terms into the class of positive terms, *i.e.*,
to treat " not butter " *as if* it named a thing and " not white "
*as if* it denoted a color. In other words, by grammatically
minimizing the difference between negative and positive terms,
ordinary language creates in some thinkers the temptation to
conceal the difference even more, to play the same game with
negative terms that the existentialist metaphysician plays with
the word " nothing ". And what a philosopher does, who is
impressed by the semantic difference between negative and
positive terms and is *opposed* to any attempts to conceal the
difference, is to *change the use of* " see " and " judge " in such a
way as to make more pronounced than it is in ordinary language
the difference between negative and positive terms. He *alters
language* for the purpose of making a linguistic difference more
conspicuous.

In his new, philosophical way of speaking, it will make
descriptive sense to say " I see butter " and " I see that the rose
is red ", but it will make no descriptive sense to say " I see no
cheese ", or " I see the absence of cheese ", and " I see that the
lily is not red ". The expressions " no cheese " and " not red "
are not to count as describing what we *see*, and this comes to

*contracting* the use of " see ", *restricting* the word to its use with positive terms. In place of using " see ", and in general " perceive ", with negative terms he uses " judge ", which is verbally *stretched* for the purpose of doing this new work, work it does not do in ordinary language. In his metaphysical language he replaces the ordinary sentences " I see that there is no cheese on the table " and " I see that the rose is not blue " by the philosophical sentences " I *judge* that there is no cheese on the table " and " I *judge* that the rose is not blue ". In this way, with the help of a contracted use of " see " and a stretched use of " judge " he is able to make more pronounced the semantic difference between negative and positive terms. The statement, " You see what each thing is, not what it is not ", informs us that in the *made-up* language of some metaphysicians the word " see " has only *part* of its ordinary use, its use with positive terms.

# CHAPTER IV. KNOWLEDGE, BELIEF AND ASSERTION.

## SOME QUESTIONS ABOUT 'KNOW' AND 'THINK'

### By A. M. MacIver

ALL the following sentences *appear* to be self-contradictory :

(A)  (1)  "*p* is true but I know that it is not."
     (2)  "*p* is true but I do not know that it is."
     (3)  "*p* is true but I think that it is not."
     (4)  "*p* is true but I have no opinion on the matter either way."
     (5)  "I know that *p* is true but I may be mistaken."
     (6)  "I think that *p* is true but I may be mistaken."
     (7)  "I know that *p* is true but I am aware that I may be mistaken."
     (8)  "I think that *p* is true but I am aware that I may be mistaken."

Now compare with these another set of sentences :

(B)  (1)  "*p* is true but the Editor of *Analysis* knows that it is not."
     (2)  "*p* is true but the Editor of *Analysis* does not know that it is."
     (3)  "*p* is true but the Editor of *Analysis* thinks that it is not."
     (4)  "*p* is true but the Editor of *Analysis* has no opinion on the matter either way."
     (5)  "The Editor of *Analysis* knows that *p* is true but he may be mistaken."
     (6)  "The Editor of *Analysis* thinks that *p* is true but he may be mistaken."
     (7)  "The Editor of *Analysis* knows that *p* is true but is aware that he may be mistaken."
     (8)  "The Editor of *Analysis* thinks that *p* is true but is aware that he may be mistaken."

Every sentence in set (B) corresponds to a sentence in set (A) ; but, of set (B), (2), (3), (4) and (6) are quite evidently self-consistent, while (1) and (5), though they are certainly self-contradictory if the word ' know ' is used in one sense, are self-consistent if it is used in another. If it is so used that "A knows *p* " always entails " *p* ", then they are plainly self-contradictory (for of course " he may be mistaken " is here equivalent to " *p* may not be true ") ; but, if ' know ' is used (as I think it sometimes is, though not generally by philosophers) in such a way that "A knows *p* " is merely equivalent to "A is convinced of *p* " (in the sense in which we most often speak of " being convinced of " something in everyday usage), then these sentences also are self-consistent (for we can often say, " You may be convinced of that but all the same you are wrong ".)

The situation is different with regard to (7), for this still seems to be a contradiction in whatever sense ' know ' is used, since (8) also seems to be a contradiction—for we are inclined to say, " If he is aware that he may be mistaken (that is, that *p* may be false), can it be said that he thinks that *p* is true? Does he think more than that *p may* be true? "—and, if (8) were a contradiction, so *a fortiori* would (7) be. (It makes no difference whether " to be aware " here means " to know " or " to think " ; the same conclusions follow.) This raises a difficulty, for propositions of this form are very often asserted ; when Oliver Cromwell made his famous request to the Scotch Calvinists (" I beseech you, in the bowels of Christ—believe it possible you may be mistaken! "), are we to say that he was asking of them a logical impossibility? But this is not the difficulty that I want to discuss here. I have only added these sentences to my list, partly to point this difficulty out in the hope that somebody else may perhaps be able to deal with it, and partly to make quite clear what I am discussing by indicating what I am *not* discussing. (For I think that these propositions have sometimes been confused with (5) and (6) in the list.)

The difficulty that I want to discuss is this. Each sentence in list (A) only differs from the corresponding sentence in list (B) in containing the pronoun ' I ' in place of the substantival phrase ' the editor of *Analysis* '. But this difference should be of purely *grammatical*, not *logical*, significance.

Sentences containing pronouns (" pronominal sentences " as I shall sometimes call them) have systematic ambiguity, in that such a sentence may express different propositions, according to the speaker who utters it or the circumstances in which it is uttered ; but what logic is concerned with is the propositions, not the sentences. To take Ramsey's example, there is no contradiction between the *sentences* " I went to Grantchester yesterday " and " I didn't go to Grantchester yesterday "—or even between the propositions which they express, so long as they are uttered by different people, or by the same person on different days ; but there *is* contradiction between the propositions which they express if they are uttered by the *same* person on the *same* day. But, if we are in any doubt as to whether the propositions expressed by such sentences (as spoken by particular people on particular occasions) are contradictory or not (or have or have not other logical relations), we can settle the matter by eliminating the ambiguity, by translating the sentences into forms in which the pronouns are replaced by nouns. For example, if the sentence, " I went to Grantchester yesterday " is uttered by Mr. Braithwaite[1] on February 15th, 1938, and the sentence, " I didn't go to Grantchester yesterday " is uttered by Dr. Ewing[1] also on February 15th, 1938, we can see that the propositions they express are not contradictory by translating them into the forms, " Mr. Braithwaite went to Grantchester on February 14th, 1938 " and " Dr. Ewing didn't go to Grantchester on February 14th, 1938," which are *obviously* not contradictory ; and again, if Mr. Braithwaite on February 15th says, " I went to Grantchester yesterday " and on February 16th says, " I didn't go to Grantchester yesterday," the propositions expressed are not contradictory, as becomes obvious when the sentences appear in translation as " Mr. Braithwaite went to Grantchester on February 14th " and " Mr. Braithwaite didn't go to Grantchester on February 15th ", but, if Mr. Braithwaite says on the same day both, " I went to Grantchester yesterday " and " I didn't go to Grantchester yesterday ", then the propositions expressed *are* contradictory, for the sentences appear in translation as " Mr. Braithwaite went to Grantchester on February 14th " and " Mr. Braithwaite didn't go to Grantchester on February 14th ", in which the contradiction is obvious. (In the same way there is no contradiction between

---

[1] I hope that both the gentlemen concerned will forgive my taking their names in vain.

" I went to Grantchester yesterday ", and " You didn't go to Grantchester yesterday " if they are both uttered, even on the same day, by Mr. Braithwaite, say, to Dr. Ewing, but there *is* contradiction if the first is addressed by Mr. Braithwaite to Dr. Ewing and the second by Dr. Ewing to Mr. Braithwaite, and this appears when the pronouns are eliminated in translation ; there is no contradiction between " Mr. Braithwaite went to Grantchester " and " Dr. Ewing didn't go to Grantchester ", but there *is* between " Mr. Braithwaite went to Grantchester " and "*Mr. Braithwaite* didn't go to Grantchester.") But this assumes that a sentence containing pronouns, as used by a particular speaker on a particular occasion, (e.g. " I went to Grantchester yesterday " as uttered by Mr. Braithwaite on February 15th) and a sentence not containing pronouns (e.g. " Mr. Braithwaite went to Grantchester on February 14th ") express the same proposition, and that logical relations (such as contradiction) hold between the *propositions*, not between the *sentences*. When the pronouns are eliminated by translation, it is shown what logical relations hold between the propositions expressed by the original sentences containing the pronouns, because, though ambiguity is removed, the meaning of the pronominal sentence as used on a particular occasion is not altered.

But now consider any sentence in list (B) above—other than (1) and (5) when the word ' know ' is used in certain senses, and perhaps (7) and (8) ; the propositions which they express are quite evidently self-consistent. And then consider the corresponding sentences in list (A) ; these are apparently self-contradictory. But, if we suppose the latter uttered by the Editor of *Analysis* himself—a perfectly conceivable supposition—then each of these sentences expresses the same proposition as the corresponding sentence in list (B). And how can the proposition expressed by one form of words be self-contradictory, if the same proposition, when expressed by another form of words, is clearly self-consistent?

The answer that I want to suggest is that none of the sentences in list (A)—always with the exception of (1) and (5) in certain senses of the word ' know ', and perhaps of (7) and (8)—is in fact a contradiction at all. The appearance of contradiction is due to the confusion of contradiction with something else.

Let us take a concrete example, such as " Mussolini is having a bath but I do not know whether he is or not ". This seems to be self-contradictory. (And it makes no difference here if we substitute ' think ' for ' know ' and say " Mussolini is having a bath but I neither think that he is nor think that he is not "— that is, " I have no opinion on the matter " ; the appearance of contradiction remains ; it would be said that " Mussolini is having a bath " *implies* both " I know that he is " and, *a fortiori*, " I think that he is."[1]) And let us suppose the speaker to be the Editor of *Analysis* ; *he* then will seem to be contradicting himself. But, if we only translate the sentence so as to eliminate the pronoun, we find that all that is being asserted is " Mussolini is having a bath but the Editor of *Analysis* does not know that he is "—which would not, I think, seem to be self-contradictory to anyone ; in fact, unless either Mussolini *never* has a bath or the Editor of *Analysis* possesses the powers of a clairvoyant, it has probably on many occasions been actually *true*.[2] How then can we maintain that " Mussolini is having a bath but *I* do not know that he is ", as uttered by the Editor of *Analysis*, is self-contradictory?

The only way out would seem to be to distinguish the *proposition* and the *assertion* of it, and say that, though this proposition is perfectly self-consistent, and can be asserted by anyone *except* the Editor of *Analysis*, yet the Editor *himself* cannot assert it. But then what do we mean here by " cannot assert? " Not that he cannot make the noises, for clearly he *could*. I can perfectly well say (make the noises) " Mussolini is having a bath but I do not know whether he is or not ", and the Editor of *Analysis* does

---

[1] Lest I should be accused of attacking a position nobody holds, I may point out that Mr. Duncan-Jones (in " Lewy's Remarks on Analysis ", *Analysis* Vol. 5, p. 10) treats the similar case of " I think *p* but not-*p* " (which is only the obverted form of my (A) (3) as a contradiction. It is true that he calls it a " quite different *form* of contradiction " (my italics) from " the already obvious contradiction of asserting not-*p* along with an assertion which entails *p* ", but he seems to have no doubt that it is equally a form of *contradiction*. I seem to detect the same assumption in the doctrine which Miss MacDonald, in *Arist. Soc. Supp. Vol.* XVI, p. 30, attributes to Professor Moore, but I admit that her statement is capable of several interpretations.

[2] This sentence is still pronominal as involving tense (for *tense*, unless a date is definitely expressed, must be regarded as a " pronoun "), which is why we can speak of it as being " true on some occasions though not on others ", meaning that, as uttered on some occasions, it expresses true propositions, though, as uttered on other occasions, it expresses false propositions.

not, so far as I know, suffer from any form of aphasia which prevents him from doing the same thing (nor would it make any difference to the argument if he did).

Shall we then say that he cannot utter the noises *meaning anything by them* ? But now what do we mean by "meaning anything by them?." The words ' Mussolini is having a bath ', as spoken at any particular time, have a perfectly definite meaning according to the rules of the English language (barring any difficulties that may be raised about the proper name, which are not relevant here)—they express a perfectly definite proposition, which may be true—and so do the words ' I do not know whether Mussolini is having a bath or not ', as spoken by any particular *person* at any particular time ; and, as the two propositions are not inconsistent (for it is quite conceivable that Mussolini should take a bath without anybody except Mussolini himself knowing that he was doing so, and logically possible that he should do so in a fit of complete absent-mindedness, so that not even *he* knew it), the words ' Mussolini is having a bath but I do not know whether he is or not ', as spoken by any particular person at any particular time, also have a quite definite meaning according to the rules of the English language—express a definite conjunctive proposition, which again may perfectly well be true. Nor is anyone who tries to utter these words immediately smitten with a sudden *amnesia* for the meanings of English words and constructions which he knew before. In any ordinary sense of " knowing what words mean ", I can perfectly well utter these words *knowing exactly what they mean*, and so can anyone else (such as the Editor of *Analysis*).

Nor can we say that, though anyone could utter these words, they are *meaningless to him* because no experience of *his* could verify them. We are told—it is a favourite example with the Verificationists—that the statement " There are mountains 10,000 feet high on the other side of the moon " is significant to us now, although we cannot at present tell whether it is true or not, because we can describe an experiment which would settle the matter (such as going to the other side of the moon and measuring) though we are not at present in a position to perform the experiment ; but the very same experimental results which would verify *this* statement would also verify the statement, " There are mountains 10,000 feet high on the other side of the moon though we do not at present know whether there are or not ". To return to our former example, suppose the Editor of *Analysis* at midday on February 15th, 1938 (out of the blue, without rhyme or reason) to utter the words, " Mussolini is now having a bath though I do not know whether he is or not " ; although he has no authority for his assertion (any more than, in the other example, we have any authority for asserting, "There are mountains 10,000 feet high on the other side of the moon "), still he is asserting something which is *significant to him*, even by the verification test, for by the same time on February 16th he might well be in possession of evidence, of the kind (whatever it may be) which at present justifies us in making statements about the past, which would entitle him to say then "Amazingly enough, what I said yesterday has turned out to have been true ; exactly twenty-four hours ago Mussolini *was* having a bath though I didn't then know whether he was or not ". And there is no reason why he should not, at the time when he *made* the statement, have *described* the way in which it might be verified, though of course he would have to wait before he could *perform* the verification ; but (as Schlick said[1]) " *waiting* is a perfectly legitimate method of verification ".

So we are forced to the conclusion that sentences of the form ' *p* but I do not know *p* ' are not in fact *contradictory* at all. And the same applies to the other sentence-forms that I have mentioned ; they are none of them contradictory. Why then have people ever thought that they *were ?* The reason, I think, lies in the tendency of philosophers (especially present-day " analytical " philosophers) to consider Language apart from its *use*. The result is that (as applied to forms of words) " to have no use " tends to be equated with " to make no sense ". But these are not in fact the same thing. Such a form of words as ' Mussolini is having a bath but I do not know whether he is or not ' *makes sense*—as used on any particular occasion by any particular person it expresses a proposition which is self-consistent, may be true, and may later be *found* to be true ; the only objection to it— and it is a serious one—is that nevertheless it *has no use*.

The whole purpose of making a statement (at least if language is being used in the " scientific " way, which is the only use that

1 *Gesammelte Aufsätze* 1926-1936, p. 345.

is here in question) is " to communicate information "—that is, that the hearer should be inclined by the speaker's authority to decide in favour of what is stated being true. But this will only follow if the hearer supposes that the speaker *knows*, or at the very least *thinks*, that what he says is true. For this reason it comes to the same thing in practice to say "*p*" and to say "I know that *p*": not that the two statements have the same meaning—for the first might be true and the second false—but what a hearer will be led to believe by them, if he is led to believe anything, will be the same in both cases. (It is true that, in some cases, "I know that *p*" will be more persuasive than "*p*", especially if emphasis is laid on the word 'know'; for example, if I say "Mussolini is having a bath", a hearer may remain sceptical until I add "I *know* that he is"; but this is irrelevant, because I might produce exactly the same effect by repeating emphatically "He *is*": all that I am trying to do here is to convince him that I am in earnest—which I might even do simply by my *expression* or *tone of voice*.) If, however, I say "*p* but I don't know *p*" ("Mussolini is having a bath but I don't know whether he is or not")—and still more, of course, if I say "*p* but I don't *think p*" ("Mussolini is having a bath but I have no opinion on the question whether he is or not") or "*p* but I think not-*p*" ("Mussolini is having a bath but I think he isn't")—the second half of what I say makes the *saying* of the first half *pointless*. To append to any statement " —but I don't know whether this is so or not" is equivalent in *effect* to prefixing to it, "Don't attend to what I am going to say next because it is not meant seriously". It is expressly to disclaim the authority which must be assumed by the hearer if he is to consider the remark worth attending to, and therefore if it is to be worth making.

This, I think, is what people have had in mind when they have regarded sentences of such forms as '*p* but I don't know *p*' as contradictory. But it is one thing to say that a statement is *not worth making*—another to say that it is *self-contradictory* or *meaningless*. (Of course there is contradiction involved in the situation of *making* such an assertion, but it is not contradiction *in what is asserted*; it is contradiction between part of what is asserted and what must be assumed by the hearer if the other part is to be worth attending to.) It may be *more important* to know whether a sentence is worth uttering than to know whether it is significant ; but that is another question. It is certainly a very important fact about sentences of these forms that they are not only not worth uttering on certain occasions (as " It is raining " is not worth saying to someone in the open air in the middle of a downpour) but, by their very nature, *never* worth uttering (except as examples in a philosophical discussion). But, even so, no harm is done—and a little clarity is gained—by recognizing that they are *not contradictions*. (Or, if the word ' contradiction ' is so used as to cover both kinds of case—which seems to me anyhow a bad practice—at least it should be made clear that it is being used in two quite different senses.)

## FURTHER QUESTIONS ABOUT ' KNOW ' AND ' THINK '

### By AUSTIN DUNCAN-JONES

A. M. MacIver criticises the view that sentences of such forms as ' *p* but I think not-*p* ' are self-contradictory ; he also criticises incidentally a remark which I made[1] to the effect that ' I think *p* but not-*p* ' is a " form of contradiction ".

I don't propose to discuss MacIver's paper exhaustively, or to defend my own remark, which certainly needs elucidation : I propose to discuss two points in MacIver's paper on which I think he is undoubtedly mistaken.

MacIver starts by listing two sets, (A) and (B), of eight sentences each. I shall be obliged to reproduce his list (A), which is as follows.

" (A) (1) ' *p* is true but I know that it is not.'

(2) ' *p* is true but I do not know that it is.'

(3) ' *p* is true but I think that it is not.'

(4) ' *p* is true but I have no opinion on the matter either way.'

(5) ' I know that *p* is true but I may be mistaken.'

(6) ' I think that *p* is true but I may be mistaken.'

(7) ' I know that *p* is true but I am aware that I may be mistaken.'

(8) ' I think that *p* is true but I am aware that I may be mistaken.' "

---

[1] *Analysis*, Vol. 5, p. 10.

List (B) differs from (A) only in that in sentences (1) to (4) the phrase ' the editor of *Analysis* ' is substituted for ' I ', and the verb governed by ' I ' is changed from the first to the third person : and that in (5) to (8) a corresponding change is made, except that the second ' I ' is replaced by ' he '.

My first point is very simple. MacIver says[1] that each of the sentences (A) (1–8) "*appears* to be self-contradictory". Here MacIver seems to have been led into an obvious mistake by excessive schematism. For (A) (6) and (8) don't even appear to be self-contradictory. If we use ' think ' in the sense it would ordinarily have in this kind of context, " I think that *p* is true " is, paradoxically, equivalent to " I *am inclined* to think *p* is true ". For instance " I think the economic theory of the causes of the great war is true " is equivalent to " the economic theory is the one which I am inclined to accept " : and this statement almost calls for the addition " but (I am aware that) I may be mistaken ", which simply amplifies what has been said already. But was MacIver perhaps using ' think ' in a peculiar sense?

I think it is just possible that he was. He distinguishes[2] two possible meanings of ' know ' : one, such that " 'A knows *p*' always entails '*p*' " ; the other such that " 'A knows *p*' is merely equivalent to 'A is convinced of *p*' ". It seems just possible that MacIver was treating ' think ' as equivalent to ' know ' in the second sense. Further on[3] he says " it would be said that " Mussolini is having a bath " *implies* both ' I know that he is ' and, *a fortiori*, ' I think that he is ' ". MacIver denies that " Mussolini is having a bath " implies " I know that he is " : but he doesn't seem to question that if I know *p* then, *a fortiori*, I think *p*.[4] Yet obviously, if " I think *p* " is used in the colloquial way, as equivalent to " I am inclined to think *p* ", it doesn't follow from " I know *p*" at all, but is inconsistent with it. Admittedly " I think *p* " might be used as a sort of emphatic meiosis by somebody who really felt quite sure of *p* : if, for instance, somebody said something I disagreed with, and I banged on the table and said "*I think not*" in an angry tone. But this is a freak usage. So if MacIver's statement that (A) (6) and (8) appear to be self-contradictory was not simply a blunder—if

[1] p. 88.　　　　[2] p. 89.　　　　[3] p. 92.
[4] Yet people often say " I don't think, I know ".

there are some sentences of similar form which he has good reason for saying appear self-contradictory—he should, I think, have chosen a different form of words.

My second point is more complicated and more interesting. Apart from the two sentences I have already discussed, I do not propose to raise the question whether the sentences in list (A) are self-contradictory. But I want to say something about an argument by which MacIver claims to show that certain of them are not. MacIver admits that certain (A) sentences, and the corresponding (B) sentences, may be self-contradictory, at any rate on one interpretation : but he argues that each (A) sentence, if used by a certain person, expresses the same proposition as the corresponding (B) sentence, and that consequently, if a given (B) sentence is not self-contradictory, it follows that the corresponding (A) sentence is also not self-contradictory ; and he argues that some of the (B) sentences, and therefore the corresponding (A) sentences, are in fact not self-contradictory.

MacIver describes a procedure of " translating " sentences containing pronouns (or " pronominal sentences ") " into forms in which the pronouns are replaced by nouns ".[1] When the pronoun in question is ' I ', this is done by substituting for ' I ' the name or a description of the user of the sentence. The two sentences then " express the same proposition " —MacIver says this is " assumed " ; but he doesn't seem to regard it as a questionable assumption) : and " the meaning of the pronominal sentence as used on a particular occasion is not altered ". Accordingly if one of MacIver's (A) sentences were uttered by the person who is in fact editor of *Analysis* it would express the same proposition and have the same meaning as the corresponding (B) sentence. Yet certain of the (B) sentences are quite obviously not self-contradictory, and it follows that the corresponding (A) sentences are also not self-contradictory.

Part of this argument is very plausible. It does seem natural to say that if two sentences express the same proposition, or have the same meaning, they must have the same modality (that is, both be self-contradictory, or necessary, or contingent). (MacIver does indeed say[2] that " logical relations (such as contradiction) "—and therefore, I suppose, also logical characters,

---

[1] p. 90          [2] *Ibid.*

such as modality—apply to propositions, not to sentences. But as he frequently speaks of sentences contradicting one another, or being self-contradictory, I don't think this limitation need be taken very seriously. I shall assume that it will be generally intelligible to talk of modalities and logical relations, not only in relation to propositions, but also in relation to sentences, and I won't waste time by justifying or explaining this practice.) There may also be a certain temptation to say that " I went to Grantchester yesterday " (to take MacIver's example[1], as spoken by A, expresses the same proposition, and has the same meaning, as "A went to Grantchester yesterday ", said on the same day by somebody else. The two sentences would, with certain qualifications, convey the same information.

But these assumptions, and the conclusion which seems to follow, only seem plausible as long as we don't reflect on the meaning of ' express the same proposition ' or ' have the same meaning '. I propose to confine my attention to ' express the same proposition ', which is slightly the simpler of the two. I hope to show that sentences of the types which MacIver says express the same proposition actually don't, if ' proposition ' is used in the ordinary way. In that case one half of MacIver's argument breaks down. But my contention is not easy to prove, because the meaning of ' proposition ' is not so precise and unambiguous, in the ordinary usage of philosophers, that a single simple criterion can be given for deciding whether two sentences express the same proposition. To take a simple and relevant example : it's permissible to talk about '*the* proposition " I am hungry " ' ; but it's also permissible to say that the sentence ' I am hungry ' expresses different propositions when used by different people, or by the same person on different occasions. (MacIver's argument of course depends on using the word ' proposition ' in the latter of these ways.) However, I shall also try to show that MacIver uses the word ' proposition ' in such a way that two sentences may express the same proposition although they have not got the same modality, although, for instance, one is self-contradictory and the other is not. And in that case the other half of MacIver's argument breaks down.

MacIver holds that when a sentence containing the word ' I '

[1] p. 90.

is used by someone, say A, who is applying ' I ' to himself, other sentences may be formed by substituting for ' I ' A's name, or a definite description which stands for A, which will express the same proposition as the original sentence as used by A. He doesn't distinguish the cases in which he replaces ' I ' by a name from those in which he replaces it by a description, so presumably either is always allowed. Presumably also the relation of express-ing the same proposition is transitive ; in which case different sentences, containing a name or different descriptions, all of which in fact apply to the same person, and which differ in no other way, will express the same proposition. MacIver also gives an example of replacing a word like ' yesterday '[1] by a phrase standing for a definite date: but it will not be necessary for me to consider any pronominal expressions except the word ' I '.

(1) When ' $p$ ' and ' $q$ ' differ only in respect of their subject-expressions, we should not usually say that they express the same proposition unless the two subject-expressions have the same meaning. If 'A' and ' B ' are the subject-expressions, 'A is identical with B ' must be an analytic proposition. For instance, ' the present king of England '[2] does mean the same as ' the present occupant of the English throne ', and we are therefore prepared to say that, for instance, ' the present king of England is fond of horses ' expresses the same proposition as ' the present occupant of the English throne is fond of horses '. But we shouldn't say that either of these expresses the same proposition as ' the second son of George V is fond of horses ' ; and if the person who actually is king of England were to say ' I am fond of horses ', we shouldn't say that the sentence he was using expressed the same proposition as any of the other sentences I have mentioned. (Of course in a way ' I ' as used by the person who actually is king of England *has* the same meaning as ' the second son of George V ', or ' the present king of England '— the same denotation, perhaps? But ' I am king of England ' as used by the person who is king of England would not be an analytic but a synthetic proposition.) Or again, from " the present king of England is not fond of horses " it certainly doesn't follow that " the second son of George V is fond of horses[2] " is false.

(2) The next point arises naturally from the first. Suppose

---

[1] *loc cit.*        [2] I.e. in 1938 viz. George VI

'$p$', '$q$', and '$r$' are sentences which differ only in that '$p$' contains the word 'I', '$q$' contains the name of a person who has in fact used '$p$', and '$r$' contains a description which in fact applies to the person named in '$q$'. Then it is always logically possible, and often possible in practice, for someone to know the proposition expressed by '$p$', as used by the person in question, and not know the proposition expressed by '$q$' or the proposition expressed by '$r$'; or to know the proposition expressed by '$q$' but not that expressed by '$r$', or vice versa. (There is a certain difficulty about saying that he might know the proposition expressed by '$q$' or '$r$' but not that expressed by '$p$', to which I shall return later.) Suppose '$p$' is 'I live in Cambridge', '$q$' is 'Professor Moore lives in Cambridge', and '$r$' is 'the editor of *Mind* lives in Cambridge'[1]. In that case, there probably are people who know the proposition expressed by '$q$' but don't know the proposition expressed by '$r$' and there may be people who know the proposition expressed by '$r$' but not that expressed by '$q$'. And if a stranger heard Professor Moore say '$p$' ('I live in Cambridge'), in circumstances which gave no reason for doubting his statement, we should say that he knew the proposition which Professor Moore's words expressed, although perhaps he didn't know the proposition expressed by '$q$' or by '$r$'. According to MacIver, '$p$', '$q$', and '$r$' would all express the same proposition. But we certainly don't use the word 'proposition' in such a way that the same person can at the same time both know and not know a certain proposition.

(3) MacIver confines his attention to proper names and descriptions which apply to some actual person. It is worth considering the position of descriptions which apply to nobody. On MacIver's view, the proposition expressed by 'the editor of *Mind* lives in Cambridge' can also be expressed by 'I live in Cambridge' as uttered by Professor Moore. But the proposition expressed by 'the editor of *Philosophical Gossip* lives in Oxford' can't be expressed by 'I live in Oxford', since, I presume, there is no one to utter this sentence. It is very strange if, in order to discover whether a proposition can be expressed in a certain form of words, we have to know whether it is true.

(4) There is a certain temptation to say that '$p$', '$q$', and '$r$'

[1] Professor G. E. Moore was Editor of *Mind* 1921–1947.

(under heading (2) above) must express the same proposition, because they all refer to the same fact. In a sense of course they do—but only, I think, if this means the same completely determinate or " non-general " fact. The non-general fact in question will have to be a very complicated fact, relating to every detail of somebody's life. But this fact will also be referred to by a great many other sentences, such as ' I caught the 9.30 train this morning ', which nobody would dream of saying expressed the same proposition as ' $p$ ', ' $q$ ', or ' $r$ '.

I think it would be very undesirable to say that they all refer to the same general fact ; but I can't give reasons for this without a long and probably unprofitable discussion of the use of the word ' fact '.

But there is a closely related point which is worth mentioning. To say that ' $p$ ', ' $q$ ', and ' $r$ ' refer to the same fact might mean that they have to be verified in the same way. And this is patently false. The process of verifying ' $p$ ', ' $q$ ', and ' $r$ ' might well in practice be quite different, and must necessarily be partly different. I might, of course, verify both ' $q$ ' (' Professor Moore lives in Cambridge ') and ' $r$ ' (' the editor of *Mind* lives in Cambridge ') by the single process of looking at a copy of *Mind* and seeing Professor Moore's address. But even then, one aspect of this process would be relevant only to ' $q$ ' and another aspect would be relevant only to ' $r$ '. Thus, on MacIver's view, a holder of any form of the principle that " the meaning of a sentence is the method of its verification " would have to admit that two sentences might have different meanings and yet express the same proposition. Of course if two sentences have different meanings we shall almost certainly also say that they express different propositions. And even apart from the verification principle there would probably be fairly wide agreement that if two sentences have to be verified in different ways it follows that they express different propositions.

I think these considerations make it fairly clear that sentences interrelated in the same way as ' $p$ ', ' $q$ ', and ' $r$ ' in my example don't in any ordinary sense express the same proposition, but three different propositions. In that case MacIver is mistaken in arguing that each of his (A) sentences expresses the same proposition as the corresponding (B) sentence, and his proof that

certain of his (A) sentences are not self-contradictory is therefore
not valid. But if the foregoing considerations are not found
convincing, there is another way of disproving MacIver's
argument.

Consider the sentences (*a*) ' I am not an editor ', (*b*) ' Professor
Moore is not an editor ', (*c*) ' the editor of *Mind* is not an editor '.
Of these sentences, (*c*) i's obviously self-contradictory, while
(*a*) and (*b*) as obviously are not—and (*a*) would not be even if
it were said by Professor Moore. Yet on MacIver's view (*a*), if
uttered by Professor Moore, (*b*) and (*c*) must all express the same
proposition. If a proposition has the same logical character as
the sentences which express it, it follows that the same proposition
may both be and not be self-contradictory. In any event, it
follows that the same proposition may be expressed both by a
self-contradictory and by a self-consistent sentence. In either
case, it follows that even if each of MacIver's (A) sentences
expresses the same proposition as the corresponding (B) sentence
it is quite possible for one to be self-consistent and the other to
be self-contradictory.

Enough has I think been said to show that MacIver's claim to
prove that certain (A) sentences are not self-contradictory is
completely untenable, in so far as it rests on the argument that
they express the same propositions as the corresponding (B)
sentences, and that these are obviously not self-contradictory.

In the latter part of his paper, MacIver argues that the inclination to call sentences of such forms as ' *p* but I think not-*p* '
self-contradictory really arises from the fact that the saying of
them must always be pointless : and that there really is a contradiction, not in the sentence, but " between part of what is asserted
and what must be assumed by the hearer if the other part is to
be worth attending to "[1]: the point is, I suppose, that the
hearer must assume " the speaker believes what he is saying ",
that is " believes *p* ", and this conflicts with the speaker's statement
" I think not-*p* "). This suggestion seems to be independent of
the argument I have been criticising, and I don't feel at all sure
that it is not the right account of what I previously called a
" form of contradiction ". I don't, however, feel quite sure
that it is. MacIver accuses philosophers, especially " analytical "

[1] p. 95.

philosophers, of " considering language apart from its use "[1]. He adds the curious statement that, as a result, " ' to have no use ' tends to be equated with ' to make no sense ' ". I should have thought this would be a natural result, not of separating language from its use, but of considering it only in relation to its use. I can't help suspecting that MacIver is perhaps himself guilty of " considering language apart from its use ", when he talks of the " pointlessness " of making a certain statement. I can only put this point very vaguely. MacIver attempts to distinguish between a proposition which is self-contradictory, and a proposition whose assertion is, from its own nature, pointless, because " there is a contradiction involved in the situation of *making* such an assertion " : I have a suspicion that this distinction may rest on a fictitious separation of the properties which symbols possess " in themselves ", and the practical purposes for which they can be used in different kinds of situation. I recognise that this fiction, if it is a fiction, is probably just as deep-rooted in my own mind as it is in MacIver's.

There is an incidental point connected with the interchangeability of pronouns, names, and descriptions which is interesting. When I was trying to show that sentences containing pronouns don't express the same propositions as corresponding sentences containing names or descriptions, there is another argument which I might have used. Pronouns and their equivalents work, as symbols, in a different way from descriptions and proper names.[2] In an obvious sense—quite different from Russell's—a pronominal sentence is an incomplete symbol : it can't be understood unless it is completed in some way by circumstances. In an equally obvious sense a non-pronominal sentence is complete in itself. It might be argued that a complete and an incomplete symbol could never express the same proposition, and that accordingly none of MacIver's (B) sentences can express the same proposition as any of his (A) sentences. But could any reason be given for this principle except that in fact no instance of a complete and an incomplete symbol which express the same proposition can be found? If this is the only reason which could

---

[1] p. 94.

[2] I think Russell was right, as far as he went, in saying that ordinary proper names were equivalent to descriptions ; but that isn't very far. It was confusing to say that we attach different descriptions to them on different occasions ; for obviously in some sense they mean the same for everyone.

be given, the argument is circular. For it presupposes that a criterion already exists for deciding whether '$p$' and '$q$' express the same proposition : it can't therefore be used in establishing such a criterion.

I feel, however, that there is some additional ground for saying that a complete and an incomplete symbol can't express the same proposition, but I don't know whether I can justify this feeling. Suppose '$p$' and '$q$' are sentences which differ only in that '$p$' contains '1' and '$q$' contains a name or description standing for somebody who has in fact used '$p$'. It might be argued that if '$p$' and '$q$' expressed the same proposition it should be possible for anyone who knew the language to which '$p$' and '$q$' belong to use either '$p$' or '$q$' indifferently : but actually '$q$' can be used by anyone, while '$p$' can only be used, to convey the same information, by one person. But compare this case with a slightly different case. Suppose there were a symbolism which involved writing characters in different colours. Suppose '$p$' involved the use of a red character, and '$q$' didn't. I might then be able to write '$q$', but unable to write '$p$' because I had no red ink. But we clearly shouldn't regard this as a sufficient reason for saying '$p$' and '$q$' couldn't express the same proposition. We feel, however, that in this case the impossibility of my using '$p$' is accidental; whereas in the former case the impossibility of my using '$p$', if I were not the person named or described in '$q$', would be essential.

I argued above, under (2), that someone might know the proposition expressed by a pronominal sentence without knowing the proposition expressed by a corresponding non-pronominal sentence ; but suggested that there was a difficulty about saying that someone might know the proposition expressed by the non-pronominal sentence without knowing that expressed by the pronominal sentence. The difficulty is that he might know the proposition expressed by '$q$' (used as above) but not understand the proposition expressed by '$p$' : it would of course follow that in one sense he didn't know the proposition expressed by '$p$'— because he could't know it : but in a different sense from that in which he doesn't know a proposition which he does understand, and could know. It might be argued that '$p$' can be understood only by those who hear it—if it's spoken—because the speaker is himself part of the symbolism. The complete symbol of which the incomplete symbol ' *p* ' is part can't be reported, as complete verbal symbols can. It can of course be described and imagined, and so, in a sense, understood by those who didn't hear it. But in another sense it can't be understood. When I understand a non-pronominal sentence, the complete symbol is before me. But when I understand an ' I ' sentence, as spoken on some occasion on which I wasn't present, only part of the symbol is before me, and part is merely imagined.

I raise these points about " incomplete symbols " simply for the sake of suggesting certain puzzles, not with the intention of putting forward any positive view. Similar puzzles can of course be found for other reported pronominal sentences—compare, for instance, the reported sentence ' this colour is darker than that '.

## REPLY TO MR. DUNCAN-JONES

### By A. M. MacIver

I AM afraid that Mr. Duncan-Jones is being a little pedantic, in the sense of demanding greater precision than a particular context requires. All that my argument required was that the proposition expressed by a sentence in the first person should always be in principle expressible by a sentence in the third person. There was no need for the examples I used to be more than suggestive, to induce readers to reflect that, if this were done with sentences of such forms as " *p* but I don't think *p* ", it would be seen that they did not express contradictions. Since it is quite possible that Mussolini should be having a bath at a time when Mr. Duncan-Jones did not think that he was, it follows that, if Mr. Duncan-Jones were to say " Mussolini is having a bath but I don't think he is ", he would be asserting a proposition that was not self-contradictory. This seems to me to be one of those points which are quite obvious when attended to and yet so often neglected as to lead to common philosophical muddles, and I am sorry that Mr. Duncan-Jones should sidetrack the discussion into the irrelevant question (however interesting in itself) how far sentences of different grammatical forms can exactly coincide in meaning.

But there is one thing which I should like to point out about this, and that is that we get different answers to the question what proposition such-and-such a sentence expresses, according as we consider the sentence purely in itself or as used in a given context.[1] Take one of Mr. Duncan-Jone's examples, the sentence 'Professor Moore lives in Cambridge'. Of course this has no meaning at all apart from the conventions of some language—when Mr. Duncan-Jones speaks of the properties which symbols possess " in themselves " (his inverted commas), I presume that he must mean the properties which belong to them by convention, as distinguished from those attributed to them in use on a particular occasion—but the meaning which belongs to it merely by the conventions of the English language is much vaguer than that which may be understood from it when addressed by a particular speaker to a particular hearer. All that it represents purely by the conventions of the language is the very general proposition that somebody of the rank of professor and name of Moore lives in some place called Cambridge (of which I find nine in the index of my atlas). From the sentence as used by Mr. Duncan-Jones any reader of *Analysis* will understand a much more definite proposition than this, but only because we know something about Mr. Duncan-Jones (namely that he is a British philosopher of the first half of the twentieth century) and something about contemporary philosophy. In other circumstances the same sentence (that is, another token of the same sentence-type) might convey the quite different proposition that some American professor of the name of Moore lived in Cambridge, Massachusetts.

When Mr. Duncan-Jones talks about " the proposition which a sentence expresses ", he clearly does not mean the very general proposition which it represents purely conventionally ; he means the much more definite proposition which it would convey in some supposed circumstances. He is saying that there are circumstances in which what would be conveyed by " I live in Cambridge ", even if the speaker was Professor Moore (that is, the particular Professor Moore to whom Mr. Duncan-Jones is referring), would not be the same proposition as would be

---

[1] The *systematic* dependence of meaning on context which we find in *pronominal* sentence-forms is something over and above what I am discussing here.

conveyed by " Professor Moore lives in Cambridge " or " The editor of *Mind* lives in Cambridge ". For example, the hearer might not know that the speaker was Professor Moore, or that Professor Moore was editor of *Mind*. But we can also suppose circumstances in which each of these sentences would convey the same proposition as either of the others. Suppose I have been introduced to Professor Moore and then hear him say " I live in Cambridge " ; what I shall then understand will be just what I should understand if someone else said " Professor Moore lives in Cambridge ". Or suppose that a man has been pointed out to me as the editor of *Mind* but I do not know what his name is or anything else about him ; what I shall then understand if I hear him say " I live in Cambridge " will be just what I should understand if I heard someone else say " The editor of *Mind* lives in Cambridge ". Or suppose I know that Professor Moore is the editor of *Mind* but know nothing else about him ; then what I shall understand from " Professor Moore lives in Cambridge " will be just what I should understand from " The editor of *Mind* lives in Cambridge ".

I believe that, if Mr. Duncan-Jones had observed this, he would never have thought that his arguments were valid against my paper. For, if there are any circumstances in which one sentence would convey the same proposition as another sentence, then, if the proposition conveyed by one of those sentences is obviously self-consistent, the proposition conveyed by the other cannot be self-contradictory. The fact that the same sentences in other circumstances might convey different propositions is simply irrelevant. In my paper I took certain circumstances for granted. Of course " Mr. Braithwaite went to Grantchester on February 14th, 1938 " would only convey the same proposition as " I went to Grantchester yesterday " to a hearer who knew that the latter was spoken by Mr. Braithwaite on February 15th, 1938. The point is that in those circumstances (which I took for granted) the same proposition would be conveyed by either sentence. The consequences which I drew then follow (or at least it has not yet been shown that they don't.)

# SAYING AND DISBELIEVING

## By Max Black

IF Thomas were to say "Mushrooms are poisonous but I don't believe it ", would he be contradicting himself? This question has been discussed by many writers,[1] all of whom agree that no self-contradiction would occur. According to them Thomas expresses the very same proposition that would be expressed if somebody else were to say "Mushrooms are poisonous, but Thomas does not believe that they are ". The latter proposition is obviously not self-contradictory, and might very well be true; mushrooms might really be poisonous and Thomas need not believe that they are.

Those who have discussed the question agree, however, that it would be " perfectly absurd "[2] for Thomas to make such a remark, and they give a number of explanations of the source of this absurdity. It seems to me that all these accounts contain the same mistake : in arguing that Thomas would be expressing the same proposition that would be expressed by the sentence referring to Thomas by his name, they all assume that he would be expressing *some* proposition, i.e., that he would be making an *assertion*. I think this is wrong, and I shall try to show why.

I shall begin by considering what Moore says. His view is that when Thomas pronounces the words " Mushrooms are poisonous " his words " imply " that Thomas believes mushrooms to be poisonous. What the word " imply " means, Moore explains as follows :—

" There seems to be nothing mysterious about this sense of ' imply ' in which if you assert that you went to the pictures last Tuesday, you *imply*, though you don't *assert*, that you *believe* or know that you did ; and in which, if you assert that Brutus'

[1] A. M. MacIver, " Some questions about ' know ' and ' think '," this collection, pp. 88–95, G. E. Moore, *Ethics* (1912), 125, *The Philosophy of G. E. Moore* (ed. P. A. Schilpp, 1942), 541–3, *The Philosophy of Bertrand Russell* (ed. P. A. Schilpp, 1944), 203–4. See also, C. H. Langford in *The Philosophy of G. E. Moore*, 332–3, Y. Bar-Hillel in *Mind* 55 (1946), 333–7, P. F. Strawson in *Mind* 59 (1950), 330–3, Norman Malcolm in *Philosophical Analysis* (ed. M. Black, 1950), 259–61.
[2] See the next quotation from Moore.

action was right, you *imply*, but don't *assert*, that you approve of Brutus' action. In the first case, that you do imply this proposition about your present attitude, although it is not implied by (i.e. does not follow from) *what* you assert, simply arises from the fact, which we all learn by experience, that in the immense majority of cases a man who makes such an assertion as this does believe or know what he asserts : lying, though common enough, is vastly exceptional. And this is why to say such a thing as ' I went to the pictures last Tuesday, but I don't believe that I did ' is a perfectly absurd thing to say, although what is asserted is something perfectly possible logically . . ." [1]

In an earlier discussion, Moore says :

" There is an important distinction, which is not always observed, between what a man *means* by a given assertion and what he *expresses* by it. Whenever we make any assertion whatever (unless we do not mean what we say) we are always *expressing* one or other of two things—namely, either that we *think* the thing in question to be so, or that we *know* it to be so."

And a few lines later, he adds :

" Even when I do not mean what I say, my words may be said to *imply* either that I think that *A* is *B* or that I know it, since they will commonly lead people to suppose that one or other of these things is the case." [2]

Moore's latest statement of the point is as follows :

" To say such a thing as ' I believe he has gone out, but he has not ' is absurd. This, though absurd, is not self-contradictory; for it may quite well be true. But it is absurd, because by saying 'he has not gone out' we *imply* that we do *not* believe that he has gone out, though we neither assert this, nor does it follow from anything we do assert. That we *imply* it means only, I think, something which results from the fact that people, in general, do not make a positive assertion, unless they do not believe that the opposite is true : people, in general, would not assert positively ' he has not gone out ', if they believed that he had gone out. And it results from this general truth, that a hearer who hears me say ' he has not gone out ', will, in general,

[1] *The Philosophy of G. E. Moore*, 542-3.
[2] *Ethics*, 125.

assume that I don't believe he has gone out, although I have neither asserted that I don't, nor does it follow, from what I have asserted, that I don't. Since people will, in general, assume this, I may be said to *imply* it by saying ' he has not gone out ', since the effect of my saying so will, in general, be to make people believe it, and since 1 know quite well that my saying it will have this effect."[1]

From these remarks of Moore, we can derive the following explanation of the way in which he is here using the word " imply " : Suppose (i) a speaker is using an expression, $E$, (ii) people do not generally use $E$ unless some related proposition $p_E$ is true, (iii) people hearing the speaker use the expression $E$ will generally believe $p_E$ to be true, and, finally (iv) the speaker knows all this—then if these four conditions are met, the speaker's words may be said to *imply* $p_E$.

The following examples will fit this explanation :

(a) A man will not normally say " Damn! " unless he is annoyed, and people hearing him swear will normally believe him to be annoyed, and he knows this ; so if a man says " Damn!" he *implies* that he is annoyed.

(b) Only a woman will normally say " I am going to have my dress lengthened ", and anybody hearing these words will believe that a woman is speaking, and the speaker herself knows this ; so anybody using those words implies that she is a woman.

(c) Nobody who utters an English sentence is usually unable to speak English, and this is a matter of common knowledge, both to the speaker and to his hearers ; hence anybody who utters an English sentence *implies* that he can speak English.

(d) If anybody makes any remark at all, he is normally awake, and people will know him to be awake and he knows that they will know it ; so if I make any remark at all, I *imply* that I am awake.

If any of these implications happens to be false, some more or less usual event has occurred—a man has used an oath without being annoyed, or has talked about " my dress " although he is a man, or has uttered an English sentence without being able to speak English, or has been talking in his sleep.

[1] *The Philosophy of Bertrand Russell*, p. 204.

On this view, what Thomas said, when he said " Mushrooms are poisonous, but I don't believe it ", was not self-contradictory, but only wildly implausible and contrary to what experience would lead us to expect. The absurdity of his remark is a *factual* absurdity, such as would be involved in saying : " I know my Christian name, but I simply cannot remember my surname " or " I feel perfectly well, yet I never sleep at all " or " The inside of my body is a vacuum ". All of these remarks are wildly implausible ; they are all absurd because they are incredible and known by the speaker to be incredible.

Moore said that lying—and we might add, joking—is " vastly exceptional ". But the speaker might be a congenital liar like Pecksniff, so that we would be really amazed to find him telling the *truth*. Of course a man who says " *p*, but I don't believe *p* " immediately blows the gaff upon himself, and this is no doubt rarer than unabashed and unqualified lying—as rare, perhaps, as the spectacle of a man's walking on his hands. We might say that the absurdity of a man's walking on his hands arose from the apparent *pointlessness* of the performance ; but if the man in question said that he was practising acrobatics, we would understand the point of what he was doing, and would no longer describe his performance as absurd. But can we even imagine what it would be like for the utterance in good faith of " *p*, but I don't believe *p* " to have a point? If Moore is right, the mistake made by Thomas is in spinning a yarn which we normally have every reason to disbelieve ; there is no logical discrepancy between the two clauses of Thomas's statement. In practice, however, we do treat the apparent discrepancy between " *p* " and " I believe that not-*p* " as a logical discrepancy. Suppose we hear a public speaker say, at one point in his remarks, " There will be another World War within a decade " and then hear the same speaker say, later on, " I believe there will not be another World War within the next ten years ". It would be natural, and reasonable, to ask him to *reconcile* these two remarks ; we treat each as telling against the truth of the other, and we assume that both ought not to be asserted simultaneously. Suppose now the speaker in question were to answer our demand by saying " You know how irresponsible I am! I said there would be a war within ten years in order to shock the audience. But I don't really believe what I said, you know!" This explanation would tell us *why* he said what he did, and remove the surprise we may have felt at his saying it. Yet it would confer no licence upon him to continue to assert both "$p$" and "I believe that not-$p$" in the future. To the charge that one assertion contradicts another, it is no defense to say "I was lying when I said '$p$'". This may explain how the speaker came to say "$p$, but also not-$p$"; it has no tendency at all to show the two propositions are consistent.

Moore's account assumed that somebody could at any rate *assert* "I went to the pictures last Tuesday, but I don't believe that I did". This assumption needs to be examined. Let us first consider what our response would be if we heard somebody pronounce these words in an assertive tone of voice.

The first difficulty is to imagine any context in which this performance would not leave us flabbergasted and utterly at a loss to know what to think. Of course, philosophers can say anything, and if a member of the Aristotelian Society were overhead intoning these words, we might be sympathetic rather than surprised. But if an ordinary man in ordinary circumstances were to burst out with "I went to the pictures last Tuesday, but I don't believe that I did", our best surmise might be that he was reciting a line of verse, or pulling our leg, or "simply saying the words" without meaning what he said. If he assured us that he was in earnest, however, and that he meant what he said; and if he even repeated the extraordinary remark with added vehemence, we might think a further effort of interpretation worth making.

Now ordinary language is so pliable that almost any sentence can be *made* to bear a meaning. A man who seriously said "I went to the pictures yesterday, but I don't believe it" might mean something like this : "There is evidence to show that I went to the pictures yesterday (people claim to have seen me there, here is my ticket stub, etc.)—I suppose I must have been there—yet I can't remember a thing about it. I seem to remember playing chess that night—I still can't believe it".

In this interpretation, the words, "I went to the pictures yesterday", have been replaced by the weaker sentence "I suppose I must have gone to the pictures yesterday" which *fall short* of making the original assertion. By weakening the first clause of the original paradoxical remark, we succeed in making good though unusual sense of that remark.

A psychologist or a philosopher might offer a second interpretation, somewhat on the following lines : " Yes, I went to the pictures yesterday. But I would hardly dignify my attitude toward that fact by using the impressive word ' belief '. I take the fact for granted, act as though it were a fact, but there's none of the effort and tension that are a sign of genuine active belief ". In this interpretation, the second clause of the original paradoxical remark (i.e., " I don't believe I went to the pictures yesterday ") has been given a weaker meaning than it would normally have. " I don't believe " has been construed as meaning the same as " I don't *actively* believe ". This second interpretation, like the first, makes good, though still more unusual, sense of the original paradoxical remark.

Both interpretations are strained or forced. If we were to impose them on the speaker's words, we would be entertaining extraordinary hypotheses about what the speaker was trying to say. Only if we had some good independent reason to suppose he was speaking responsibly would we feel justified in making such extraordinary efforts to make sense of what, on first hearing, was quite unintelligible.

Imagine now that the speaker rejects all such ingenious attempts to put a reasonable, if far-fetched, interpretation upon his language. Perhaps he retorts : " This is all very ingenious, but quite irrelevant. I meant exactly what I said, and I was using words in their familiar ordinary meanings. There is no question of mere evidence that I went to the pictures yesterday —I actually went. And I don't assume or take for granted that I did—I don't believe it, I actively *dis*believe it! " If this should happen, all that would be left for us to say would be the exasperated " He *can't* be serious ". This is not an expression of incredulity, like the " I don't believe it " of the man who first met a giraffe. My contention is that it would be *wrong* to say that the original paradoxical remark was an assertion at all.

Let us consider, for the sake of comparison and contrast, the following case. A man, of average height, on being asked how tall he is, replies, apparently in all seriousness, " Two feet ".

Further investigation seems to show that he is not joking, that he means his words to be understood literally, in their familiar non-metaphorical senses, that he clearly understood the original question, knows what he is saying, and so on. These considerations would incline us to say he *is* honestly asserting that he is two feet tall. On the other hand we would be just as strongly disinclined to say that he could be honestly asserting what he seemed to be asserting.

I have argued in another paper[1] that it is a " presupposition " of the expression " honest assertion " that there shall be a certain accordance between the speaker's performance (the words he uses) and his " state of mind " (among other things, his knowledge that he is not two feet tall). In an abnormal case like the present one in which the presupposition is falsified, the expression lacks a use, and the question whether or not an honest assertion was made fails to arise. This is what happens when a man of normal height says he is two feet tall.

Thus the sentence " He honestly asserted that he was two feet tall " has no application in the situation described. It would be wrong either to say that the speaker did honestly assert that he was two feet tall or that he did not honestly assert that he was two feet tall. It would be wrong to *use* the expression " honestly assert " at all in this case. (If we like, we can say that a case of a man's uttering the paradoxical sentence in the situation described is *not* a case of making an honest assertion—provided we understand this to mean only that we cannot use the expression " honest assertion " for that type of case.)

If all else failed, we would probably say of a man who seemed to be honestly asserting he was two feet tall, in the circumstances described, that he must be insane. But this judgment would not be a clinical diagnosis (though the speaker's extraordinary remark might be the first entry in a medical dossier). Even if he never behaved otherwise than normally in all subsequent occasions we would be tempted to say that he must have been *momentarily* insane. This is like saying that an act for which we have no explanation is " due to chance ", where we provide only the

---

[1] " Definition, presupposition, and assertion," *The Philosophical Review*. 61 (1952), 532—550. In that paper I have tried to explain in detail what I mean by " presuppositions ".

illusion of an explanation. By shrugging our speaker off as insane, we excuse ourselves from having to choose between "He asserted" and "He did not assert"; we banish the instance from the realm of logical adjudication.

Parallel considerations apply to the case of a speaker who seems to be honestly asserting something expressed by the words, "I went to the pictures yesterday, but I don't believe that I did", and to be using those words, non-figuratively, in their ordinary senses. If evidence points to the man's being in earnest, understanding what he says, and so on, a presupposition of the term "honestly asserts" is falsified. It would be wrong to say that he made an honest assertion and wrong to deny that he made an honest assertion. And to say he must have been insane would be simply a way of parrying a demand to choose between the two judgments.

It seems to me that the meaning of the word "assertion" is to be understood in terms of the meaning of the expression "honest assertion", and not *vice versa*.[1] A man who lies is trying to deceive his hearers by behaving like somebody who makes an honest assertion. Now if it is improper to say that a man could make an honest assertion by means of a certain statement, it would seem to follow that it must be improper to say that a man could lie when using that statement. I hold, therefore, that it would be wrong to describe a normal man who said "I am two feet tall" as lying, or, indeed, as making an assertion at all.

The sentence "I am two feet tall" might be used, in exceptional circumstances, to make an honest assertion. A midget might say it and a philosopher who followed Alice down the rabbit hole might have to say it. No circumstances can be described, however, in which it would be proper to make an honest assertion by means of the words "Oysters are edible, but I don't believe it"—to change the illustration—so long as those words were being used in their familiar ordinary senses.

I think we can see why the form of words, "Oysters are edible, but I don't believe it", is always improper. When the words "Oysters are edible" are pronounced assertively, the tone of voice used, together with the choice of the appropriate

---

[1] This is defended in the paper referred to in the previous footnote.

copula ('are', not 'may be', or 'conceivably might be' or one of the other alternatives available) is a *conventional sign* of what we might call "good faith". In order to use the English language correctly, one has to learn that to pronounce the sentence "Oysters are edible" in a certain tone of voice is to *represent oneself* as knowing, or believing, or at least not disbelieving what is being said. (To write a cheque is to represent oneself as having money in the bank to honour the cheque). Perhaps the tone in question was once the natural and untutored way in which conviction would manifest itself. But whether this is so or not, that tone has become a *conventional* sign. So that, whether the man who asserts "Oysters are edible" in fact believes what he is saying or is deliberately lying, he signifies that he knows, or believes, or at least does not disbelieve what he says. (If this were not so, lying would be more difficult than it is. A liar trades upon the conventional signification of his linguistic act to produce a deceptive impression).

In saying that an utterance in a certain tone of voice *conventionally* signifies "good faith" on the speaker's part, I mean that the making of such an utterance in the absence of the corresponding knowledge or belief is properly treated as a violation of the language. If a man began a sentence with the words "After Columbus landed at San Salvador . . . " while believing that Columbus never did land at San Salvador, he would be misusing the words as much as if he deliberately used the word "red" to describe something blue. A liar who speaks earnestly is faking a mere manifestation of belief (like a man who tries to appear younger by wearing a wig); but a man who says "$p$" while disbelieving $p$ is breaking a rule about a conventional sign (like an unmarried women who wears a wedding ring).

I have said that the speaker *signifies* that he does not disbelieve what he says. It would be incorrect to say that he *says* so, since in such contexts we commonly use the word 'say' to refer only to what is explicitly formulated by a declarative sentence—or what is entailed by the proposition expressed. The speaker says that oysters are edible (and whatever logically follows from the truth of that proposition) but nothing more. In this sense of 'say', a man who utters a command has "said" nothing whatever, for he has not explicitly formulated any declarative sentence. Yet he has certainly *communicated* a certain intention by the use of a conventional sign. A certain tone of voice in conjunction with the choice of the imperative mood conventionally signifies that the speaker desires the action he is describing to be performed.

Logicians have almost invariably neglected the *signification,* as distinct from the *meaning*, of utterances, with the result that they have been led to overlook the possibility of conflicts between significations. If I say " Close that door, but don't close it! " it would be improper to say that I am uttering a self-contradiction in the logicians' sense of that term. Yet the utterance " Close that door! " contains a conventional sign whose signification is incompatible with the signification of " Do *not* close that door! " If I had said " I want you to close that door, but I do not want you to close that door " there would be a plain logical contradiction in what I was saying. But part of the signification conventionally conveyed by the utterance " Close that door, but don't close it! " is exactly the same as would be conveyed by the self-contradictory indicative sentence. The two imperatives have *incompatible* significations.

Consider now our response to the words " Close that door! I don't want you to do it, however ". Here we would properly regard the indicative sentence (" I don't want you to do it ") as cancelling the imperative—and if the command were to be reiterated we should be unable to make sense of the communication. There is a conflict here between the conventional signification of the imperative tone and what is said by the indicative sentence that follows ; the signification of the sign is incompatible with the meaning of the words that follow. A similar case occurs when an attempt is made to use the words " Oysters are edible, but I don't believe that they are ". The pronouncing of the first three words conventionally signifies that the speaker does not disbelieve what he says ; this signification is incompatible with what is explicitly said by the clause that follows ; hence the whole sentence fails to have a use.

It follows that to pronounce, in an assertive tone of voice, the sentence " Jones honestly asserted that he went to the pictures but that he did not believe that he went ", without the intention of giving the words an unusual meaning, would be to *misuse* language. It would not be the kind of misuse involved in pronouncing assertively the words " Runcibles are chuffable " ; nor the kind of misuse involved in saying " Every triangle has exactly two sides " ; nor the kind of misuse involved in announcing without qualification "A virus is non-animate ". It is not a case of nonsense, or logical contradiction, or unqualified application of a term to a border-line case. The sentence in question might be called " inoperative ", because its truth would require the falsification of one of its own presuppositions. We could *give* it a sense, if we chose. But that would require a change in our language.

# CHAPTER V. SAYING AND ASSERTING.

## SOME NOTES ON ASSERTION

### By C. LEWY

[Although this paper still seems to me to contain some points which are worth making, I now think that it contains a number of mistakes ; but it would be impossible to correct them without writing, in effect, a new paper. C. L. (1954).]

I DO not propose to consider in this paper the so-called problem of assertion in any detail. All I wish to do is to make some critical remarks on what Mr. Wisdom says on the subject in his recent paper in *Mind*,[1] and to discuss briefly a few related points.

Moore has discussed the whole problem in great detail[2] and many of the things I'm going to say are due to him. On the other hand, I should, perhaps, mention that the chief point I'm about to discuss occurred to me before I heard Moore's comment on Wisdom's paper.

Wisdom says (*op. cit.* p. 463) that " statements about propositions and characteristics such as ' He asserted the proposition that Africa is hot ', ' She is chic ', can be turned into statements about words ' He uttered the sentence "Africa is hot " ', ' She is what the French call " chic " ', if, and only if the verbal statements are so used that we say that a man understands them only if he understands not merely the expression 'the sentence "Africa is hot " ', but also understands that sentence and similarly understands the word ' chic ' ".

This statement may in a way be regarded as an attempt to correct a now famous mistake of Carnap, who used to hold that " Babylon was treated of in yesterday's lecture " can be translated into " the word ' Babylon ' occurred in yesterday's lecture ",[3] and analogously of course that the proposition "*A* asserted that Africa is hot " can be translated into "*A* uttered the sentence 'Africa is hot ' ".

These are examples of the translation from the so-called " material mode of speech " to " the formal mode ".

---

[1] ' Metaphysics and Verification,' *Mind*, October 1938    [2] In lectures.
[3] Cf. *Logical Syntax of Language*, p. 286.

Now, it has been pointed out by Moore (and probably by others) that this won't do. For a parrot can utter the words "Africa is hot" but no-one (except possibly Carnap) would say that a parrot can *assert* that Africa is hot.

The passage quoted from Wisdom doesn't make it *quite* clear that the same objection wouldn't be relevant to his own view : for it isn't plain whether the words " . . . we say that *a man* understands them only if . . . " refer to the hearer or to the speaker. If they were intended to refer to the hearer then the objection would be relevant (and so would a similar one : suppose a German who didn't know any English uttered the words "Africa is hot" ; we should not say that he asserted that Africa is hot). But if, as I think is the case, Wisdom was referring to the speaker, these objections are not valid.

But although Wisdom seems to have avoided Carnap's error, his own claim that the two propositions are logically equivalent is, I think, unjustified. I shall try to express my criticism by considering first what conditions must be satisfied if $A$ is to assert anything.

Following Moore I shall formulate them as follows :

(1) $A$ must use some *token* or other,

(2) $A$ must use some token with some meaning or other (*or* $A$ must attach some meaning to some token which he uses).

These two conditions are *necessary* but not sufficient.

[*Note* : Moore mentions two other conditions which some philosophers regard as necessary but which, according to him, are not necessary.

The first is that in order to assert $p$ $A$ should either believe $p$ or know $p$. To state this as a necessary condition is wrong because one can certainly assert $p$ and be lying. Furthermore we couldn't lie at all *without* asserting something or other. On the other hand the temptation to state this condition as a necessary one is, I think, excusable. For there is, I think, a tendency to say that $A$ didn't really assert $p$, if he was lying. But I have no time to develop this point here.

The second condition which some people *mistakenly*, according to Moore, regard as necessary is that in order to assert $p$ one must use a token of $p$ or a token of an expression which has the same meaning as $p$. Moore denies this, and the sort of example he

gives in support of his view is this.[1] Suppose I make an arrangement with Smith that if I go to the Union I shall leave on my
desk a white sheet of paper with a cross in the middle. Suppose
I do leave such a sheet of paper on my desk, but instead of
going to the Union go to the University Library. Then Smith
could rightly accuse me of breaking the arrangement, and say
" You *said* that you were going to the Union ". I agree with the
example but deny that it supports Moore's claim. For in this
case I should be introducing a new language (or a new language-
arrangement) in which leaving a white sheet of paper with a cross
in the middle *would* mean the same as the words " I am going to
the Union " mean in English. Thus I should be using a token
of an expression which has the same meaning as *p*. I may,
perhaps, be extending in this case Moore's use of ' expression '
and of ' token ' but this seems to be unimportant. All that can
rightly be said is, I think, that it is not necessary in order to
assert *p* to use a token of *p* or a token of an expression which has
the same meaning as *p in any of the existing languages* (like French
or German).]

Wisdom's description satisfies the conditions (1) and (2), and
it satisfies further another condition (which in itself is neither
necessary nor sufficient), namely that *A* attached the *ordinary*
meaning to *p*.

But even all this is not enough to justify his claim that " He
asserted the proposition that Africa is hot " means the same as
" He uttered the sentence 'Africa is hot ' if and only if etc. ".

This can be brought out in the following way. I now write
down the proposition " The Labour Party will win the next
General Election ". I attach to all the words occuring in the
sentence expressing this proposition their ordinary meanings
etc., but can it be said that I have *asserted* that the Labour Party
will win the next General Election? Obviously not. I may have
been merely *considering* this proposition.

Similarly an actor on the stage is not asserting any propositions
expressed by the sentences which he utters. The members of
the chorus in Auden and Isherwood's " On the Frontier " were
not *asserting*

---

[1] This is not actually his example, though modelled on his.

> Perhaps we shall die by a firing squad,
> Perhaps they will kill us, that won't be odd,
> But when we lie down with earth on our face,
> There will be ten men much better to fight in our place!

Nor am I asserting anything, to take yet another example, when I read aloud a poem.

I conclude therefore that " He asserted the proposition that Africa is hot " *cannot* be translated into " He uttered the sentence 'Africa is hot'" as Carnap has claimed; nor can this be done on the more complicated lines suggested by Wisdom.

Both for Carnap and Wisdom, however, the alleged possibility of making this translation is important. The importance of it, in the case of Wisdom, lies in the fact that he wishes to say that for every statement about abstract entities—propositions, characteristics—there is a verbal statement which makes the same factual claims though its meaning is different.

This may suggest to us that what Wisdom meant by saying " ' He asserted $p$ ' can be turned into ' He uttered " $p$ " ' if, and only if, etc.", was not that the two statements mean the same but that they make the same factual claims. This however wouldn't do either. For one of the " factual claims " made by the sentence " He asserted that Africa is hot " is that he either knew that Africa is hot, or believed this, or was lying; whereas " He uttered the sentence 'Africa is hot'" (even if this is used in the sense which Wisdom has explained) does not make this claim because he might have been merely considering the proposition.

I have mentioned two conditions necessary for saying that A has asserted $p$, but said that they were not sufficient. Can we find a condition which in conjunction with these two would make a sufficient set? I think we can. There is a certain way of speaking which may be called " an assertive way ". And what distinguishes asserting a proposition (in speaking) from merely considering it is the assertive way in which it is said.

Thus Wisdom should have said that the statement " He asserted that Africa is hot " can be turned into " He uttered

*assertively* the sentence 'Africa is hot' if, and only if, etc.".
Whether this would serve his purpose I don't know.

What makes a way " an assertive way " (of saying things in a language)? There is a tendency to ask this question thinking that it's possible to give one or more characteristics which are essential, i.e. both necessary and sufficient.

I cannot do this. I can however describe this way indirectly by saying that a parrot does *not* utter sentences assertively, nor does an actor on the stage, nor does a person reading aloud a poem or a novel. But if, trying to describe it " more directly ", we ask : Is it a particular tone of voice? or is it " a feeling of conviction " accompanying the uttering of the sentence? or is it perhaps just the uttering of the sentence plus having a certain image before " the mind's eye "?—we see that none of these will do in all cases.

For do we always utter a sentence in one particular tone of voice when we assert it? Does " a feeling of conviction " always accompany our assertions? (And in any case the fact that we can assert something and be lying shows that this won't do.) Do we always have a certain image when we assert a proposition? And even if this were so, couldn't we have the same (or an exactly similar) image while merely considering it?

We may then try to describe an assertive way of speaking by reference to the effects which it produces. The characteristic one has in mind in this connection is that if I say $p$ in an assertive way I tend to make my hearers believe $p$ or tend to convince them that I believe $p$. A short reflection will show that this again is neither necessary nor sufficient. I can assert $p$ without making my hearers believe it or even without convincing them that I believe it (when I assert $p$ but my hearers take me to be making an ironical remark). Conversely, I can by uttering $p$ make my hearers think that I believe it and yet not be asserting $p$ at all (e.g. when I make a joke which my hearers take seriously).

Thus I cannot give any one characteristic which must be present if a way of speaking is to be assertive, but I think that enough has been said to make the meaning of this expression perfectly clear.

# ON CARNAP'S ANALYSIS OF STATEMENTS OF ASSERTION AND BELIEF[1]

## By ALONZO CHURCH

### I

FOR statements such as (1) *Seneca said that man is a rational animal* and (A) *Columbus believed the world to be round,* the most obvious analysis makes them statements about certain abstract entities which we shall call ' propositions ' (though this is not the same as Carnap's use of the term), namely the proposition that man is a rational animal and the proposition that the world is round ; and these propositions are taken as having been respectively the object of an assertion by Seneca and the object of a belief by Columbus. We shall not discuss this obvious analysis here except to admit that it threatens difficulties and complications of its own, which appear as soon as the attempt is made to formulate systematically the syntax of a language in which statements like (1) and (A) are possible. But our purpose is to point out what we believe may be an insuperable objection against alternative analyses that undertake to do away with propositions in favour of such more concrete things as sentences.

As attempts which have been or might be made to analyze (1) in terms in sentences we cite : (2) *Seneca wrote the words ' Man is a rational animal ' ;* (3) *Seneca wrote the words ' Rationale enim animal est homo ' ;* (4) *Seneca wrote words whose translation from Latin into English is 'Man is a rational animal' ;* (5) *Seneca wrote words whose translation from some language S' into English is ' Man is a rational animal' ;* (6) *There is a language S' such that Seneca wrote as sentence of S' words whose translation from S' into English is ' Man is a rational animal '.* In each case, ' wrote ' is to be understood in the sense, " wrote with assertive intent." And to simplify the discussion, we ignore the existence of spoken languages, and treat all languages as written.

Of these proposed analyses of (1), we must reject (2) on the ground that it is no doubt false although (1) is true. And each of (3)—(6), though having the same truth-value as (1), must be

[1] Presented to the Association for Symbolic Logic, December 28, 1949.

rejected on the ground that it does not convey the same information as (1). Thus (1) conveys the content of what Seneca said without revealing his actual words, while (3) reproduces Seneca's words without saying what meaning was attached to them. In (4) the crucial information is omitted (without which (1) is not even a consequence) that Seneca intended his words as a Latin sentence, rather than as a sentence of some other language in which conceivably the identical words ' Rationale enim animal est homo ' might have some quite different meaning. To (5) the objection is the same as to (4), and indeed if we take ' language' in the abstract sense of Carnap's ' semantical system ' (so that it is not part of the concept of a language that a language must have been used in historical fact by some human kindred or tribe), then (5) is L-equivalent merely to the statement that Seneca once wrote something.

(5) and (6) are closely similar to the analysis of belief statements which is offered by Carnap in " Meaning and Necessity," and although he does not say so explicitly it seems clear that Carnap must have intended also such an analysis as this for statements of assertion. However, (6) is likewise unacceptable as an analysis of (1). For it is not even possible to infer (1) as a consequence of (6), on logical grounds alone—but only by making use of the item of factual information, not contained in (6), that ' Man is a rational animal ' means in English that man is a rational animal.

Following a suggestion of Langford[1] we may bring out more sharply the inadequacy of (6) as an analysis of (1) by translating into another language, say German, and observing that the two translated statements would obviously convey different meanings to a German (whom we may suppose to have no knowledge of English). The German translation of (1) is (1') *Seneca hat gesagt, dass der Mensch ein vernünftiges Tier sei.* In translating (6), of course ' English ' must be translated as ' Englisch ' (not as ' Deutsch ') and ' ' Man is a rational animal ' ' must be translated as ' ' Man is a rational animal ' ' (not as ' ' Der Mensch ist ein vernünftiges Tier ' ').

Replacing the use of translation (as it appears in (6)) by the stronger requirement of intensional isomorphism, Carnap would

[1] In The *The Journal of Symbolic Logic*, vol. 2, p. 53.

analyze the belief statement (A) as follows : (B) *There is a sentence* $\mathfrak{S}_i$ *in a semantical system S' such that (a)* $\mathfrak{S}_i$ *is intensionally isomorphic to ' The world is round ' and (b) Columbus was disposed to an affirmative response to* $\mathfrak{S}_i$. However, intensional isomorphism, as appears from Carnap's definition of it, is a relation between ordered pairs consisting each of a sentence and a semantical system. Hence (B) must be rewritten as : (C) *There is a sentence* $\mathfrak{S}_i$ *in a semantical system S' such that (a)* $\mathfrak{S}_i$ *as sentence of S' is intensionally isomorphic to ' The world is round ' as English sentence and (b) Columbus was disposed to an affirmative response to* $\mathfrak{S}_i$ *as sentence of S'*.

For the analysis of (1), the analogue of (C) would seem to be : (7) *There is a sentence* $\mathfrak{S}_i$ *in a semantical system S' such that (a)* $\mathfrak{S}_i$ *as sentence of S' is intensionally isomorphic to ' Man is a rational animal ' as English sentence and (b) Seneca wrote* $\mathfrak{S}_i$ *as sentence of S'*.

Again Langford's device of translation makes evident the untenability of (C) as an analysis of (A), and of (7) as an analysis of (1).

## II

The foregoing assumes that the word ' English ' in English and the word ' Englisch ' in German have a sense which includes a reference to matters of pragmatics (in the sense of Morris and Carnap)—something like, e.g., " the language which was current in Great Britain and the United States in 1949 A.D. "

As an alternative we might consider taking the sense of these words to be something like " the language for which such and such semantical rules hold," a sufficient list of rules being given to ensure that there is only one language satisfying the description. The objection would then be less immediate that (1) is not a logical consequence of (6) or (7), and it is possible that it would disappear.

In order to meet this latter alternative without discussing in detail the list of semantical rules which would be required, we modify as follows the objection to (7) as an analysis of (1). Analogous to the proposal, for English, to analyze (1) as (7), we have, for German, the proposal to analyze (1') as (7") *Es gibt einen Satz* $\mathfrak{S}_i$ *auf einem semantischen System S', so dass (a)* $\mathfrak{S}_i$ *als Satz von S' intensional isomorph zu ' Der Mensch ist ein vernünftiges Tier ' als deutscher Satz ist, und (b) Seneca* $\mathfrak{S}_i$, *als Satz von S' geschrieben hat*.

Because of the exact parallelism between them, the two proposals stand or fall together. Yet (7′) in German and (7) in English are not in any acceptable sense translations of each other. In particular, they are not intensionally isomorphic. And if we consider the English sentence (α) *John believes that Seneca said that man is a rational animal* and its German translation (α′), we see that the sentences to which we are led as supposed analyses of (α) and (α′) may even have opposite truth-values in their respective languages ; for John, though knowing the semantical rules of both English and German, may nevertheless fail to draw certain of their logical (or other) consequences.

# ON BELIEF SENTENCES

## REPLY TO ALONZO CHURCH

### By RUDOLF CARNAP

CHURCH's paper[1] raises objections against the explication of belief sentences which I had proposed in my book *Meaning and Necessity*. The first part of Church's paper does not apply to my analysis because the latter does not refer to historically given languages, but rather to semantical systems, which are defined by their rules. Thus only the objection stated in Church's last paragraph applies. This objection is correct, but it can be met by a modification in my explication of belief sentences, suggested by Putnam.[2] I shall not discuss this point here, because at present I am inclined, for general reasons, to make a more radical change in that explication.

It seems best to reconstruct the language of science in such a way that terms like ' temperature ' in physics or 'anger' or ' belief ' in psychology are introduced as theoretical constructs rather than as intervening variables of the observation language. This means that a sentence containing a term of this kind can neither be translated into a sentence of the language of observables nor deduced from such sentences, but at best inferred with high

[1] In this volume, pp. 125-128.
[2] Hilary Putnam, " Synonymity and the analysis of belief sentences ", *Analysis*, Vol. 14 pp. 114-122.

probability. I think, this view is at present shared by most logical empiricists; it has been expounded with great clarity and convincing arguments by Feigl[1] and Hempel.[2]

In application to belief sentences, this means that a sentence like

(i) John believes that the earth is round,

is to be interpreted in such a way that it can be inferred from a suitable sentence describing John's behaviour at best with probability, but not with certainty, e.g., from

(ii) John makes an affirmative response to "the earth is round" as an English sentence.

When I wrote my book, I had already developed the general view mentioned above, concerning the nature of sentences in physics and psychology. However, I believed then erroneously that for the intended semantical analysis the simplification involved in taking a response as a conclusive evidence for a belief, would not essentially change the problem. It seems that Benson Mates[3] was the first to see the difficulty involved, although not its solution. He pointed out (l.c., p. 215) that any two different sentences, no matter how similar, could evoke different psychological responses. He argued that therefore my explication of synonymity, and likewise any other one, would lead to difficulties, e.g., in the case of the following two sentences :

(iii) Whoever believes that $D$, believes that $D$,

(iv) Whoever believes that $D$, believes that $D'$,

where '$D$' and '$D'$' are abbreviations for two different but synonymous sentences. Then (iii) and (iv) would themselves be synonymous. However, while (iii) is certainly true and beyond doubt, (iv) may be false or, at least, it is conceivable that somebody may doubt it. This is indeed a serious difficulty, but only as long as we regard an affirmative response to '$D$' as a conclusive indication of belief in $D$.

Church pointed out to me that Mates' paradoxical result concerning (iii) and (iv) disappears if we give up that view. We may then

[1] H. Feigl, "Existential hypotheses", Phil. of Science, 17, 1950, 35–62 ; " Principles and problems of theory construction in psychology ", in *Current trends in psychological theory*, University of Pittsburgh Press, 1951, pp. 179–213.

[2] C. G. Hempel, *Fundamentals of concept formation in empirical science*, Encycl. Unified Science, Vol. II, No. 7, 1952.

[3] Mates, " Synonymity ", in : *Meaning and Interpretation*, Univ. of California Publications in Philos., Vol. XXV, 1950, pp. 201–226.

take (iv) as logically true, just like (iii). If somebody responds affirmatively to ' $D$ ', but negatively to ' $D'$ ', we shall merely conclude that one of his responses is non-indicative, perhaps due to his momentary confusion.

While I agree with Church in this point, there remains a divergence of view with respect to the question of the best form for belief sentences in a formalized language of science. One form uses indirect discourse in analogy to the form (i) of ordinary language. The other form avoids indirect discourse ; here a belief sentence does not like (i) contain a partial sentence expressing the content of the belief, but instead the name of such a sentence, for example :

(v) John has the relation $B$ to " the earth is round " as a sentence in English.

It is to be noted that, according to the new interpretation explained above, (v) is not deducible from (ii) but is merely confirmed by it to some degree. ' $B$ ' is a theoretical construct, not definable in terms of overt behaviour, be it linguistic or non-linguistic. The rules for ' $B$ ' would be such that (v) does not imply that John knows English or any language whatsoever. On the other hand, the reference to an English sentence in (v) may be replaced by a reference to any other synonymous sentence in any language ; e.g., (v) is taken to be L-equivalent with :

(vi) John has the relation $B$ to " die Erde ist rund " as a sentence in German.

As an explication of synonymity we may use here the relation of intensional isomorphism as proposed in my book ; it holds, if the two expressions are constructed in the same way out of signs with the same intensions ; as an alternative, a slightly stronger relation, suggested by Putnam, may be used, which requires that the two expressions have, in addition, the same syntactical structure.

Church entertains the view that a belief must be construed as a relation between a person and a proposition, not a sentence, and that therefore only the first form, like (i), is adequate, not the second, like (v). I do not reject the first form, but regard both forms as possible. I do not think that the arguments offered by Church so far show the impossibility of the second form. Both forms must be further investigated before we can decide which one is preferable. It must be admitted that the second form has certain disadvantages ; it abolishes the customary and convenient device of indirect discourse, it uses the metalanguage, and it becomes cumbersome in cases of iteration (e.g., " James asserts that John believes that . . . " would be replaced by a sentence about a sentence about a sentence). The main disadvantage of the first form is the complexity of the logical structure of the language, whereas the language for the second form may be extensional and therefore very simple. The introduction of logical modalities produces already considerable complications, but the use of indirect discourse increases them still more. The greatest complexity would result from the use of the Frege-Church method, according to which an expression has infinitely many senses depending upon the text (see my book pp. 129 ff.). Church believes that these complications are inevitable, but I am not convinced of it. I regard it as possible to construct a language of the first form in such a way that every expression has always the same sense and that therefore two expressions which fulfill a certain criterion of synonymity are synonymous in any context, including contexts of simple or iterated indirect discourse. But many more investigations and tentative constructions of languages will have to be made before we can see the whole situation clearly and make a well-founded decision as to the choice of the language form.

# CHAPTER VI. LOGIC: PSYCHO-ANALYSIS AND MORALS.

## THE LOGICAL STATUS OF PSYCHO-ANALYSIS[1]

### By Stephen Toulmin

Philosophy has always flourished on half-fledged sciences. The great periods in the history of Western Philosophy have been periods in which new modes of thought and new ways of reasoning were being developed, and their history is at least partly a record of the teething-troubles of these new instruments. As long as new ideas remain unfamiliar, their scope and nature tend to be misunderstood, and their use hampered by misplaced and fruitless controversy. At the best, the result is Descartes ; but a great deal of the more transitory kind of philosophy trades on these misunderstandings, and satisfies the public taste for conjuring, mystification and paradox by a fine display of technicalities, which on closer examination are found simply to sugar-coat a series of dotty answers to screwy questions. In the past this has happened chiefly to physics and biology, but nowadays the main victim is psycho-analysis. Although it is fifty years since Freud's pioneer work, and although psycho-analytic techniques are in regular therapeutic use, the position of psycho-analysis as an intellectual discipline is still not established. It may therefore be prudent for once to enquire how far the mystery surrounding the subject comes from a desire to ask the wrong questions about it, and how far a better understanding of the nature and logic of psycho-analysis will, by itself, dispel the fog.

From the way in which popularisers of psycho-analysis, many psycho-analysts, and even Freud himself, have talked and written, one gets a very confused idea of psycho-analytic procedure, and consequently (as I want to shew) a distorted picture of the implications of psycho-analytic discoveries for philosophy and for our everyday lives. To begin with, Freud's discovery is presented to us as a double one. First, it is suggested, he discovered the ' unconscious mind ', in a way strictly comparable to

[1] The substance of this paper was delivered as a report to the Tenth International Congress of Philosophy, Amsterdam, on August 16th, 1948.

Columbus' discovery of America or Harvey's discovery of the circulation of the blood. And then, we are given to understand, Freud *also* discovered that, by revealing to the mentally-ill the contents of their unconscious minds, he could often cure them of their distresses. Taking the portmanteau notion of ' discovery ' at its face-value, we are at once amazed, mystified and, after a little reflection, dismayed. We are amazed that any man should have the genius to make *two* such discoveries; we are mystified both by the very notion of an ' unconscious mind ' and by the strange and apparently arbitrary fact that a revelation of its contents is often enough to relieve mental illness ; and, finally, we are dismayed because the discovery seems bound to destroy our few remaining shreds of belief in free-will, having drawn back the last, kindly veil which up to now had hidden from us the inexorable machinery of cause-and-effect governing what we had liked to call our own, ' personal ' decisions.

" What *kind* of thing is the ' unconscious mind ' ? " " Can an analyst really discover the *causes* of mental illness? ", " If that is what he claims to do, are not the ' explanations ' he gives often highly speculative? ", " Further, how can he in some cases ' explain ' neuroses in terms of ' traumatic experiences ' which never in fact occurred? ", " Finally—and this in some ways is the most mysterious question of all—how on earth is it that the revelation of the ' unconscious mind ' can *cure* neuroses at all? " : such questions prompt themselves insistently, and the answers generally given are of little assistance. Take the last as an illustration. Why do psycho-analytic cures work at all? And are they better in principle than drugs, or hypnotic suggestion? No, say the sceptics, just a mixture of flukes and common sense. Yes, says Freud, but proceeds to give this flowery and metaphorical explanation of *why* they are better :

Painting, says Leonardo, works *per via di porre*, for it applies a substance—particles of colour—where there was nothing before, on the colourless canvas ; sculpture, however, proceeds *per via di levare*, since it takes away from the rough stone all that hides the surface of the statue contained in it. The technique of suggestion aims in a similar way at proceeding *per via di porre* ; it is not concerned with the origin, strength and meaning of the morbid symptoms, but instead, it superimposes something—a suggestion—and expects this to be strong enough to restrain the pathogenic idea from coming to expression. Analytic therapy, on the other hand, does not seek to add or to introduce anything new, but to take away something, to bring out something; and to this end concerns itself with the genesis of the morbid symptoms and the psychical context of the pathogenic idea which it seeks to remove. . . Besides all this, I have another reproach against [suggestion], namely, that it conceals from us all insight into the play of mental forces ".[1]

The metaphor Freud chooses for his ' explanation ' is particularly unfortunate. It could hardly be said that a given block of stone ' contained ' only *one* statue, so we are left with the apparently arbitrary nature of analytic psycho-therapy still unexplained.

In this paper, I want to suggest that our troubles arise from thinking of psycho-analysis too much on the analogy of the natural sciences. I shall point out that (ethics and religion apart) we are accustomed to giving several logically distinct types of explanation of human conduct ; and that the decision, which type of explanation is appropriate in any particular situation, depends upon our purpose in asking for an ' explanation '. In order to achieve a balanced view of psycho-analysis, it is necessary to compare psycho-analytic explanation with at least *three* of these more familiar types. When this is done, the very features of psycho-analysis which are apt to appear most puzzling become intelligible ; and the scope and status of the subject become clearer.

Consider three logically distinct types of ' explanation ' of human conduct :

E1, the ' stated reason ' which one oneself gives, in reply to the question, " Why did you do that? "—e.g. " Because it's time for bed and I want to go home ".

E2, the ' reported reason ' to which one refers in answering the question, " Why did he do that? ", asked of a third person— e.g. " Because it's time for bed and he wants to go home ".

E3, the ' causal explanation ' which one can sometimes give of an action—one's own or somebody's else's—e.g. " Because he was given an injection of cocaine twenty minutes ago ".

[1] See " On Psychotherapy " (1904), in Freud's *Collected Papers*, Vol. I, p. 254 : the notion of ' mental forces ' is one to which I shall have to return at the very end of this paper.

These three types of ' explanation ' are logically related to three distinct forms of speech—to the ' psychological signal ' S1 (e.g. " I am in pain "), to the ' psychological report ' S2 (e.g. " He is in pain "), and to the ' statement of material fact ' S3 (e.g. " They went to the cinema "). The logical distinctions between these three classes are as follows. Over S1 and E1, there is no question of ' giving one's evidence ' or of ' making a mistake '. If I call out, " I want you to come here ", it makes no sense for you to ask, " How do you know ? " or "Are you sure? ", for I might as well have said, " Come here! ", or have waved to you to come—indeed, I must at one time or another have learnt to use all these three as methods of summoning people. Over S2 and E2, it makes sense to talk of ' evidence ' and of ' mistakes ' ; but what the person himself says constitutes conclusive evidence. Over S3 and E3, one can again talk of ' mistakes ' and of ' evidence ', but the evidence is now a matter of factual observations neutral between all observers, including the person under discussion.[1]

Although a logical distinction can be drawn between the first-person present indicative ' signal ' (" I want a drink ") and the ' psychological report ' (" He wants a drink "), they are united *in use*, firstly, by the kinds of situation in which they are appropriate and, secondly, by the purposes they normally serve. For instance, the statement " X wants a drink " finds its normal use in situations where, if X is given a drink, X will accept it with satisfaction : this holds good whether X be ' I ' or ' he ', whether the statement be a ' signal ' or a ' report '. The same considerations apply to the stated and reported reasons for an action. And it is this which makes us want to say that the use of the signal expresses the ' same ' thing about oneself that others express by the use of the report.

It is important to remark at this stage on the connection between the notion of a ' reason ' or ' motive ' for an action and that of ' satisfaction '. When considering what practical account we ought to take of a man's actions, we do not need a full causal analysis—even if one could be given : it is a knowledge of his motives, his reasons—the wishes behind his actions——that we

---

[1] The difference between S1 and S3 is the difference between " I am going to give you a good hiding " and " I am going to be sick ".

need. It is, indeed, to play a part in this job that the forms of speech I have called 'psychological signals and reports' are introduced and must be understood.

Consider next the relation between 'psycho-analytic explanation' and our three simpler types of explanation, E1 to E3. In everyday situations of several different kinds, we find it natural to describe or explain people's conduct (even our own) in ways which are of interest to a psycho-analyst. (Remember Freud's *Psychopathology of Everyday Life*). These accounts may bear a resemblance to any of the three types of explanation discussed so far : logically speaking, they may be regarded as intermediate between E1, E2 and E3 and the typical psycho-analytic explanation, which may be called E4. For instance, one may say

E14, "I found myself wishing that I was alone with her " : this is a 'signal' as much as S1 and E1, for there is no question of 'giving evidence' or 'making mistakes '—in fact the description given in such cases seems to be uniquely appropriate.

E24, "He behaved for the moment as though he hated the sight of her " : this is the corresponding type of 'report' but, significantly, what the person himself says is now less conclusive as evidence than in the case of E2.

E34, "He behaves like that because his father used to beat him violently as a child " : this is a genuinely 'causal' explanation if the evidence considered as relevant is (i) a correlation between a cruel upbringing and subsequent behaviour of this type and (ii) the fact that he actually was beaten violently when young.

None of these three explanations (E14, E24, E34) is, strictly speaking, a 'psycho-analytic' one, but each is of more interest to an analyst than the corresponding simple explanation, E1, E2 or E3. It is suggestive to display the logical characteristics of the different types of explanation diagrammatically, representing the typical explanation of each type by a point and the rough boundaries of each class by circles (*see diagram on p.* 137). This means of representation will lead us to expect, for instance, that the logical differences between a psycho-analytic explanation (E4) and a strictly causal one (E3) will be similar to, though less marked than those between stated or reported reasons (E1 or E2) and E3.

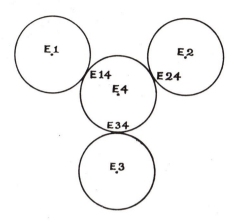

This is what we find, and it is these differences which are a source of much of the mystification about psycho-analysis. The typical psycho-analytic explanation E4 (as presented by an analyst at the end of a series of consultations) has something in common with each of the other three types of explanation. Firstly, the patient must come to recognise it as a natural (indeed, as *the* natural) expression of his neurotic state of mind : it must, that is, provide him with a plausible ' stated motive '. Secondly, third parties who are familiar with the case-history must accept it as a description of his conduct : it must, that is provide a plausible ' reported motive '. Thirdly, such ' facts of early life ' as it invokes must be of a kind which could have led to this kind of conduct : the explanation must include a plausible ' causal history ' of the neurosis.

It is not essential, however, that the ' causal history ' should refer only to authentic facts, and this distinguishes psycho-analysis from other types of investigation. A psycho-analytic explanation may be accepted (provisionally, at any rate) as ' correct ', even though the ' facts ' cited as causes never occurred.[1]

---

[1] " Few episodes in the history of scientific research provide a more dramatic test of true genius than the occasion on which Professor Freud made the devastating discovery that many of the traumas to which he had been *obliged to attach aetiological significance* had never occurred outside the imagination of the patients." Ernest Jones, Preface to Freud's *Collected Papers*. (My italics.)

This is reflected in the analyst's procedure. He is largely in-different to what independent witnesses have to say about his patient's early life : what the patient himself says about it is what counts. In this respect the psycho-analytic explanation (E4) resembles an account of *motives* (such as E1 or E2) rather than one of *causes* (such as E3). An explanation in terms of a ' fantasy-trauma ' is, however, less satisfactory than one in terms of authenticated facts and, if its fictitious nature is detected by the analyst, it can be accepted only as provisional, and eventually comes to be regarded as a symptom on its own account. Where there is a choice, the fantasy is rejected, shewing that the difference between E4 and E3 is less marked than that between E1 or E2 and E3.

It is this continuity of E4 with the other three types of explana-tion of conduct which gives us grounds for regarding the tech-niques of psycho-analysis as potentially ' rational ', in a way in which hypnotic suggestion, brain surgery and insulin treatment cannot be. The kernel of Freud's discovery is the introduction of a technique in which the psycho-therapist begins by studying the *motives for*, rather than the *causes of* neurotic behaviour. It is illuminating to regard his early ' law of dream-interpretation ' (" Every dream is the fulfilment of a suppressed wish ") as a methodological reminder, rather than as an empirical generalisa-tion, rewording it as " It's the *motive for* dreaming that matters to the psycho-therapist ".

There need be nothing mysterious, either, about the thera-peutic success of psycho-analysis. Firstly, the technique can be regarded as an extension of the more familiar technique of giving ' reasons ' for actions—a technique which, as we saw, is itself to be understood in connection with the fulfilment of the agent's aims. Secondly, if a fully-fledged analytic explanation is not a part of a successful cure, we do not regard it as a ' correct ' explanation : therapeutic failure is as fatal to an explanation in psycho-analysis as predictive failure is to an explanation in physics.

Once the distinction between the typically causal explanation (E3) and the analytic one (E4) is appreciated, the deterministic worry also loses much of its bite. A man who can give in detail his reasons for acting as he does is (roughly speaking) the one whose conduct we should regard as least ' determined '. The

success of psycho-analysis, so far from destroying the last grounds
—or loop-hole, if you prefer it—for belief in free-will, should
re-emphasise the importance of ' reasons for action ', as opposed
to ' causes of action ', and so the possibility of free choice.
Indeed, as a practical technique, psycho-analysis already provides
a means of judging the *degree* of freedom involved in a particular
action—how far it was consciously planned, and how far it was
compulsive. It may indeed be true, as Freud claimed, that psycho-
analysis does more than hypnosis or insulin to reveal " the play
of mental forces ", but these ' forces ' are as much akin to the
' reasons ' for a decision as they are to the ' stresses ' in a machine :
they are as much the ' motives ' as the ' motive-power ' behind our
behaviour.

## PSYCHOANALYTIC EXPLANATION

*By* ANTONY FLEW

### FOREWORD (1954)

[It now (Dec. 1953) seems to me that I exaggerated in pre-
senting the difference between psychoanalytic ' motive ' explanations and ' causal ' ones as an unbridged and unbridgable
gulf : for even the analysts themselves begin the work of explaining the relative strength and development of particular motives
in other, rather mysterious, terms. But I still think such
cartooning over-simplification was justified : to bring out how
very different the basic Freudian concepts are from those of
the more conventional scientific disciplines. Unfortunately the
controversy of which this paper was a part never touched on the
questions raised by the limitations of psychoanalytic method : the
dependence on the unsupported observation and testimony of
the analyst, the lack of objective tests of a patient's condition
before and after analysis, the need for controlled experimental
check up of theories. See e.g. R. R. Sears *Survey of Objective
Studies of Psychoanalytic Concepts* (New York : Social Science
Research Council Bulletin No. 51) ; G. S. Blum *Psychoanalytic*

*Theories of Personality* (New York: Magraw Hill, 1953), H. J. Eysenck, *Uses and Abuses of Psychology* (Pelican, 1953) Ch. 10–12. A.F.]

### PSYCHOANALYTIC EXPLANATION

TAKING as my text two chapters from Freud, I want to support, to illustrate, and in some ways to develop, the main thesis of Mr. Toulmin's illuminating article. His thesis is that, " The kernel of Freud's discovery is the introduction of a technique in studying the *motives for* rather than the *causes of* neurotic behaviour ". The two chapters in Freud are Nos. 17 and 18 in the *Introductory Lectures on Psychoanalysis* (1929 Edition). They show that the Father of psychoanalysis himself, when dealing in practice with particular cases, was concerned primarily with the *motives* for neurotic behaviour, whereas, when theorising and generalising about his work, he often thought he had been dealing with something quite different, namely, the alleged *efficient causes* of such behaviour. They thus support Mr. Toulmin's thesis about the nature of psychoanalytic explanation, and also constitute one of the major and canonical sources of the vast mass of misconceptions as to what psychoanalysts have discovered. The material in these two chapters has, besides clarity and compactness, the additional merits of being classical and fundamental. For Freud uses to illustrate his conception, or misconception, of the nature of his discoveries two case histories of obsessional neurosis. And, as he says, (p. 219), " The obsessional neurosis and hysteria are the two forms of neurotic disease upon which the study of psychoanalysis was first built up, and in the treatment of which also our therapy celebrates its triumphs ".

It is most conspicuous (at least to anyone who has read Mr. Toulmin's article) that wherever, in these two chapters, Freud is close to the particular case, he talks of finding the motives or purposes of obsessive acts, and of interpreting their meaning, whereas, whenever he starts to generalise, to begin talking theory, he writes as if he had inferred the existence of something concealed, as if he had discovered the unconscious mind " in a way ", as Mr. Toulmin has it, " strictly comparable to Columbus' discovery of America or Harvey's discovery of the circulation of the blood ".

Thus he writes, " With the first patient we have heard of the senseless obsessive act she performed and of the intimate memories she recalled in connection with it ; we also considered the relation between the two and deduced the *purpose* of the obsessive act from its connection with the memory. At first, " she could quite truly answer that she did not know what impulse led her to do it ". Then, " she found the connection and was able to tell it. But even then she knew nothing of the *purpose* she had in performing the action, the *purpose* that was to correct a painful event of the past and to raise the husband she loved in her own estimation. It took a long time and much effort for her to grasp and admit to me, that such a *motive* as this could alone have been the driving force behind the obsessive act " (p. 234, My italics). Later, after giving the two case histories, Freud insists, " I have now shown you that neurotic symptoms have meaning like errors and like dreams ". (p. 228).

He thus reinforces and sets in its context his claim that neurotic symptoms can be interpreted in terms of " meaning ", " purpose ", " intention ", " motive ", by reminding us of his earlier successes in the similar interpretation of lapses of memory and slips of the tongue (in *The Psychopathology of Everyday Life*) and in that of dreams (in *The Interpretation of Dreams*).

So far so good. But now Freud tries to draw the general conclusion that he has discovered a class of recherché items which must on no account be omitted from any inventory of the furniture of the Universe which is to maintain pretensions to exhaustiveness. Having described the case of the patient who did not know the motive or purpose of her obsessive act he deduces that, " Mental processes had been at work in her, therefore, of which the obsessive act was the effect ; she was aware in the normal manner of their effect ; but nothing of the mental antecedents of this effect had come to the knowledge of her consciousness. She was behaving exactly like a subject under hypnotism whom Bernheim had ordered to open an umbrella in the ward five minutes after he awoke, but who had no idea why he was doing it. This is the kind of occurrence we have in mind when we speak of the existence of ' unconscious mental processes ' ; we may challenge anyone in the world to give a more correctly scientific explanation of this matter, and will then gladly withdraw our inference that unconscious mental processes exist. Until they do, however, we will adhere to this inference and, when anyone objects that in a scientific sense the unconscious has no reality, that it is a mere makeshift, *une façon de parler* we must resign ourselves with a shrug to rejecting his statement as incomprehensible. Something unreal, which can nevertheless produce something so real and palpable as an obsessive action ! " (pp. 234-5). This passage, quoted at length, should alone be sufficient to show that at this period Freud himself thought that he had discovered an outré new thing which, hidden as it were behind a curtain, produced obsessive acts as a puppet master produces the jerky movements of his puppets, or as the concealed projector produces the moving pictures on the silver screen. This opinion is reinforced by other passages, " You will then understand that we cannot dispense with the unconscious part of the mind in psychoanalysis, and we are accustomed to deal with it as something actual and tangible " (p. 235) and, " he must remain content with the veriest scraps of information about what is going on unconsciously in his own mind " (p. 241).

These extensive quotations bring out sharply the contrast between what Freud is doing and knows he is doing when he actually practises psychoanalysis, and what he thinks he has been doing, when afterwards he comes to report what he thinks he has discovered. Freud as a working psychoanalyst is primarily concerned with discovering and making patients realise and admit the motives, purposes, and intentions of their neurotic behaviour, which motives, etc., are called " unconscious " because, until he has done his work, his patients have no knowledge of them. But Freud as a theoretician seems to think (at this stage) that he has *inferred* the existence of unconscious mental processes which *produce* real and palpable obsessive actions. (All statements of Freud's theoretical position have to be qualified by the phrase, " at this stage ", since it was developing constantly. In the later stages I find it increasingly difficult to understand what he did think he had discovered).

Freud's practice of psychoanalysis showed a genius which it would be almost impertinent to praise but his theory here seems to be extremely questionable. For he was apparently thinking of unconscious mental processes as the inferred efficient causes which produce obsessive acts as their effects. Thus he writes, " Mental processes had been at work in her, therefore, of which the obsessive act was the effect ", and he tells us that the unconscious cannot be " une facon de parler " because it can " produce something as real and palpable as an obsessive action ". But if these unconscious mental processes are to be taken ás the putative efficient causes of obsessive acts, then their introduction was a gratuitous multiplication of dubious entities.

They would be dubious because they would be very weak candidates for the job of efficient causation to which Freud here apparently wished to appoint them. " The unconscious part of the mind " with which, he claims, " we are accustomed to deal as something actual and tangible " (p. 235) though perhaps in some sense actual is certainly very far from being in any sense tangible. It makes no sense to ask whether it is rough or smooth, heavy or light, sweet or acrid in smell, light or dark in colour. It could not be put on any museum shelf marked " Substances ". It could not even be kept in a special bottle labelled " Invisible and spiritual substance, very elusive ". For unconscious mental processes, like conscious ones, have no position. To tell us that they go on " in the mind " is only a vexatious way of telling us that it makes no sense to ask " Where? " And this all goes to show that it is preposterous to think of them as the efficient causes which " produce " real and palpable obsessive acts. They are not sufficiently substantial to do this job.

But if unconscious mental processes, conceived of as efficient causes, are a dubious innovation they are also, and fortunately, a gratuitous one. For there are already available some gratifyingly tangible potential efficient causes in terms of which to construct causal explanations of obsessive acts (and, for that matter, of other acts which are not obsessive at all). These are the myriad neurones of the nervous system, all the paraphernalia of the neurologists, waiting, solid, visible, tangible, a sight to delight and inspire the experimentalist.

Thus if this conception of the nature of its discoveries is accepted as correct, psychoanalysis will be in a very uncomfortable position indeed. For it will have to be considered as a rival to neurology and kindred branches of physiology. It will have to be taken as offering a causal explanation, in terms of rather dubious occurrences and questionable entities, of phenomena which neurology has a very good chance of explaining in terms of quite solid and undubious neurones. Fortunately it is possible to interpret psychoanalytic discoveries in another way, as offering not rival explanations to those of neurophysiology, but as providing an altogether different kind of explanation.

Such an interpretation is strongly suggested by the fact, already noticed above, that Freud himself in describing particular cases speaks not of " causes " but of " motives ", " purposes ", and " intentions ". Now an explanation of a piece of behaviour in terms of motives is altogether different from an explanation in terms of causes. Asked why he had plunged a stiletto into Cesare's back Guiseppe might—but never would—give the physiologist's explanation. The movement of the knife was the climax of a long chain of causation. Some stimulus excited nervous impulses which set off a particular sort of commotion in the brain which resulted in the passage of further nervous impulses down to the relevant muscles. And so on. This would be a *causal* explanation. But Guiseppe might—and in fact would —explain the occurrence in terms of motives and purposes. He would explain that he wanted to inherit money under Cesare's will, or that he was jealous of his musical talent, or that he was in love with his wife. And this would be an explanation of the *motive* sort.

It is fairly obvious that psychoanalytic explanations are very much more like *motive* explanations than they are like *causal* explanations. Take for example the case already quoted from Freud. He asked himself why the patient performed certain obsessive acts. And his answer was that the patient wanted to " correct a painful event of the past and to raise the husband she loved in her estimation ". After, " a long time and much effort " she admitted that this must have been her motive. Or take any of the familiar examples from the *Psychopathology of Everyday Life*. They are all designed to show that people forget, or make slips of pen or tongue, because they want to, and to illustrate the motives which they have for such errors.[1] Or take the " law of dream

[1] Though Freud sometimes speaks of *causes* it is purposive and distinctively human concepts such as *motive, purpose, intention* which are most prominent in this book too (Pelican edition 1938, pp. 9, 12, 13, 28, 33, 34, 46, 47, 51, 56, 77, 78, 79, 82, 83, 89, 90–5, 121, 123, 162–4, 178, 181).

interpretation ", " Every dream is the fulfilment of a suppressed wish ". This law asserts that all dreams are motivated, that people dream what they wish would happen in real life, that all dreams can be explained in terms of motives. It seems that Freud's discovery of the unconscious mind, of unconscious mental processes should not be interpreted as a discovery of récherché, efficient causes, but as the discovery that much more human behaviour, especially neurotic human behaviour, is motivated, or, better, can be explained in terms of motives, than anyone had ever previously believed (Granted of course certain crucial extensions of the concept of motive, which are an essential part of Freud's discovery).[1] Common sense and artistic insight had always been prepared to recognise some unconscious motivation, as Freud himself was at pains to point out in the *Psychopathology of Everyday Life*. Freud's great achievement was to discover how much more unconscious motivation we all have than any of us knew we had, and to devise a therapy which exploits this discovery to cure certain neuroses. The difference between the psychoanalytic explanation and the ordinary everyday motive explanation is one of degree ; in the latter it is comparatively easy to induce the agent to state his motives whereas in the former the patient can be made to recognise and admit his motive only at the climax of a prolonged and laborious analysis. But there is a spectrum of possibilities stretching from the frank and normal to the pathological, from the most straightforward case,— the man who knows and will readily admit his motive, through the man who knows but will not readily confess it, right up to the extreme cases, the psychoanalytic patients whose motives are unknown to everyone else as well as to themselves until the analysis is complete.

Now someone might agree that it is better to talk of motives, purposes, wishes, intentions and the like when discussing psychoanalysis. He might agree that it is more helpful to think of mixed motives or conflicting desires[2] than of the " play of mental forces ".

---

[1] As Freud's wayward pupil Stekel puts it : To whatever school of analysis we belong Freud is the master of us all . . . who opened our eyes . . . found reason in unreason " (*Technique of Analytical Psychotherapy*).

[2] As Freud often did think : compare, for instance, the *Introductory Lectures*, pp. 361-2 and 366 with *Collected Papers*, Vol. I, p. 254 (the passage cited by Toulmin).

But he might still consider that motive explanations are " ultimately " causal, that they could in principle be reduced to causal ones. He might think that psychoanalytic explanations are a useful stopgap while we await the advances in neurology which shall put the analysts out of business. Freud himself once or twice suggested some such view. In discussing the " latent states of mental life " and whether they were " to be conceived of as unconscious mental states or as physical ones ", he writes, " Now as far as their physical characteristics are concerned, they are totally inaccessible to us ; no physiological conception nor chemical process can give us any notion of their nature " (*Collected Papers*, Vol. IV, p. 101). From which he draws the moral that psychoanalysis is, at present, the only practical method of investigating these states.

Detailed investigation of the logical liaisons of " motives " and associated words would and should provide material for a very substantial book, but perhaps a few scrappy suggestions would do something to show that a motive explanation is quite radically different from an explanation by efficient causes. *First*, motives are quite intangible and insubstantial while efficient causes notoriously have to be substantial. *Second*, it seems that a piece of behaviour can be both motivated and caused. Guiseppe's action was certainly caused and it has been suggested in outline how the causal story would run. It was also motivated and under interrogation he would no doubt admit that his motive was (as the police inferred from circumstantial evidence) that he wanted to inherit the money Cesare had imprudently willed to him. The police and Guiseppe who knew all about his motives might know nothing of the efficient causes of the action while the physiologists might know all about the efficient causes but nothing of the motives. *Third*, and this is an extension of the second point, no translation is possible from " cause language " into " motive language ". If it were we might learn physiology from logicians who would deduce the efficient causes of our behaviour from knowledge of its motives. (Similarly, if there really were necessary connections of this sort between " state " propositions and " citizen " propositions we might have deduced the guilt of Goering from the guilt of the German state without recourse to the laborious and expensive investigations revealed in the

Nuremberg trials). And if such translation is impossible then it would presumably be wrong to talk of the " cause language " and the " motive language " as if they were two languages which could be used to assert the same propositions. *Fourth*, motives may be good or bad, kindly or corrupt, vicious or saintly, reasonable or unreasonable enlightened or unenlightened but, causes can be none of these. So even if we found that as a matter of fact whenever motive proposition M was true some physical or causal proposition C was also true we could not " reduce " motives to causes or to bodily descriptions. No evidence showing that whenever Luigi was in love and wanting to marry Maria or Simonetta his body was always in such and such a state would have the slightest tendency to show that his motives or desires were " merely " complex conditions of his body. A programme that attempted to " reduce " motive propositions to cause propositions by discovering such contingent connections would therefore be as misconceived as a programme which set out to discover necessary connections by the methods of deduction. Both would be as misconceived, though not quite as popular, as the programmes which have tried to " reduce " ethics, aesthetics, or logic to psychology by the discovery of necessary or contingent connections between what are in fact quite radically different universes of discourse.[1] *Fifth*, as an indirect confirmation of the thesis that psychoanalysis provides motive explanations which are fundamentally different from causal ones it is interesting to note that novelists have been as interested and excited by the works of the psychoanalysts as they have been indifferent to or bored by the writings of the experimental psychologists and students of conditioned reflexes. The significant exception is Huxley in " Brave New World ". Novelists are primarily interested in human motives, purposes, desires, and intentions—in human beings treated as such (if the slight ethical flavour may be excused). Experimental psychologists are primarily interested in the causation of human behaviour—human beings treated like animals or machines. And so it would be natural to expect, if

---

[1] Freud characteristically expected that motives would one day be correlated with physiological states "that all our provisional ideas in psychology will some day be based on an organic substructure" *Collected Papers*, Vol. IV, p. 36. But this, of course, is, not at all the same thing as a 'logical reduction' of motives to physiological states.

this paper is on the right track, what we in fact find to be the case, that novelists would have more in common with psycho-analysts than with experimental psychologists and students of conditioned reflexes.

My two theses have been, *first*, that psychoanalytic explanations or at any rate classical Freudian ones in the first instance are "motive" and not "causal" explanations; and, *second*, that these two sorts of explanation are so radically different that they are not rivals at all.

## CURE, CAUSE AND MOTIVE

### TWO BRIEF NOTES

#### By RICHARD PETERS

I WANT to single out two points for brief comment in the series of articles on "The Logical Status of Psycho-analysis" in the hope that some methodologically conscious psychoanalyst will venture to clear up some of my perplexities about these articles.

First of all Mr. Toulmin maintains that "therapeutic failure is as fatal to an explanation in psycho-analysis as predictive failure is to an explanation in physics".[1] This is a rather startling pronouncement which seems to assume an over-simple view of cure in psycho-analysis. It also is made more plausible by a failure to distinguish certain aspects of pschyo-analytic practice. These two defects in Mr. Toulmin's treatment are connected.

Consider Mr. Toulmin's account of cure. He seems to equate cure with the revelation by an analyst to a patient of the 'unconscious motives', of his actions.[2] This, he maintains cautiously, '*often*' effects a cure. The use of the word 'often' suggests either that Mr. Toulmin is aware that some patients are not cured by this method or that he knows that the revelation of unconscious motives is at best to be regarded as a necessary condition of psycho-analytic cure and very seldom as a sufficient condition, other goings-on like 'transference' and 'abreaction' also being necessary. His later remarks about cure suggest that the former and less charitable interpretation of Mr. Toulmin's caution is the correct one. My knowledge of psycho-analytic

---

[1] S. Toulmin, *The Logical Status of Psycho-Analysis*, this volume p. 138.
[2] Op. cit., p. 137.

practice is not at all extensive, but I can quote Freud's own remarks on the limited importance in cure of this revelation of ' unconscious motives ', and I feel sure that Mr. Toulmin will not be offended if I quote from Freud's " Observations on ' Wild ' Psycho-analysis " ! " Telling the patient what he does not know because he has repressed it, is only one of the necessary preliminaries in the therapy. If knowledge about his unconscious were as important for the patient as the inexperienced in psycho-analysis imagine, it would be a sufficient cure for him to go to lectures or to read books. Such measures, however, have as little effect on the symptoms of nervous disease as distribution of menu-cards in time of famine has on people's hunger. The analogy goes even further than its obvious application, too ; for describing his unconscious to the patient is regularly followed by intensification of the conflict in him and exacerbation of the symptoms ".[1] So much, then, for Mr. Toulmin's equation of cure with revelation of unconscious motives.

Surely, too, Mr. Toulmin fails to make some necessary distinctions in his talk of cure and explanation. Psycho-analysis, as I understand it, is partly a theoretical system for explaining behaviour, partly a collection of historical techniques like hypnosis, free-association, narcosis, etc., for detecting cause-factors in nervous disorders, and partly a branch of technology concerned with attitude changing. These distinctions are easy to overlook because psycho-analysts are so pre-occupied with technology (attitude changing) and their preliminary detective work that they seldom make *explicit* attempts to overthrow the hypotheses which they *use* either in detection or in attitude changing.[2] Thus their cures look like *indirect* confirmations of the theoretical assumptions which they use. But this is rather ambiguous ; for the problem is to see the assumptions which are thus confirmed by their cures. A person may be a good scientist, but a poor detective or historian and a worse technologist. His fertility in framing hypotheses may be astonishing

[1] S. Freud " *Collected Papers* ", Vol. 11, p. 302.
[2] Of course there are moral as well as technical difficulties to be encountered in such an undertaking. See, for instance, Prof. Dingle's point in his reply to Mr. Toulmin on p. 65 of *Analysis*, Vol. 10, No. 1, and difficulties of the kind raised by J. F. Brown in his chapter on ' Towards an Experimental Psycho-pathology ' in his *The Psycho-dynamics of Abnormal Behaviour*, Ch. XXII.

and his testing procedures unimpeachable; but in spite of his theoretical knowledge of physics or psycho-analytic theory he may be poor at diagnosing the complaints of wireless sets and patients, and worse at building them up. Similarly, like Macchiavelli, he could be a good detective but a poor scientist and practical attitude changer. So, surely, a cure might fail in psychoanalysis for many types of reasons. I will separate out some of them :

(*a*) Psycho-analytic theory might be at worst wrong or at best poorly confirmed. Thus the theoretical assumptions used by analysts in tracking down ' motives ' and ' causal histories ' might be at fault. (Call these assumptions ABC).

(*b*) The analyst might be a poor detective. In spite of the adequacy of his theoretical assumptions (ABC) and the efficacy of his techniques for revealing the past (e.g. hypnosis, free-association, narcosis), he might fail to spot the relevant initial conditions from which, together with his theoretical assumptions (ABC), maladjustments could be predicted in individual cases.

(*c*) The theoretical assumptions (call them XYZ) about attitude-changing which the analyst uses in the technological application of his theory (e.g. about ' identification ', ' transference ', revelation of ' unconscious motives ', ' abreaction ', etc.) might be wrong or inadequate.

(*d*) The analyst might be a poor technologist in the sense that he did not possess the knack of constructing in himself or in his patient the initial conditions from which, together with assumptions XYZ, a cure or change in attitude could be predicted.

Mr. Toulmin envisages the psycho-analyst as, in the main, a kind of detective who serves up ' full-fledged analytic explanations ' of a historical character about a particular patient's ' motives ' and ' causal history '.[1] This explanation is not to be regarded as ' correct ' if it does not form part of a successful cure. Mr. Toulmin's view could be correct only if (1) the sole assumption of type XYZ used in attitude changing was that revelation of ' motives ' effects a cure, if (2) such a revelation of motives was an impersonal transaction uninfluenced by the personality and intuitive ability of the analyst and if (3) explanation in psycho-analysis were solely of the historical type and

[1] Op. cit., p. 138.

there was no way of *directly testing* psycho-analytic hypotheses
of type ABC—i.e. the indirect technological test was the sole
test available. And I do not think that any of these assumptions
is plausible.

My second comment is on Mr. Flew's distinction between
' motives ' and ' causes '[1]. Many articles could be written
showing that Freud was not over-conscious of verbal and
methodological niceties and I have no intention of replying in
detail to Mr. Flew's onslaught. I just want to select and discuss
what he says about ' motives ' and ' causes ', because this rigid
distinction seems to be rather fashionable now.[2] I shall maintain
that this is merely a way of stating in the case of a particular
sphere of interest (psychology) the well-worn distinction between
theoretical and historical explanation and that, in the proper
sense of ' causal explanation ', the gulfs suggested by Mr. Flew
are over-emphasised.

A ' motive ' explanation, as Professor Ryle points out explicitly
and Mr. Flew implies in his talk about ' motives ' being ' intangible ' and ' insubstantial ', states a law-like proposition to the effect
that if certain types of situation arise then a given person or group
of persons will respond in certain typical ways. Such explanations
are law-like in a limited sense because they do not maintain that if
certain situations arise then *anyone* will respond in certain typical
ways. Some, of course, have maintained this—e.g. those who
have maintained that man is ' by nature ' aggressive, social,
rational, political, acquisitive, and so on. But it is not plausible
to suggest that all men are e.g. jealous, kind, parsimonious,
generous. This law-like explanation, often of very limited
generality, is contrasted by Professor Ryle and Mr. Flew with
explanations in terms of ' efficient causes '. Just as we say that the
glass broke because a stone hit it, so we also say that a person
passed the salt because he heard his neighbour ask for it. Quite
rightly both Professor Ryle and Mr. Flew point out that these
types of explanation do not conflict with law-like explanations
in terms of ' brittleness ' and ' considerateness '. In fact Professor
Ryle points out that often ' efficient cause ' statements occur in
the protases of the conditional clauses which give meaning to
law-like statements.

[1] This volume p. 144.          [2] See G. Ryle, *The Concept of Mind*, Ch. IV.

I have no quarrel at all with this distinction. My only comment is that it is a way of stating within a particular sphere of interest (psychology) the well-worn distinction between theoretical and historical explanations, to use Professor Popper's terminology,[1] or between ' systematic ' and ' historico-geographical ' explanations, to use Lewin's terminology.[2] Surely the typically ' causal ' explanation is not of the historical but of the theoretical type? The gravitation law constitutes a causal explanation of the falling of the mythical apple ; Newton did not grub about like a detective trying to trace the ' efficient causes ' of the apple's fall. Scientists do not concern themselves with historical research into the ' efficient causes ' and, as Professor Popper points out, ' efficient causes ' can be viewed only as initial conditions relative to general assumptions or law-like statements, i.e. they always presuppose general assumptions often of rather a trivial character.[3]

Now it may well be true that psycho-analysts tend to behave more like historians or detectives than like theoretical scientists and therefore tend to specialize in explanations of the ' efficient cause ' type. But this is matter of emphasis and interest. The assumptions *used* by psycho-analysts in their detective work and in their technology can be set out for direct and explicit testing and the crucial question raised by Mr. Flew is whether there is in fact a great gulf between these causal explanations used by psycho-analysts and his ' motive ' explanations. I think myself that there is no such gulf, the difference being only one of different levels of generality.

Let us consider a typically Freudian causal explanation which can be extracted from his work—that certain adult motives or traits—e.g., parsimony, petulance, and pedantry are functionally dependent upon certain tendencies to react to frustrating situations at the potting period of infancy. I am not a bit concerned whether this particular explanation is a good one ; I suspect that no one knows because so few explicit attempts have been made to overthrow it. All I want to do with it is to note its general character. It attempts to deduce certain motives and traits in

---

[1] K. Popper, *The Open Society*, Ch. 25, *passim*.
[2] K. Lewin, *Principles of Topological Psychology*, p. 30.
[3] See, e.g., Popper's comments on Hume on p. 343 of his notes.

adult life (i.e. law-like statements) from a causal-genetic hypothesis. It presumes less limited generality than many ' motive '
explanations in that it is taken as a universal law and from it many
' motive ' statements are deducible. It does not seem that the
two types of statement—' motive ' and ' causal '—are fundamentally dissimilar ; they differ only in their level of generality.

' Motive ' explanation is of the Aristotelian type. Why does
the glass break? Because it is fragile. Why did Shylock demand
his pound of flesh? Because he was parsimonious. Aristotle
developed this type of explanation by trying to find ' motives '
or traits common to the whole species. Why does a king make
laws? Because man is a rational animal. We do what we do
because we are what we are. This is true but theoretically trivial
when expressed in Aristotelian form. Statistics are often used to
make this explanation seem rather less trivial ; mathematics
always lends an air of scientific respectability. Ideally, if we
stopped short of this type of explanation, we would have a vast
classificatory system like that envisaged by Aristotle. But historically this type of explanation gave way to explanation in terms of
functional dependence which was deductively more powerful.
Sugar remained ' soluble ', but its ' solubility ' as well as host of
other dispositional properties now became deducible from
chemical theory. Similarly psycho-analysts hope that, though
Shylock will remain ' parsimonious ' this ' motive ', as well as a
host of others, will be deducible from a theory about the functional dependence of adult motives and traits on our tendencies
to react in certain typical ways to typical frustrating situations
in infancy like weaning and potting. Others often resort to a
physiological theory instead of to a social environment theory in
order to explain our ' motives '. I cannot see any objection to
this which many including Mr. Flew hold to be an unspeakable
practice. Pre-frontal leucotomy, for instance, seems to show
that if certain nerve-fibres in the prefrontal region of the brain are
cut, then there will be predictable changes in social dispositions.
Changes in ' motives ' (tendencies to react to certain typical situations in typical ways) can be shown to be functionally dependent
on typical neuro-physiological changes. Why all the fuss? Why
should physiology and psychology be regarded as separate en-
quiries with separate languages and separate ' subject-matters '?

Finally, 'motive' and 'cause' explanations in psycho-analysis can be illustrated by referring to the methodological talk of working psychologists. They regard 'habits', 'drives', etc., as 'intervening variables' between certain types of response (behaviour variables) to situations (stimulus variables) and certain antecedent variables like social training, initiating physiological condition, heredity.[1] Such 'intervening variables' are meaningful if they are tied down to behaviour and to antecedent variables. 'Motive' explanations are to be seen as an attempt to correlate behaviour variables only with stimulus variables.[2] A good correlation extending over a large number of cases can be attained only if the antecedent variables of social training and heredity can be regarded as constants or rigidly controlled. Hence the limited generality of 'motive' explanations of human behaviour in contrast to the wide generality of 'drive' explanations of animal behaviour. People like Freud concentrate, it seems to me, on formulating hypotheses about the social training antecedent variables. From a theory about these they hope to be able to explain why one person's reactions to certain stimulus situations ('motives' being 'exercised') are different from another person's. Freudians try, perhaps rather confusedly, to give explanations from which 'motive' explanations can be deduced and which are therefore of a higher level of generality, 'genotypical' rather than 'phenotypical', to use the psychologist's jargon. To say that a person is 'parsimonious' postulates only a correlation, for him, between certain stimulus situations and typical responses ; to say that he has an 'anal' disposition is to relate his behaviour to a general theory about the functional dependence of motives and traits on early typical reactions to social training. Physicists did not stop at explanation in terms of 'brittleness', 'heaviness', and 'solubility'. Are psychologists to be blamed if they try to advance from explanations only in terms of 'motives'?

---

[1] See, e.g., E. Tolman *Purposive Behaviour in Animals and Men* and C. Hull, *Principles of Behaviour.*

[2] This I now think a mistake. See R. Peters, *Motives and Causes*, Proc. Aris. Soc. Supp. Vol. XXVI, 1952, Pp. 145–162. I think it important to distinguish different types of dispositional terms which Prof. Ryle includes under the term "motive". It is especially important to distinguish "motive", which is a *causal* term, from "intention" or "objective", "trait", and "attitude", which are not [R.S.P., 1954]

## POSTSCRIPT (1954)

### By STEPHEN TOULMIN

THE conflict between Mr. Peters and myself in the papers here reprinted was not as sharp as it appears. He concerned himself with the theoretical doctrines about the development of the mind which Freudians have built up from their clinical experience and invoke in their explanations, and he assumed that I had been writing about that also. But I was more interested in the actual interpretations psycho-analysts will offer of a patient's behaviour than I was in their theory of mind. Correspondingly, Mr. Peters uses the term ' motive ' in a different sense from me : for him a motive is such a thing as parsimony and a statement about motives a ' law-like ' statement, whereas I was talking of motives more in a sense akin to that of ' reasons ' for conduct. Mr. Peters' motive-explanations may not differ in any striking respect from ordinary causal (E3) explanations, but over a man's reasons for doing what he does—acknowledged or unacknowledged—the distinctions I tried to draw become vital.

As for Mr. Peters' objections to my account of cure : I gave none. It would not be possible to characterise the psycho-analytic conception of cure adequately in 2,000 words, and I assumed (unwisely perhaps) that the complexity of the subject was common knowledge. I certainly did not mean that one need only *tell* a man he has certain unconscious motives for these to be revealed to him—if there were no resistances there would be little need for analysis. None the less, the analyst tries to reveal them, and one necessary (though not sufficient) test of the correctness of his interpretations is whether the patient would, in finally coming to accept them, abandon the inappropriate attitudes manifested in the neurosis.

There has been a noticeable change of emphasis among analysts since Freud. He himself set great store by the idea of psychic *mechanism*, and he took over many of his technical terms from the neurology in which he had been trained. Many present-day analysts, however, regard talk about psychic mechanism as analogical, and recognize the danger that the physiological model may be misleading : they see it as their business rather to expose a special variety of *misconception*. Causal questions arise, of course, when we ask genetic questions, i.e. what events in a man's life can give rise to these misconceptions ; but the interpretation of a patient's present state of mind frequently involves no such causal reference. This change of emphasis, Mr. Flew and I would say, helps to bring the theory of psycho-analysis into line with what its practice has always been, and eliminates the divergence we find between Freud's meta-psychological papers and his case-reports. Since it was this divergence which gave rise to many of the philosophical misunderstandings about psycho-analysis, philosophers should welcome its disappearance.

## CONSCIENCE AND MORAL CONVICTIONS

### By GILBERT RYLE

IN discussing the conflict between Moral Sense theories of ethical knowledge (or conviction) and intellectual theories like those of Kant and Price, recently, I struck a point which was new to me. I had always vaguely supposed that ' Conscience ' is ordinarily used to signify any sort of knowledge or conviction about what is right and wrong. So that *any* verdict about the rightness or wrongness either of a particular type of conduct or of a particular piece of conduct could be called a verdict of ' Conscience '. I had also supposed that ' conscience ' was too vague and equivocal a word to enjoy any definite syntax.

But then I noticed that ' conscience ' is *not* used in this way. We limit the verdicts of conscience to judgments about the rightness or wrongness of the acts only of the owner of that conscience. It is absurd to say, ' My conscience says that *you* ought to do this or ought not to have done that '. Judgments about the morality of other people's behaviour would not be called verdicts of conscience. If asked to advise someone else on a moral point, I could not without absurdity say that I must consult my conscience. Nor, if someone else misbehaves, can *my* conscience be said to disapprove. Conscience is a *private* monitor.

True, I can set myself to imagine moral problems. I can consider how my conscience would react if I were in your shoes, doing what you have done, or meditate doing. I can say, " I could not do so and so with a clear conscience, so you ought not to do it ". But I can't say, "*My* conscience won't be clear if *you* do it ". What, then, is the difference between conscience and moral conviction which makes it absurd to regard the verdicts of my conscience as co-extensive with my moral convictions? Why can *my* conscience pass judgment only on *my* actions?

Originally, it appears, ' conscience ' generally connoted ' self-knowledge ' or ' self-consciousness '. Introspection would be an activity of ' conscientia ', whether the objects of the introspection were or were not subjects of moral predicates. With the Reformation, if not earlier, self-inspection was supposed to be the direct discovery of the requirements of God. And ' Conscience ' began to have the narrower meaning of the knowledge by self-inspection of *my* duties and faults. Butler links conscience very closely to ' reflection ' (in Locke's sense) which is equivalent to introspection. But why should my moral convictions apply differently to me, just because direct inspection by me is restricted to *my* thoughts, motives and resolves?

Certainly, I can't know directly how you feel or what you think, but I can often know well enough by inference. And in reading a novel I can know all about the motives and desires of the characters, for the novelist tells me them. Yet, though I know all about you, or about the hero of the novel, I can't say that my conscience approves or disapproves either of your conduct or of his. Conversely, introspection or self-inspection are not sources of infallible knowledge. I can misdescribe, to myself, without dishonesty, my own motives. I may, e.g. fail to find ' Schadenfreude ' in my ' serves him right ' attitudes, though it is there.

So the difference cannot derive from that between my having *knowledge* of myself and only *opinions* about other people. If God is omniscient it would still be absurd to say that *his* conscience chided me for my behaviour.

At this point it looks tempting to go back and say (with the Moral Sensationalists) that, after all, my moral verdicts about myself do record special (moral) sense-perceptions, while my moral verdicts about others, involving as they do both generalisations of rules and inferential imputation of motives, dispositions, etc. are intellectual and rational. But this will not do. My particular verdicts of conscience are applications of general rules, imperatives or codes. My conscience says, 'You aren't being *honest*' and this involves understanding both what being honest is, and that it is a general desideratum. (It is like one's prompt recognition that what one is saying is bad grammar, i.e., is a breach of a general rule. The facts that the recognition is prompt and may be unarticulated do not entail that we have a ' grammatical sense ').

I suggest that the solution of the puzzle, which, I think, is a genuine one about the syntax of ' conscience ' and of ' moral conviction ', is in this direction. What is it to *have* a moral conviction? Or, what is it to *have* principles? At first, we begin by saying that it is to know or be convinced that some general proposition is true or that some universal imperative is right, or wise. But what are the public tests of whether a person really knows or is really convinced of so and so? They are, I think, the following :

(1) That he *utters* it regularly, relevantly and without hesitation.

(2) That other things which he says regularly, relevantly and unhesitatingly, presuppose it.

(3) That he is ready or eager to try to persuade other people of it and to dissuade them of what is inconsistent with it.

(4) That he regularly and readily behaves in accordance with it, on occasions when it is relevant.

(5) That when he does not behave in accordance with it, he feels guilty, resolves to reform, etc.

We are inclined to say that (1) and (2) show that he intellectually accepts the principle ; he thinks e.g. that honesty is desirable : that (4) and (5) show that he is honest or pretty honest, and that (3) shows something between the two, namely, that he admires or respects honesty. And we should also be inclined to say that (1) and (2) taken *alone* show that he is not *really* convinced ; the principle is a part of his intellectual furniture but not of his real nature. His acceptance of it is academic. It is not operative on his volitions, emotions and behaviour. But this is rather fishy. For it sets up a queer fence between thinking, feeling and willing ; as if being a man of principle (say, being honest) differs from acknowledging honesty by the irruption of some new faculty, called will or feeling, which can accept principles, only not in the way in which thought does so. But thinking, e.g. believing, is an aspect of character or nature. The difference between not feeling qualms of doubt and not hesitating in bodily action is not a hard and fast line. *Saying* readily and *doing* readily seem to be related as species to genus, not as co-ordinate species of a higher genus. Talking to oneself or aloud is behaving. So there seems to be a sense in which *real* acceptance of a principle (does not lead to, but) *is* being disposed to behave in accordance with it. To ' know ' a rule of conduct *is* to be regulated in one's conduct. To know *properly* the rules of grammar is to be able to talk correctly, correct mistakes and to wince at those of others. A man's party manners show whether he ' knows ' the rules of etiquette ; his ability to *cite* ' Etiquette for Gentlemen ' does not.

Supposing it conceded that sometimes appropriate behaviour is part of what we *mean* by certitude or acceptance of a proposition, let us label as ' operative ' the knowledge or conviction which manifests itself in the disposition to behave—in *all* sorts of behaviour, including ' thinking '—in accordance with the principle which is said to be known or accepted. To be disposed to behave in a certain way in certain circumstances is to be prone or inclined to do so. Other things being equal a person with a certain disposition will probably behave in the given way ; that is what the word ' disposition ' means.

Now if someone has operatively accepted a certain principle, but other things are not equal, i.e. he experiences some contrary impulse, there will not only exist a conflict between the temptation and the abstract principle ; there will be actually experienced a conflict between the temptation and the disposition which is the operatively accepted principle. He will feel a tension because he *is* the two tendencies to act which are in conflict. " It goes against the grain ". And these two tendencies, with their conflict, are visible on self-inspection or inferrible from what he can introspect. His knowledge or conviction of the principle is not an external censor but an internal competitor. His knowledge how he should behave does not *cause* but *is* a nisus to behaving in that way, but it is a *felt* nisus only when it is impeded.

But in passing verdicts on the conducts of others, our conviction, so to speak, cannot be more than academic. For me to believe that you should do so and so can be only to pronounce and perhaps to try to persuade ; in the full sense of ' operative ' my conviction about your duty cannot be operative, for it cannot issue in the required behaviour. (The desire to punish, rebuke and reform seems to be a response to the inoperativeness of merely finding fault.)

Or, alternatively, my application of a principle to you can take the form only of a verdict or of advice or exhortation, with perhaps subsequent reproof or punishment. But my application of my principle to me can take the form of doing what I should. In this sense conscience is never a merely verdict-passing faculty, it is a conduct-regulating faculty. Its exercise is behaving or trying to behave and not describing or recommending. We credit conscience with *authority* as well as with knowledge. That is, we use the word ' conscience ' for those moral convictions which issue not in verdicts but in behaving or trying to behave. So it is a tautology that my conscience cannot direct the behaviour of someone else.

This has analogies elsewhere. In a certain sense, I, having read the text books and been a spectator, know how to swim ; that is, I know what actions people must take to progress in a desired direction in the water, with the nostrils clear of the water. But no-one would say that I really know how to swim or that I have swimming-skill, unless when I do it myself I usually succeed. And it would be absurd to say that I have skill or expertness in the swimming of others, though in the academic sense of the word ' know ' I may know just what mistakes they are making. The proper manifestations of my skill are my performances and not mere directions to others. And the proper manifestations of my conscience are in my good conduct, or reluctance to behave ill or remorse afterwards and resolutions to reform. Conscience is not something other than, prior to or posterior to moral convictions ; it is having those convictions in an operative degree, i.e. being disposed to behave accordingly. And it is active or calls for attention when this disposition is balked by some contrary inclination. Conscience has nothing to say when the really honest man is asked a question and when he has no temptation to deceive. He then tells the truth as he signs his name, without considering what to do or why he should do it or how to get himself to do it. Conscience is awake only when there is such a conflict. The test for the existence of such a conflict is the occurrence of attention to the problem of what is to be done. Pangs or qualms of conscience can occur only when I am both disposed to act in one way and disposed to act in another and when one of these dispositions is an operative moral principle. (And this ' can . . . only ' is logical and not causal.) Wondering what to do is a manifestation of a balked disposition to act ; if it was not balked I would act as I am disposed to act for that is what ' disposed ' means. Consulting my conscience entails attending introspectively to my conflicting dispositions to act. Hence I cannot (logically) consult my conscience about what you are to do. Having a conscience to ' consult ' is having a (partially) operative moral conviction.

Now there are convictions of rules of conduct other than moral ones. So they should in parallel circumstances engender naggings, commands, etc. parallel to those of conscience. Is this so ?

1. *Rules of Prudence.* I have learned from experience, doctors, hearsay, etc. that it is bad for me not to have a regular allowance of sleep each night. I know that I shall feel ' like death ' to-morrow afternoon if I do not have at least seven hours of sleep. And I do habitually go to bed at 12, say, to be called at 8, without thinking of the effects of not doing so. " Midnight is my bed-time " is the only thought that usually occurs to me if any thought occurs to me at all. Now, suppose, I am halfway through an exciting detective story at midnight. So I want to read on, and I am disposed to go to bed at ' my bedtime '. I do not feel guilty, but I find myself making excuses and promises for the future. Or, I tell myself that to-morrow afternoon is disengaged so I can sleep then. So I do attend to factors in the situation similar to those which are considered in questions of conscience. In certain of their uses, words like ' discretion ' and ' caution ' resemble ' conscience '. In the sense, e.g. in which my discretion guides my actions it cannot guide yours. To be cautious, provident, etc. is not just to acknowledge or enunciate certain propositions which may be true for everyone ; it is to be disposed to live cautiously, providently, etc., which though it includes such acknowledging and enunciating does not reduce to them.

2. *Rules of Etiquette, fashion and social decorum.* " We dress

for dinner at Christ Church ". When we do this, the ' done ' thing, we do not generally consider the utilities or aesthetic amenities of the practice. We just dress—i.e. it is a habit—but one which is actualised not only in dressing, but also in feeling surprised if a colleague dines in day clothes, in stopping teaching some time before dinner, etc. Our acceptance of the convention is manifested primarily by our behaving regularly and unquestion- ingly in accordance with it. Sometimes I am prevented from dressing. Then, while dining in mufti, I feel uncomfortable (though not guilty or imprudent). My sense of decorum, which is not, of course, a new mode of sense perception, nags gently. And in the sense in which I am punctilious about my own dinner uniform I cannot be punctilious about that of other people, I can be only noticing about them or critical of them.

3. *Rules of arithmetic.* The accurate computer regularly observes the rules of addition, subtraction, multiplication and division. And his observance of them is not manifested in a special momentary act of acknowledging them, declaring them or teaching them, but in all his acts of accùrate computation. His grasp of the rules is his ability and skill in working in accord- ance with them. He does not begin each morning's work by reciting an arithmetical creed. In a certain sense of ' think ' he never thinks of the rules. In another sense of the word, however, he is thinking of the rules all the time ; for he is continually applying them correctly and skilfully. The rules are now *habits* of operating. But his accuracy, flair or scrupulousness governs only his own computations. He cannot have a flair about the calculations of other people, though he knows the rules which they should keep and how these rules apply to their particular problems. But this knowledge is ' academic ' while flair is prac- tical. The former issues at most in behests and criticisms ; the latter in accurate calculations. To know *operatively* the rules is to know how to calculate, i.e. to be able to calculate correctly, swiftly and without fatigue. The fact that many good mathe- matical teachers are bad mathematicians brings out these two opposed senses of ' knowing mathematics '. Is there anything in this field analogous to either the questions or commands of conscience ? I think there is. If a computer happens to know the answer which he expects to arrive at, e.g. from reading a pass

book, he may through laziness or wishful thinking run too hastily through a column of figures and then, even though by accident his answer is correct, he feels a sense of guilt about his steps, and is inclined to go over them again more carefully. This is especially so when he gets to an answer which for some reason *must* be wrong. To locate and correct a mistake requires a special act of attention to what, say, certain figures do and do *not* add up to. His ordinary scrupulousness does not normally require the occurrence of actual scruples. But sometimes he has actually to feel scruples, which he would not feel unless he were dispositionally scrupulous, and on a given occasion has not been scrupulous enough. God would calculate (if at all) with 100 per cent scrupulousness and 0 per cent scruples. Similarly, he would always do the right thing and would never wonder what he ought to do. He would never consult his conscience and would never have pangs of conscience.

It might be said that having scruples, though they will be scruples of different sorts, is common to all cases where *real* acceptance of rules or principles is the being disposed to behave in a certain way, but where this disposition is balked of its normal actualization by some special temptation or interruption. It is like trying to mis-spell one's own signature, when writing one's own name has become an automatic habit. One *can* do it, but there is a resistance. One may compare also the practised cyclist trying to control a tricycle. His normal responses, e.g. in turning or in tilting are balked by the abnormal situation. He knows (academically) what to do, but does not *really*, i.e. operatively know how to do it. But as cycling well does not involve acknowledging or being able to cite laws of dynamics, one can scarcely speak of cycling scrupulously. Roughly, *this* sort of habit is a reflex and not an observance.

Conscience, then, is one species, among others, of scrupulousness ; and scrupulousness is the operative acceptance of a rule or principle which consists in the disposition to behave, in all modes of behaviour, including saying to oneself and others, teaching, chiding, etc., in accordance with the rule. Scruples, whether of conscience or of any other species of scrupulousness, occur only when the normal actualisation of the disposition is impeded or balked. And they, too, are only a special way in which the disposition is actualised, viz. when it cannot be *normally* actualised. The reason why my conscience is not spoken of as either judging or commanding other people is the same as the reason why, in general, a man can be described as scrupulous only about his own acts, namely, that full operative acceptance of the rule can (logically) take the form only of conducting oneself in accordance with the rule. Your actions can't (logically) be exercises of or exhibit *my* skill, readiness, capacity, enthusiasm etc.

This answer to the original puzzle will, of course, provoke the objection that it denies the hallowed distinctions between cognition, emotion and volition. For I am saying that in one sense, and a very important sense, of the word, my being ' convinced ' of something or my ' knowing ' it do not *cause* but *consist* in my tending to feel certain feelings and to enact certain actions. It will be said that a thought may *engender* dispositions to feel and to act, but that these dispositions are not the causes of themselves.

I reply : (1) Then must it also be said that when I think in words, my saying so and so to myself is the *effect* of the thinking and not a constituent of it, that I first think and then tell myself what I have thought? But then I must think also what to tell myself and how to tell it, and this thinking must also have its own articulation which must in its turn be premeditated and so on . . . . Thinking *is* talking sensibly, but then why should it not equally be *behaving* sensibly?

(2) The present view, that among the criteria (*not* the symptoms) of belief and knowledge are dispositions to feel certain emotions and perform certain actions does not entail that ' thinking ', ' feeling ' and ' doing ' are synonymous. It is still necessary to distinguish impulsive, reflex and automatic from intelligent, careful, purposive, deliberate and scrupulous actions ; and silly from sensible, careless from careful, deliberate from unpremeditated, behaviour. Similarly, feeling indignant, shocked, awed, amused, thwarted, respectful differ from feeling uneasy, angry, or sleepy. Only rational beings in rational states of mind (i.e. not drunk, in a panic, or infantile) can (logically) feel the former, while animals and infants can feel the latter. Was Kant's obscure doctrine about " Practical Reason " something like this view, and Aristotle's φρόνησις which manifests itself sometimes in *acting*

from premisses and which is internally connected with ἠθικὴ ἀρετή ? What do we *mean* by ' judicious behaviour ', ' scrupulous conduct ', ' skilful or careful action '? They can't mean ' acting in consequence of certain " sententious thinking " ' ; for we can also say that the choice and control of the sentences in which we think, when we think ' sententiously ' can be judicious and careful. Nor could the alleged causal connections between thinking and doing (or feeling) have been discovered by the people who speak of ' judicious behaviour' as an effect of ' sententious thinking ', for whatever trained psychologists may do, the plain man cannot find the pure thinkings which are to be inductively correlated with the supposedly resultant actions or feelings. So his use of phrases like ' judicious behaviour' do not signify instances of such correlations.

I have not tried to show what the differences are between conscience and other sorts of scrupulousness. That is not my present puzzle. Nor have I tried to list all the varieties of conduct which can be described as ' scrupulous '. There are plenty of others besides those mentioned ; those, e.g. of good discipline in the Army and Navy, observance of Committee and Parliamentary procedure, keeping to the principles of good chess, bridge, grammar, strategy, style, prosody, and of the judge adhering to the rules of admissible evidence. None of these adherences is ' mere ' acknowledgement of general truths or imperatives. They are fully adopted in habitual observance and in feeling scruples about breaking the habits.

# CHAPTER VII. EVENTS, TIME AND TENSE

## FUGITIVE PROPOSITIONS

### By Austin Duncan-Jones

MANY of the propositions we commonly entertain have an odd
yet obvious feature which does not seem to have been much
remarked on. This feature belongs to many empirical propositions which imply the existence of some event or class of events.
It does not belong to *a priori* propositions, or to genuine universals
of law. And it is that the proposition in question cannot be entertained twice. In other words, the usual assumption that every
proposition has what D. R. Cousin calls " spatio-temporal
neutrality "[1] is mistaken.

This feature of propositions is made clear at once by formulating them in a tenseless language, in which date is expressed
by a variable or constant time coefficient. Instead of

$$\text{" Brutus killed Caesar ",} \tag{1}$$

we might say

$$\text{" Brutus kills Caesar at } T \text{ ",} \tag{2}$$

in which the present tense is used in a timeless sense. But (2) is
not an adequate rendering of (1) unless we explain the meaning
of " $T$ ". The obvious way to do so is as follows.

$$\text{" For some } t \text{, Brutus kills Caesar at } t \text{, and } t \text{ is before now ", (3)}$$

where " now " is the proper name of a moment. Whenever I
use (3) on different occasions to express a proposition which I
entertain, one element of the proposition entertained is different :
therefore on each occasion the proposition entertained is different.

This is not a self-contained oddity. For it follows that no
proposition susceptible of the kind of analysis illustrated in
(3) can ever be a matter for deliberation or controversy. If
historian A uses (3) on a given occasion, and historian B wishes
to disagree with him, B will not be able to express the proposition
he rejects, for the moment he needs to name will have passed.

---

[1] *Proc. Arist. Soc.*, 1948–49, p. 153, " Propositions ".

To produce this absurdity I have to some extent distorted the customary use of the word " proposition ". For given that the names are used in the same way it is part of the customary usage that people who say " Brutus killed Caesar " on different occasions *do* express the same proposition. But it is also part of the customary usage that if, when a sentence is used on two occasions, some part of it has different meanings on the two occasions, the sentence cannot express the same proposition on each occasion. And if S1 and S2 are sentences with the same meaning, and if S1 expresses different propositions on different occasions, then S2 expresses different propositions on different occasions. Therefore, if (3) is an adequate rendering of (1), the accepted usage of " proposition " is not consistent.

If we seek to retain the convention that historians *do* always express the same proposition by (1), we shall have to allow sentences with different meanings to express the same proposition. In that case a counterpart of our paradox will arise about meanings. Let us assume that (3) is an adequate rendering of (1), in the sense that anyone who uses (1) could have used (3), on the same occasion, to express what he meant by (1). Then if A uses (1) on a given occasion it will never be open to B on a later occasion to reject what A meant by (1).

I suppose we could remove the difficulty by a heroic semantic device which I shall not develop in detail. We could define B's rejection at $t_2$ of A's assertion at $t_1$ in a special way. We could say that B does not assert the contradictory of A's proposition, but asserts a proposition of higher order, to the effect that a certain proposition, which he describes as having been asserted by A at $t_1$, and as having a certain content, was false. Such an unwieldy piece of machinery seems disproportionate.

It might be argued that propositions mentioning a more or less definite date can be freed from paradox by non-hierarchical methods. For example, in

" Caesar died in 44 B.C.",                    (4)

the reference to the birth of Christ can be interpreted as an abbreviation for a circumstantial history told in the Gospels. And we might take it as part of what is asserted in (4) that one and only one event, throughout the whole of past and future time, corresponds to this history. The whole proposition can then be taken as asserting a time interval between two described events, without reference to the moment of assertion. I do not think this analysis is plausible. For it implies that (4) might refer indifferently to past or future events. It seems to me that from what we mean by (4) it is deducible that Caesar is dead.

I think in recent philosophy analysis of the meaning of time expressions has been either neglected or dealt with perfunctorily, although a generation or two has passed since, in other ways, philosophers began, in Alexander's words, to " take time seriously ". We lack a simple standard method of expressing time relations more explicitly than they are expressed in (1), which will enable us to keep as much as possible of the customary usage of the phrases " same proposition " and " different proposition ". I have carried my account of the customary usage only far enough to display my difficulty, and have ignored much of its subtlety.

The time with which we are concerned is the crude time of common sense.

## FUGITIVE PROPOSITIONS

### By Patrick Nowell Smith

Mr. Duncan-Jones raises a pretty paradox about those sentences in which tense plays a part. He offers no solution, but suggests that the solution lies in discovering " a simple standard method of expressing time-relations more explicitly than they are expressed in (1) " below. I am going to suggest that this way out is radically wrong, on the grounds that the time-element cannot be made explicit in a tensed sentence. My reason is, briefly, that such sentences contain an implicit reference to the context in which they are used, and that paradoxes must arise from trying to make the context of a sentence explicit in the sentence itself. If I am right, Duncan-Jones' paradox is of the same family as those which the theory of types was designed to solve.

To simplify and sharpen the issue I shall change his example to " Caesar died ". His first three sentences then become :—

| Caesar died | (1) |
| Caesar dies at $t$ | (2) |
| For some $t$, Caesar dies at $t$, and $t$ is before now | (3) |

To these we may add :—

| Caesar is dead | (4) |

The paradox arises if we try to make the tense-element in (1) explicit. Our first shot is (2); but this won't do. For the truth of (1) and of (4), which follows from (1), is a function of the time of its use. If Lot had said (1) or (4) to his wife it would have been false; if I say either of them now they are true. But (2) is not a proposition at all until a value is given for $t$. It then becomes eternally true (or false), as true for Lot as for me. To allow for the fact that (1) and (4) seem to become true from being false, we have to try something like (3). But this has the queer result of making it impossible for any historian to understand—still less affirm or deny—what another has written. (3), and therefore (1), if (3) is a correct analysis, is a 'fugitive' proposition that cannot be entertained twice. By giving an ' adequate rendering ' of (1) we make this clear.

Since this is a paradox about one of the words that have been called ' egocentric ', let us see if any light can be thrown on it by considering another such word. Suppose that on the first of December, 1949, I say " I am ill ". Taken in its context this means " N-S is ill on 1 Dec. 1949 ". This can easily be seen by showing that (*a*) this is what every English-speaking person would take it to mean and (*b*) the correct deductions follow from it ; e.g. " N-S should see a doctor ", " N-S has only himself to blame ", etc. Now the obvious objections to this analysis are (i) " I am ill " cannot *mean* " N-S is ill ", since the words might have been uttered by Duncan-Jones or anyone else. (ii) The alleged deductions do not follow from " I am ill ", but from " N-S is ill ". Both these objections rest on the assumption that " I am ill " ' has a meaning ' apart from its context ; and this is false. " I am ill " has no meaning apart from its context ; and the only grounds for supposing that it has are (as far as I can see), either some a priori theory that all properly constructed sentences must ' have a meaning ' or that there are some deductions that always follow from " I am ill ", such as " I am not well ". I see no reason for accepting the a priori theory ; and as to the deductions, it is obvious that they are in the same boat. No one supposes that " I am not well ", spoken by Duncan-Jones follows from " I am ill " spoken by N-S.

" I am ill " has no meaning apart from its context ; but in its context its meaning is clear and unambiguous. (This point is sometimes made by saying that such sentences are ' systematically ambiguous '. Nothing could be more unfortunate. For the meaning of such a sentence is never ambiguous ; and this way of putting the matter only reinforces the view that sentences have meanings, albeit ambiguous ones, in isolation.)

There is nothing mysterious about sentences that have no meaning in isolation and a different meaning each time they are used. This does not prevent people understanding, affirming or denying them. What is peculiar about these sentences is that they can be neither understood, asserted or denied by anyone unless that person knows the context. This he can do either by hearing the sentence used or by otherwise learning what its context was. When he knows this, he can substitute a sentence which contains no egocentric word, which is precisely equivalent to the original sentence and which gives rise to no paradox. That this is true is shown by the fact that you would not understand a telegram which said " I am ill " if you had no clue as to its author. To ask whether such a telegram ' means anything ' is to ask an incomplete question. We must ask whether it means anything to a particular recipient on a particular occasion.

Returning to the original example, we can now see that (1) has no meaning in isolation and that nothing follows from it. If it is argued that (4) still follows from it, the answer is that (4) only follows from (1) if contexts are given for both and the contexts are suitably related. (4) cannot follow from (1), if (1) is said by me and (4) is said by Lot to his wife ; since in this case (1) is true and (4) false. What makes us think that (4) always follows from (1) is the fact that, if different contexts are not specified, we assume that the context is the same for both ; and it is true that for any context, (4) follows from (1). We must not, however, assume that what is true for all contexts is true for none.

I am not quite sure what Duncan-Jones means by an 'adequate rendering ' : but I assume he means something like this : " S2 is an adequate rendering of S1, if and only if (*a*) S2 means the same as S1 and (*b*) everything that is implicit in S1 is made explicit in S2." If this is (at least roughly), what he means, then (3) is indeed an adequate rendering of (1) ; but it is a philosophical mistake to try to render (1) adequately. For the notion of an ' adequate rendering ' now involves two assumptions, both of which are doubtful : (i) that one proposition can ' have the same meaning ' as another, with the corollary that propositions ' have meanings ' outside contexts ; (ii) that a proposition can explicitly refer to its own context.

If I am right, tensed propositions do not voyage through time carrying their meanings with them ; but this does not make them ' fugitive ' in any embarrassing sense ; it means merely that we cannot understand them unless we know something about the context of their use.

Duncan-Jones' paradox is interesting because it brings out two points that are of much wider importance (i) It is often held that the meaning of a proposition is given when its elements and their order are given. This is a plausible view if we think of the ' meaning of a proposition ' as (vaguely) ' what the proposition says ' or what it ' contains '. But, if we accept this view, we must add that, to understand a proposition, we must sometimes know more than ' what it means ', in this sense. We must know facts about its context that cannot be contained in it.

(ii) Words and sentences do not ' apply to ', ' refer to ' or ' imply ' anything. It is *we* who apply words to things, refer to things by means of words and sometimes imply more than we say. No doubt it is sometimes convenient to forget this and to say that a word ' has such and such a meaning ', when we mean to say that any suitably qualified person would use or understand the word in this way. But the active voice here is a device for avoiding reference to particular people. It is an obvious mistake to suppose that, because " something is red " does not tell us what is red, it could be true even if no particular thing were red. It is a precisely similar mistake to suppose that, because a word or sentence means the same thing for everybody, it ' has a meaning ' even if nobody ever uses it.

## POSTSCRIPT (1954)

To say that sentences (and other expressions) have no meaning in isolation was, perhaps, an error on my part. I certainly did not wish to suggest that they are meaningless or nonsensical. Of course everyone who knows English knows what ' Caesar died ' means and of course we can discover the meanings of words from ·dictionaries ; but this is because certain expressions have accepted uses in standard contexts to which we tacitly refer. I tried to guard against the criticism that Mr. Cohen[1] makes by saying later that if we think of meaning as something ' contained in ' or belonging to an expression, we must, in order to *understand* it, sometimes know more than what it means ; and in the case of token-reflexive sentences we must know to what some of the expressions refer.

Mr. Cohen's own analysis escapes the objection that I raised against Mr. Duncan-Jones' precisely because it makes the analysis ·of tensed sentences as incomplete as the analysanda ; but for this reason also it seems to me not to meet the original demand. This is no objection to it, since the original demand is, if I am right, self-contradictory. It is the demand that a sentence-*type* which contains token-reflexive expressions should be analysed into a sentence-type which does not contain them. Nevertheless Mr. Cohen's analysis does seem to me erroneous in one way. He is explicitly and rightly trying to analyse a sentence-type ; but his analysis involves reference to " the class consisting of this and of all other past-referring tokens which would normally be thought to be in direct agreement with it ". But as he says nothing about ' direct agreement ' I am not sure how this class is to be determined. To take his own example, if Smith says " The hydrogen bomb has been exploded " shortly before, and Jones says it shortly after the first explosion, are their tokens in direct agreement? If we consider the *sentences* they use, their grammatical form, physical shape etc., we must say that they are. The disagreement only appears when we bring in the occasion of their

---

[1] See this collection pp. 180–190.

use and it consists in the fact that Jones' statement is true, while Smith's is false. It would therefore seem that, under the guise of giving an analysis of a sentence-type, Mr. Cohen is really telling us something about *statements* ; and if this is so there is little disagreement between us.

In general, I do not think that meaning can be elucidated in terms of sentence-types alone (irrespective of the statements, questions, etc., for which the sentence-tokens are used), since without reference to the uses we cannot determine which tokens belong to the same type. The view which I here oppose seems to have arisen from an appreciation of the fact that, in many cases, to understand a statement it is not necessary to know to what it refers. But, in the case of token-reflexive statements and statements containing pronouns, this does seem to me necessary. If I hear someone, reading a novel, say " She fainted on the sofa ", have I understood what was said? Yes and No. I know that some woman (or perhaps bitch) has fainted on the sofa ; but this is not what the author's statement means, nor what the English sentence means. (P.H.N.S.)

## EVENTS AND LANGUAGE

### By BERNARD MAYO

I SHALL maintain that logicians have not dealt at all adequately with sentences referring to events ; that this has been due primarily to a preoccupation with sentences in which nouns and adjectives are more prominent than verbs and adverbs ; and that this, in turn, is due to an insufficiently thorough revision of the traditional propositional logic.

### I

I begin by considering a situation that would be difficult for what I may call an orthodox logical analysis. The sentence " This stone was laid by King George V " does not appear at first sight to offer any difficulty. A typical treatment of this sentence would be to say that it expresses, or asserts, a proposition which is true if King George V laid the stone, and false otherwise. It would be added, in contrast with the traditional analysis into subject, copula and predicate (" King George V is a layer of this stone ") that what is asserted is not a property of King George V (or of the stone) but a relation between the two. Moreover, if the sentence were " This stone was laid by King George V on July 9, 1929 " it would have to be added that there is also asserted a second relation, namely the relation between the one event, the stone-laying, and other events, including the birth of Christ and certain astronomical observations. It should be noticed that both these relations are timeless, in the sense that the truth of their assertion is independent of the time at which any statement containing such an assertion is made. (This is not always so : for example, it is not with " It will rain in Manchester to-morrow ", where the truth of what is asserted is dependent on the time at which the statement is made). Consequently, the analysis has failed to analyse the meaning or function of the past tense of the verb (' was laid ').

Imagine a rather eccentric architect having the stone inscribed at the time when it was quarried : the inscription might then be " This stone will be laid by King George V ". When the time comes for the ceremony, the sentence will need to be altered. The engraver will alter the words ' will be ' to ' is being '. (Or, less outrageously, imagine the new sentence to be, " This stone is being laid by King George V ", uttered by a television commentator). Finally, when the ceremony is over, the words ' is being ' are altered to ' was '. For practical reasons, the first two stages, and the two alterations, are of course omitted ; but their logical aptness brings it home to us that in the third and familiar stage, just as in the other two, the tense of the verb is determined, not by the *meaning* of the sentence, but by the circumstances in which it is uttered. (By a pardonable metaphor, the stone may by said to ' utter ' a sentence whenever someone reads it).

The circumstances which are relevant to determining the tense are, thus, the pastness, presence or futurity of the *event*, the stone-laying. But pastness of an event is not part of what is asserted. No one expects to be told that a stone, obviously forming part of an existing building, *was* laid. And this is not a gratuitous intrusion of psychology into logic : it is the result of an enquiry of the type " To what sort of questions is the given statement an answer ? " Nor is what I am saying true only of stones and buildings, in virtue of some peculiar property of these objects ; there is a practically unlimited choice of situations in which it would be equally clear that, in a sentence in which a past tense occurred, pastness was not part of what was asserted. What, then, *is* asserted? The logical analysis I have been following so far speaks of a relation being asserted. If asked what in the ordinary sense the sentence was *about*, anyone would answer that it was about an event. But the usual logical analysis cannot allow that the sentence " This stone was laid by King George V " is *about* anything other than this stone and King George V, the entities between which a relation is asserted. Even in " This stone was laid by King George V on July 9, 1929 ", only part of what is asserted is about an event, namely the sub-statement asserting a temporal relation between the stone-laying and other events.

If the suggested logical analysis is right, then, there is a sense of ' about ' in which the sentence " This stone was laid by King George V " is not about an event ; and if common sense is right, there is another sense of ' about ' in which the sentence *is* about an event. The technical sense of ' about ' is the sense in which, according to the logical analysis, the sentence does not assert anything *of* an event. And this is true : what the sentence mainly does is not to assert anything at all, but to *record* something, namely an event. The vulgar use of ' about ' includes the sense in which a sentence records as well as the sense in which a sentence asserts.

I have to admit, of course, that the distinction between asserting and recording cannot be drawn with absolute precision. There might, for example, be circumstances in which the sentence " This stone was laid by King George V " would make an assertion : if, for instance, it were uttered in reply to someone interested in the relation of this particular stone to the founder of the building. What I want to bring out is that it is the normal function of inscriptions to record events ; and since I am going to maintain that recording is an important function of other kinds of sentence too, I wanted to begin by drawing attention to the sentences occurring in inscriptions whose recording function is beyond dispute. Of course the normal function of inscriptions includes more than mere recording : there is usually, for example, also a spatial relation between the event recorded and the site of the recording inscription. But there are other and scarcely less obvious kinds of records, such as log-books, ledgers, diaries and some history books. The typical sentences occurring in such works all have in common the fact that they record events. No doubt they often also assert relations, but this happens only in so far as the sentences are assertions as well as records.

What distinguishes the ' recording ' features of such sentences from their ' fact-stating ' features is usually the tense of the verb. The sentence " Caesar invaded Britain " is both an assertion and a record. Both functions are performed by the single word standing for the verb, and can be distinguished as follows. The ' fact-stating ' part of the sentence can be retained when the tense-form of the verb is eliminated, if, for instance, we write " Caesar inv Britain ". (This will be familiar to people who take notes at history lectures.) But lest it may be considered an objection that, in all such instances, it is known already that ' inv ' is short for ' invaded ', I want to make it quite clear that the formula would be an assertion even if this were not so. Suppose there were a language in which ' inv ' (or some other symbol) represented an indeterminate tense of the indicative mood. It is, after all, arguable that if their memories were different from what they are human beings would require a grammatical form of the verb which would allow them to assert the occurrence of a certain event without a definite reference to past, present or future. In such a language, the expression " Caesar inv Britain " would be an assertion, even though there is no tense either explicit or implicit; it would be a statement which would be true or false in virtue of precisely the same facts as the statement " Caesar invaded Britain ". (Virtually tenseless verbs are already used in formulating universal statements like " Bees make honey "). So much, then, for the ' fact-stating ' feature of my sentence, to which the time-reference of tense is irrelevant.

The feature of the sentence which records an event in time is the tense of the verb. It is now becoming clear what the occurrence of a certain tense-form does do, if it doesn't assert anything. What it does is part of the recording process. It

' dates ' the record. The present tense indicates that the event and the utterance of the sentences recording the event, are nearly simultaneous ; the past tense indicates that the record is posterior to the event.

I am not suggesting that recording events is the only function of all the tenses. Difficulty would arise about the future tense, since it is not usual to speak of ' recording ' future events. I must also admit that I am beginning to stretch the dictionary meaning of ' record ', which is to record in writing ; but I think I am justified in going back to an earlier meaning which did not so restrict the medium of expression. Some modern logicians adopt this procedure without thinking it necessary to justify the departure from ordinary usage.[1]

No doubt, in everyday life, ' recording ' features of sentences interest people much less than their ' fact-stating ' features. This is because they are not often interested in unique and solitary events, but in the relations between events. Thus it is not the bare event, Caesar invading Britain, that interests historians, but the relation of this event to other events and in particular to other events in the life of Caesar and in contemporary British history. But events cannot be studied at all until they have been recorded. And I think we are inclined to emphasise the ' fact-stating ' features of sentences, at the expense of their ' recording ' features, even more than is justified by practical needs. Logicians have followed this tendency and intensified it. This can perhaps be made clear by considering a class of sentences in which adverbs as well as verbs play an important part.

## II

The sentence " Charles struck Peter violently " is different from the examples considered so far. " Charles struck Peter " *could* be like " Caesar invaded Britain ", which asserts a relation between two objects ; and " Charles struck Peter on the morning after the ceremony " *could* be like " Caesar invaded Britain in 54 B.C. ", which asserts a relation between the event, Caesar invading Britain, and the event, the birth of Christ. But " Charles

---

[1] E.g. ' Let us call a proposition which records an actual or possible observation an experiential proposition.' (A. J. Ayer, *Language, Truth and Logic*, p. 38).

struck Peter violently " does not assert a relation between Charles and Peter, or a relation between the event, Charles striking Peter, and something else.

The trouble arises because of the time-honoured terminology of logic. The usual context in which the word ' assert ' is used is the context in which I assert $y$ of $x$ : this is clearly consistent with the traditional logic of propositions, $y$ being a predicate asserted of $x$, a subject. Consequently, where logicians have considered verbs and adverbs at all, they have tended to assimilate them to the noun-adjective pattern. Saying of a process that it occurred in a certain way is like saying of an object that it has a certain property. The temptation to do this is increased by the syntactical rules of English and some other languages which make sentences of the one form readily translatable into sentences of the other. Thus the sentence " Charles struck Peter violently " can be translated " Charles dealt Peter a violent blow ", or, more formally, " The event, Charles striking Peter, was violent ". Sentences of this form look exactly analogous, logically as well as grammatically, to sentences of the form, " The object, *Victory*, is wooden ". But they are not *logically* analogous. To say that the object *Victory* is wooden is to say of an entity known as having certain properties that it also has a further property, that of being wooden. To say that an event, Charles striking Peter, was violent, *looks* as if it is to say of an event known as having certain ' properties ' that it has also a further ' property ' : that of being violent. This might be possible in certain circumstances, for instance, if someone had asked, " How did Charles strike Peter ? " But if the sentence occurred, as it normally would, in a context of action, say in a novel, or a police report, it would not be possible to say that the event, Charles striking Peter, already known, was being described as violent. It would not even be possible to say, without gross distortion of the facts, that the sentence first states that a certain event occurred, namely Charles striking Peter, and then further states that this event had the ' property ' of being violent. Because what is mentioned (and, I should want to say, *recorded*) is simply an event, namely the event, Charles striking Peter violently. The violence is not an attribute of the event. It is just that a record of the event which mentioned striking but which did not mention violence would be an inadequate, incomplete or misleading record. It would not be *false* (it would, as a matter of fact, be true) but it would be unsatisfactory. And, as logicians are coming to recognise, being false is only one kind of unsatisfactoriness in sentences.

It can, then, be said that a fundamental logical difference between sentences about objects and properties, involving nouns and adjectives, and sentences about events, involving verbs and adverbs, is that the verb-adverb combination is a very much tighter unit than the noun-adjective combination. A full analysis of the differences between the object-situation and the event-situation would have to go very much further than this. I have not been able to do much more than draw attention, by the use of inverted commas, to the queerness of the concept of property as applied to an event. But all that is needed for my point here is to show that the subject-predicate analysis of propositions, though applicable with very little modification to sentences of the noun-adjective type, is totally inapplicable to at least some sentences of the verb-adverb type.

I shall now consider what is implied by the syntactical possibility of translation already mentioned. The events referred to as " Charles striking Peter " and " Caesar invading Britain " are, in ordinary English, referred to as ' the striking of Peter by Charles ' and ' the invasion of Britain by Caesar '. In these forms the expressions function grammatically as nouns, and indeed they are parsed as noun-phrases. An attempt to analyse these noun-phrases according to the modern logical theory of descriptions, would, I think, result in a curious confirmation of my suggestion that logicians have been remarkably negligent of such expressions. According to the theory of (definite) descriptions sentences containing a phrase of the form ' the so-and-so ' can be translated into sentences in which there occurs no such phrase, but only sub-sentences asserting that one object, and only one, possesses a certain property. I cannot see how the theory can be reformulated so as to accommodate events as well as objects. " The death of Scott was sudden " is not analysable in the same way as " The author of *Waverley* was Scottish ". For the latter is equivalent to "At least one object wrote *Waverley* ; at most one object wrote *Waverley* ; no object both wrote *Waverley* and was not Scottish ". But the former sentence has no such equivalent. In the latter,

' having written *Waverley* ' and ' being Scottish ' are both properties of an object ; and although ' the author of *Waverley* ' looks as
if it refers to an object, it refers only to a property asserted, by
implication, to belong to some object. But in the former, ' the
death of Scott ' does refer to an event, not merely to a ' property '
asserted to belong to some event ; and ' sudden ' does not refer
to a further ' property ' of the event, but is itself part of what is
asserted as having occurred, as constituting the event. Hence
Russell's theory of descriptions does not apply to all phrases of the
form ' the so-and-so ', but only at most to those phrases of that
form which refer to objects and not to events.[1]

# TENSE USAGE AND PROPOSITIONS

## By L. JONATHAN COHEN

I WISH to suggest an analysis of sentences in a determinate tense
which will avoid the disadvantages apparent in the analyses that
I have seen published hitherto. These fall into three groups :—

i. Professor G. E. Moore,[1] Mr. C. H. Langford,[2] Lord Russell,[3]
Professor Hans Reichenbach[4] and Mr. A. E. Duncan-Jones[5]
hold that the meaning of propositions which sentences like
" Brutus killed Caesar " are used to state is given by an analysans
like " For some *t*, Brutus kills Caesar at *t*, and *t* is before now ",
provided that the present tense of the analysans is assumed to
have no temporal reference. On this view " now " in the analysans is the proper name of a moment ; and consequently the
analysis conflicts, as Mr. Duncan-Jones has pointed out, with the
custom that historians who utter the sentence " Brutus killed
Caesar " on different occasions are taken to agree with one
another and thus to be asserting the same proposition.

ii. Mr. B. Mayo[6] holds that sentences in, say, the past tense,
like " Brutus killed Caesar ", do two different jobs. They assert
a fact ; and they record its pastness. The time-reference of its

[1] *Proceedings of the Aristotelian Society.* Supplementary Vol. VII (1927), p. 185.
[2] *Symbolic Logic,* C. I. Lewis and C. H. Langford, 1932, p. 315.
[3] *Inquiry into Meaning and Truth,* 1940, p. 108.
[4] *Elements of Symbolic Logic,* 1948, pp. 287, 288.
[5] This collection pp. 166–168.          [6] This collection, pp. 173–180.

tense is irrelevant to the " fact-stating " feature of such a sentence, and merely " indicates that the record is posterior to the event ". " It doesn't assert anything . . . It dates the record ". But I am not quite clear about the implications of this theory. There seem to be three main possibilities :

A. Although this distinction between the " fact-stating " and " time-indicating " features of a sentence in a determinate tense may be illuminating in other respects, it is misleading if it suggests to anyone (although Mr. Mayo does not make this suggestion explicitly) that the latter feature cannot be used as an assertion of what is true or false, and therefore that agreement or disagreement with, say, a past tense utterance can only be agreement or disagreement about the " fact " asserted and cannot be concerned at all with the " time " indicated. For instance, if Mr. X says to me to-day (May 16, 1950) in the course of a conversation about world politics " The hydrogen-bomb was exploded by mistake ", I might want to disagree with the " indication " that the bomb has already been exploded, without denying the " fact " that it may one day be exploded. I should probably say " The hydrogen-bomb has not yet been exploded at all ", using the perfect tense to emphasise my disagreement about the appropriate temporal indication.

B. On the other hand, if Mr. Mayo's theory does allow the possibility of agreement or disagreement about the time " indicated ", this time is on his theory presumably the date of Mr. X's record. But I think it could only be a Looking-Glass-World creature who might say that I was disagreeing with Mr. X about the dating of his record. We both know its date perfectly well, *viz.* May 16, 1950 ; and we are in complete agreement about this date. What I am disagreeing with him about is the dating of the hydrogen-bomb explosion relative to the date of his record.

C. Finally, if Mr. Mayo's theory does (as it should) allow the possibility that agreement or disagreement with the utterance is agreement or disagreement about the dating of the fact stated, his distinction between " fact-stating " and " time-indicating " does nothing to differentiate it from the theory of Professor G. E. Moore and the others mentioned in (i) above. And it is then open to Mr. Duncan-Jones' objection. An example will perhaps bring out the force of this objection. Mr. Y might say next week (May 23, 1950) " Yes, the hydrogen-bomb was exploded by mistake " ; and, if he were commenting on the views of Mr. X and said nothing else in this connection, he would be taken to be agreeing with him, both about the " fact " stated and also about the time " indicated ", *viz.* a date prior to May 16, not one merely prior to May 23. But this excludes any date between May 16 and May 23 and so it conflicts with the theory that past tense utterances merely " indicate " a time prior to that at which they themselves occur.

iii. Mr. P. Nowell Smith[1] treats this problem as a special case of the problem presented by all token-reflexive sentences ; and he objects not so much to the details of the orthodox Moore-Russell analysis, as to any attempt to carry out such an analysis for token-reflexive sentences. He holds that " paradoxes must arise from trying to make the context of a sentence explicit in the sentence itself ", and that these paradoxes are " of the same family as those which the theory of types is designed to solve ". Moreover, to ask what a token-reflexive sentence means is " to ask an incomplete question ". We must ask what it means " to a particular recipient on a particular occasion ". Such sentences " have no meaning in isolation ". If I understand him correctly, Mr. Nowell Smith concludes that, although we can always replace any token-reflexive *token* by a non-token-reflexive equivalent, we should not seek to discover analysing equivalents for token-reflexive *types*. But this view seems to me to be open to three fatal objections :

A. It is possible to produce an analysans which does not give rise to the paradox pointed out by Mr. Duncan-Jones, as I shall try to show below.

B. The paradox which arises from the usual improper analysis is not of the same family as those which the theory of types is designed to solve. It is a peculiarity of all token-reflexive sentences like " I am brown-eyed " that when we *mention* one we can only specify or entertain an incomplete proposition,[2] since no

---

[1] This collection p. 168.

[2] Some may prefer to use the word " proposition " in such a way that " incomplete proposition " is a contradictio in adjecto. But in the way in which I am here using the word we can say, for instance, that all propositional functions and many aposiopeses in the indicative mood involve the use of a sentence to express an incomplete proposition.

particular individual is said to be brown-eyed, whereas when we use the sentence in an appropriate context we assert a complete proposition in virtue of the very fact that we are so using it. (If, on the other hand, we wish to specify or entertain the complete proposition, or to include the incomplete one in an assertion, we must write or utter a non-token-reflexive sentence, e.g. " Cohen is brown-eyed " or " If any person is brown-eyed, etc. ", respectively). It follows that both the analysans and the analysandum of a type of token-reflexive sentence-usage will express incomplete propositions, since in analysing a sentence we mention but do not use it. Accordingly, no type fallacy can occur in the process of analysis since, so far from completing an incomplete proposition improperly, which is the way in which the relevant logical paradoxes arise, the process of analysis actually entails rendering the proposition expressed incomplete. Moreover, when we use either the analysans or analysandum it is the context of its use which completes the proposition expressed, and this is no more type-fallacious in the case of " For some $t$, Brutus kills Caesar at $t$ and $t$ is before now " than it is in the case of " I am brown-eyed ".[1] Mr. Nowell Smith's mistake arises, I think, from using the word " sentence " first for " sentence-token " and then for " sentence-type " when he talks about making " the context of a sentence explicit in the sentence itself "[2]. He seems to believe that he is talking about self-referent sentence-types, which might indeed give rise to logical paradoxes like those which the theory of types is designed to solve (e.g. " No-one uses a preposition to end an English sentence with "). But what he should be talking about are token-referent sentence-types, and if properly analysed these no more lead to paradoxes than do mirror-types.

C. If we can be told what a token-reflexive sentence means " to a particular recipient on a particular occasion ", there may well be some general principles according to which this information is forthcoming. It is for these general principles that we ask when we seek an analysis of a token-reflexive sentence-type.

[1] I have dealt elsewhere (in *Mind*, Vol. 59, No. 233, of January 1950, p. 85) with the paradoxes that seem to arise from statements like " I am not speaking ".
[2] He also introduces an additional confusion by apparently using the words " sentence " and " proposition " interchangeably.

Mr. Nowell Smith wrongly holds such a search to be a " philosophical mistake ", because he wrongly believes that a token-
reflexive sentence-type can have no meaning at all outside a
particular context in which it is used. Anyone who has ever
understood any token-reflexive sentence-type mentioned (but
not used) by a grammarian, lexicographer or logician knows
that this belief is an error for the usual broad variety of senses
of the word " meaning ". Moreover, it is an error of a kind
which has unfortunately been all too common in analytical
philosophy. It can be defended only by putting an unusually
narrow interpretation on the word " meaning " and excusing
this eccentricity on the ground that it draws attention to a difference of logical form. Mr. Nowell Smith is prepared to allow
meaningfulness to token-reflexive sentence-types when *used* for
the statement of propositions, but holds that they are meaningless
when anyone *mentions* them. His theory is a good illustration of
the precept that we should always suspect error or eccentricity
when a philosopher cries " meaningless! " or " nonsense! "

I shall now suggest an analysis of the token-reflexive expression of an incomplete proposition ' " Brutus killed Caesar " '[1]
which seems to avoid the difficulties met with by the above
three theories. In doing so I shall adopt Professor Reichenbach's
distinction between the point or period of time referred to by an
utterance and the point or period of time at which the event
described took place.[2] The tense structure of sentences in most
developed languages cannot be adequately analysed without
making this distinction, because it is only thus that we can
distinguish between, say, the past and the perfect, or between the
future and the future perfect. And I shall use the present tense
in a timeless sense. In a preliminary, simplified form the analysans
will be :

' " For some *t*, Brutus kills Caesar at *t*, *t* is the point or period
of time under reference, and the time under reference is prior
to the time at which any member of the following class of tokens
is uttered, written or thought, *viz.* the class consisting of this
and of all other past-referring tokens which would normally be
thought to be in direct agreement with it " '.(1)

---

[1] These double quotation marks should of course have been used by Mr. Duncan
Jones originally.                                                [2] *Op. cit.*, p. 288 ff.

The analysans (1) expresses an incomplete proposition like its analysandum, because I am mentioning and not using a sentence-type. When this sentence-type is used and not just mentioned, the indeterminate reference (*viz.* " the class consisting of this token and of all other past tense tokens which would normally be thought to be in direct agreement with it ") is determined by the context in which it is used, and thus the proposition asserted *may* be different in different contexts. But it *need not* be different in every context. Whether or not it is different will depend upon customary usage. Thus, if, for instance, Plutarch's and Mommsen's translators have in different centuries said " Brutus killed Caesar ", and if they would normally be thought to be agreeing with one another, (1) is intended to elucidate how they would be using that sentence-type to state the same proposition. Moreover, it is also clear, if we apply the criterion of (1), that a man who said " Brutus killed Caesar " or " Brutus Caesarem interfecit " on the day before the Ides of March, 44 B.C., did not assert the same proposition as Plutarch's and Mommsen's translators. We should not normally think they agreed with him. Indeed, it seems to be the case that the proposition which he used the sentence to assert is false, while theirs is true. *Mr. Duncan Jones' paradox arises if we accept an analysis like Professor Moore's which determines the meaning of a token without reference to what would normally be thought to be in agreement or disagreement with it. The paradox disappears when we replace such an analysis by one which includes this reference.*

Of course, sentence-types in the past tense can be used to express the same proposition much more often than those in the present tense. Indeed, it might be argued that in each context in which it is used the sentence-type " Brutus is killing Caesar " is used to state a different proposition. But I think that this would be an exaggeration. The analysans for ' " Brutus is killing Caesar " ' would be :

' " For some *t*, Brutus kills Caesar at *t*, *t* is the time under reference and the time under reference is the same as the time at which any member of the following class of tokens is uttered, written or thought, *viz.* the class consisting of this token and of all other present-referring tokens which would normally be thought to be in direct agreement with it " ' (2).

If anyone actually said on that fatal occasion in 44 B.C. " Brutus Caesarem interficit " there may well have been someone else who murmured his agreement a moment later. Accordingly, on the only occasion on which the sentence-type could have been used to state a true proposition the class referred to in the analysans might have had at least two members. However, it does seem impossible to enunciate any precise set of principles which invariably control the composition of such classes. In general, perhaps, the size of these classes seems, in the case of present-tense sentence-types, to vary with the degree of continuity of the event or process described. I doubt if it is possible to say more about them.[1]

I have, of course, considerably simplified my analysis by treating " Brutus kills Caesar " as the expression of a single, simple proposition, in order to bring out the main point at issue. This point remains unaffected if I substitute a more thorough analysis for (1) (and analogously for (2)) in order to cope with awkward sentence-types like ' " Napoleon killed Caesar " ', ' "Alexander killed Caesar " ' or ' " The gryphons killed the unicorns " ' :—

' " For some one, and one only, $t$, $x$, $y$, $z$, $x$ is Brutus, $x$ kills $z$ at $t^a$, $z$ is $y$, $y$ is killed at $t^b$, $y$ is Caesar, $t$ is $t^a$, $t$ is $t^b$, $t$ is the time under reference, and the time under reference is prior to the time at which any member of the following class of tokens is uttered, written or thought, viz. the class consisting of this token and of all other past-referring tokens which would normally be thought to be in direct agreement with the whole or any significant part of it that includes a token-reflexive specification of time " '.(3)

Against my analysis I can conceive of at least three possible objections :—

i. " Your last analysans (3) shows how absurd is your whole procedure. Instead of clarifying the problem by providing substitute-expressions in ordinary language which are free from paradox you make matters worse by introducing a lot of technical jargon which the ordinary man can hardly be expected to under-

---

[1] Cf. *Language Dissertations of the Linguistic Society of America*, No. 21, April–June 1936, for a thorough treatment of this subject by Mr. O. E. Johnson in *Tense Significance as the Time of the Action* : he too holds (p. 90) that the time referred to by " now " varies in extent according to the material content of " the predicate ".

stand ". But this would be a silly objection. That hero of philosophical mythology, the ordinary man, requires not the slightest help in his use of sentence-types in a determinate tense. All I have done is to try to make explicit the principles implicit in his usage, in order to help logicians who may be worried by it. I am not recommending the jargon sentence-types (1), (2) and (3) for use instead of their respective analysanda nor claiming that they are so used. I have introduced them only in order to show that neither they nor their analysanda need give rise to paradox. They are, I think, logically equivalent to their respective analysanda, in the sense that, on any occasion on which the sentence-type mentioned in, say, (3) is used to express a complete proposition, this proposition entails and is entailed by the proposition expressed by using the sentence-type " Brutus killed Caesar " on the same occasion. Of course, there are senses of " meaning " in which these two utterances might be taken to have different meanings from one another. In particular, one seems to be *about* Brutus, Caesar and a time of death only, whereas the other is *about* these and also *about* a class of tokens. But an analysans is not illuminating at all if there is not some sense of " meaning " in which it is true to say that it differs in meaning from its analysandum.[1] The type of analysis which we make varies in accordance with the two senses of " meaning " in which our analysans can truly be said to differ from its analysandum in meaning, and to resemble it in this, respectively. In order to elucidate a paradox in a technical journal we may surely use the type of analysis which is best suited to our purpose, even though there may be other purposes which would be best served by providing an analysans in the form of a substitute-expression in ordinary language.[2]

---

[1] Cf. Professor Moore's discussion of C. H. Langford's paradox of analysis in *The Philosophy of G. E. Moore*, ed. P. A. Schilpp, 1942, p. 665.

[2] By ordinary language in this context I mean the completely unspecialised vocabulary and syntax—English, French or other—in which most people converse about matters of general interest and in which most novels, newspapers and private-letters are written. I intend to distinguish it here from two other modes of expression. The first of these (let us call it " technical language ") arises out of ordinary language when, in use, technical terms and idioms are implicitly or explicitly introduced into it either by special restrictions on the use of some familiar words and grammatical constructions or by the addition of new words or symbols to its vocabulary. It is in such technical language that parliamentary statutes, stamp catalogues, text-books of anatomy and a very great deal else are written or discussed,

ii. " The analyses are circular because they presuppose recognition of a class of tokens expressing agreement with one another, whereas the purpose of a good analysis should be to facilitate this recognition for its readers ". But the normal subject-matter of analysis consists of sentence-types and their usages (or sometimes of propositional families of sentence-types), not of individual sentence-tokens. Accordingly, the recognition of a class of tokens normally thought to express agreement with one another is a prerequisite of any analysis. Without it we have nothing to analyse. But with it we know at least some of the contents of the class of tokens referred to in (1), (2) or (3), for instance ; so that there is no ground for objecting that these analyses are circular.

iii. " Your analysis is no improvement on the orthodox one, as far as Mr. Duncan-Jones' objection is concerned. The meaning of ' this token ' will vary just as much as the meaning of ' now '." But this would be a quibble. On my analysis the class of tokens referred to is always the same for any one proposition although the class is specified by reference to a different one of its members on each occasion that the proposition is uttered. In other words, the proposition is completed in the same sense on each of these occasions  although they are different occasions.

### POSTSCRIPT (1954)

Mr. F. B. Ebersole[1] objects that my analysis violates the language-level ' theory ', because it refers to a class of tokens which would normally (in their respective contexts) be thought to agree with one another and thus implies a reference to the equisignificance of these tokens. But the language-level ' theory ' is designed to avoid the deducibility of contradictions in logico-semantical systems. It is not a rule either of ordinary language or of most technical language (including mine here), so that it is quite impossible for my analyses to

and my analyses, too, are intended to be in an appropriate kind of technical language, viz : a modification of ordinary language which can articulate what we must take the narrative and predictive statements of ordinary language to mean if we are to maintain the valuable convention that on all matters what is in all important respects the same statement can be made at different times. The other relevant type of non-ordinary language (let us call it a " logico-semantical system ") is constructed by adding interpretative semantical rules, i.e. rules of designation and rules of truth, to a logistic system, as in Reichenbach's analysis of conversational language (*op. cit.* p. 251 *ff.*)

[1] *Analysis*, xii, 1952, p. 109.

violate it. Of course, any philosopher worried by the so-called 'semantical antinomies' as well as by Mr. Duncan-Jones' paradox might seek to construct a logico-semantical system free from both troubles, and Mr. Ebersole has well shown how complicated and unilluminating this would be.

Indeed, such a system would be misleading if it were claimed as a model for historical narrative. By reconstructing a physicist's theory as a logico-semantical system we might shed some light on the intellectual ideal which he had, perhaps half-consciously, set himself. But by reconstructing Plutarch's biography of Brutus, say, in this way we should suggest that Plutarch and other historians set themselves an ideal of exact and unmetaphorical language to which their subject-matter—the indefinite variety of human action and experience—is intrinsically alien.

In my technical language of analysis, then, as in ordinary language, no grammatical rules preclude the formation of sentences that could be used to express self-contradictory statements, whether this self-contradiction be explicit as in 'Caesar is not Caesar' or implicit as in 'This statement is false'. But since neither ordinary language nor my technical language of analysis is a deductive system this grammatical tolerance in no way vitiates either of them as an instrument of thought. In fact, no worries are created for historians or such-like folk by this feature of ordinary language because they do not find it difficult to avoid contradicting themselves. And I do not think that any of my analyses are either explicitly or implicitly self-contradictory.

Accordingly, what Mr. Ebersole's criticism emphasises is not that there is any logical flaw in my analyses, as he seems to suggest, but that a technical language in which we can make a logically articulate reconstruction of tensed statements referring to a definite point or period of time must also be adequate for referring to instances of equisignificance among utterances in that very language. However, philosophers should not be too shocked by this conclusion. For firstly, though a logico-semantical system certainly needs to be carefully restricted in regard to the formation of sentences about its own sentences, the theories for which these systems may provide an illuminating reconstruction are not normally expressed by tensed sentences referring to a definite point or period of time. In an informal statement of

Newton's law of gravity, for instance, we should use the so-called timeless present. So that in setting up a logico-semantical system for the reconstruction of Newton's theory we need not make any linguistic provision for reference to definite points or periods of time. Secondly, there are other important patterns of ordinary discourse (notably counter-factual conditionals) which cannot, I think, be adequately analysed by logically sophisticated reconstruction in a technical language unless we can talk within that language, as we constantly do in ordinary English, French, etc., about relationships of equisignificance between actual utterances in it. (L.J.C.).

# CHAPTER VIII.  PROBABILITY AND NATURAL LAWS.

## TWO OF THE SENSES OF 'PROBABLE'

### By J. O. URMSON

I

CONSIDER such statements as

" The probability of heads is $\frac{1}{2}$."

" The probability of a man of eighty living ten more years low."

" The probability of suicide is higher in peace than in war."

These may be considered as samples of a group of statements typically made in games of chance, in insurance business, in biology, and in quantum physics. They seem to resemble common sense generalizations and invariant scientific laws in that they are based on the observations of regularity and extrapolate from observed regularity. They differ in that ordinary generalizations assert an unvarying conjunction or functional relationship between characteristics, while this type of probability statement seems to assert that a constant proportion of instances of one characteristic are instances of another characteristic. We may say that both types assert a regularity, but one an unvarying, the other a proportionate regularity.

Now often we do not feel that the observed regularity is sufficiently good ground to generalize from it unreservedly. In such cases instead of generalizing to " all A is B ", we may say " probably on the available evidence all A is B "; and instead of making a generalization of proportionate regularity we may say " in the light of available data it is probable that the probability of suicide is higher in peace than in war ".

It seems to me, therefore, that we have already clearly here two quite different senses of 'probable'. In one case (henceforth called " type one probability statements ") we use the word *in* a generalization to indicate that it asserts a proportional regularity (is a statistical generalization); in the other case (henceforth called " type two probability statements ") we use the word *about* a generalization which may itself be a type one probability statement. This seems quite clearly correct to me. But as some (e.g. Keynes) regard all probability statements as being essentially type two, others (e.g. von Wright) regard them all as being essentially type one, I shall devote the rest of this paper to indicating some of the differences between the two kinds of usage. I hope that some of these will raise points which are also of independent interest.

2

The first point I would like to make in favour of the distinction is this. Let G be a generalization which is not completely established. Then we may make the type two statement; " Probably G ". In such a case we think that it is possible for us to get further evidence in the light of which we shall be able to say " Certainly G " or at least " Very, very probably G ", or else "Certainly not G", or " Very improbably G ". Generally, the probability of G increases with favourable evidence and decreases or vanishes at zero with unfavourable evidence. But suppose we make a type one statement, e.g. " The probability of five peas in a pod is $\frac{1}{2}$ ". Here further favourable evidence instead of raising the probability confirms that the probability is $\frac{1}{2}$. On the other hand further unfavourable evidence might show that we had set the probability too low. It might also of course show that we had set the probability too high, or it might indicate that there was no dependable regularity in the number of peas in a pod, no assignable probability of getting five peas at all. To " show that there is no assignable probability at all " does not here, of course, mean the same as " show that the probability is zero ". Thus we have here our first tell-tale piece of evidence. *Favourable evidence confirms probabilities in the case of type one probability statements, unfavourable evidence decreases or increases or destroys such probabilities, For type two statements favourable evidence increases. unfavourable evidence decreases, the probability.*

A further sign of the difference between type one and type two probability statements is the difference in the relation in which they stand to their evidence. It is a point which has often been made that if one man says " Probably G " and another says

" Probably not G " it is not necessarily the case that one of them is mistaken. For perhaps G is probable on one set of evidence and improbable on another set. Very little reflection is required to see that the question whether G is really probable in itself, apart from questions of evidence, is not a real question. This state of affairs has been commonly signified by the statement "probabilities are relative to evidence" or the statement that " Probably G " is incomplete since probability is a relative notion. People have tended to generalize this view, which seems obviously correct for some usages of ' probable ', to cover all usages. But this again seems to me to be incorrect. I wish to say that while it is correct for the case of type two probability statements, and possibly some other usages which we are not considering, it is definitely incorrect in the case of type one probability statements. For surely it is no more improper for me to say that the probability of an A being B is P, to assert a proportional regularity, without specifying my evidence for this assertion, than it is improper for me to say "All As are B " without specifying my evidence for *that* statement. To state simply that the chance of throwing six with a die is $\frac{1}{6}$ does not involve an ellipse of the statistics gleaned from gambling dens. However pardonable the mistake of a man who had seen an extraordinary run of sixes would be if he were to assert that the probability of throwing 6 is, say $\frac{1}{2}$, it would be a mistake. There is one and one only absolute probability of throwing six.

I think that an opponent would have to admit that this distinction is at least plausible. But perhaps he still has a kick left in him. Perhaps he would ask me to admit, as I would admit, that the statement " The probability of a European understanding the word ' waistcoat ' is P " is an example of a type one probability statement. Now, it will be said, it must surely be admitted that the probability of a European understanding the word ' waistcoat ' relative to the evidence that he is an Englishman is very high, while relative to the evidence that he is a Croatian peasant, it is very low. Thus, it will be said, there is no single correct value for P, no absolute probability; its value must depend, as in other cases, on the evidence. Similarly the probability of a die falling six uppermost will have different values relative to the evidence that it is a true die and relative to the evidence that it is the property of a highly successful professional gambler.

I shall admit the facts alleged, but deny that they have implications which are not consonant with the view which I am putting forward. This is so because an interesting ambiguity of the word ' evidence ' is involved. To see this, let us compare the following statements.

1. The probability of a European understanding the word ' waistcoat ' is very high relative to the evidence that he is an adult Englishman.

2. The probability of an adult European understanding the word ' waistcoat ' is very high relative to the evidence that he is an Englishman.

3. The probability of an Englishman understanding the word ' waistcoat ' is very high on the evidence that he is an adult.

4. The probability of an adult Englishman understanding the word ' waistcoat ' is very high.

It is surely clear that these four statements, three of which verbally assert a probability of a different proposition on different evidence, and one apparently asserts an absolute probability, are in fact simply four different ways of formulating one and the same proposition.

Notice also that an essential reason for our belief that this proposition is true is the tacitly assumed evidence which is in our possession that the word ' waistcoat ' is a common English word. And this is just a disguised way of stating the statistical fact that nearly all Englishmen understand the word ' waistcoat '. Knowing that the Europeans in questions are English is no reason for thinking it likely that they will understand the word ' waistcoat ' without the information that the word ' waistcoat ' is a common English word. To ask for the probability of a European understanding the word ' waistcoat ', first on the evidence that he is English, second on the evidence that, he is a Croatian peasant, is simply to set in an idiomatic fashion two different problems. The evidence, on the other hand, that ' waistcoat ' is a common English word does not alter the character of the problem, it presents a clue for solving it.

We may perhaps sum up the point which has just been illustrated as follows. There is one type of evidence which does not function as a clue to the value of the probability but which helps to specify the class of events whose probability is in question. In the language of the frequency theorists, it is a part of the specification of the collective or reference class. We may call this specificatory evidence. A statement may always be recast, as I did in my four sentences, to eliminate specificatory evidence, or increase it or alter it without a real change of meaning. Evidence which does serve to determine the probability in question does not further specify the question, and a type one probability statement, though it may be idiomatically expressed to contain specificatory evidence is complete without the provision of any of this type of evidence,' though it would no doubt be unwarranted if we did not possess such evidence.

If what I have called specificatory evidence did help to solve problems of probability it would be a delightful situation, for only a slight literary dexterity is required to manufacture specificatory evidence. If, for example, we want to know the probability of a European living to be a hundred years old, and we are told that we must provide evidence if we want an answer, then, if specificatory evidence will do, we could say " Very well, forget that question. Tell us instead the probability of a man living to be a hundred years old on the evidence that he's a European. Or if it's easier to answer questions with more evidence than that, tell us the probability of an organism living to be a hundred years old on the evidence that it is a vertebrate mammal of the genus *homo sapiens* and a native of Europe."

In terms of this distinction, I can now say that *type one probability statements are only relative to evidence if the evidence is specificatory evidence*. They can therefore always be restated in a form in which evidence is not mentioned. *On the other hand. type two probability statements are relative to evidence of the substantial non-specificatory type*. Incidentally, I think that the failure to recognize these two senses of " evidence " accounts at least partially for the failure of some theorists to recognize the predominantly statistical character of the evidence in the substantial sense for type one probability statements.

They have seen, for example, that in the case of the question " What is the probability of rain within 24 hours " the evidence that the barometer is falling or rising is highly relevant and is not statistical. They have, however, failed to see that it is relevant simply because it alters the question in which we would naturally be interested either to " What is the probability of rain following a fall of barometric pressure within 24 hours " or to " What is the probability of rain following a rise of barometric pressure within 24 hours ". These are different questions, and, in the main, meteorological statistics are our ultimate means of answering them both.

It is, unfortunately, true that substantial evidence can be introduced as though it were part of the question at issue and not as evidence. I have said that we can reformulate " What is the probability of a European understanding the word ' waistcoat ' on the evidence that he is English? " to eliminate the specificatory evidence by saying " What is the probability of an Englishman understanding the word ' waistcoast '? " But we can also reformulate " What is the probability of an Englishman understanding the word ' waistcoat ' on the evidence that ' waistcoat ' is a common English word? " to read " What is the probability of an Englishman understanding the common English word ' waistcoat '? " But this question and the simple question " What is the probability of an Englishman understanding the word 'waistcoat' ? " would only specify different questions if we used the phrase " common English word " to distinguish one usage of ' waistcoat ' from another uncommon usage. And that is clearly not the case. If substantial evidence is stated as part of the question and not as evidence, then, unlike specificatory evidence, it makes no difference to the nature of the question.

I hope I have not over-elaborated this point, but I am very anxious to make it clear because I want to use it in order to make clear the third difference which I find between type one and type two probability statements. I think this is a very interesting difference because it raises a difficult problem which I do not here try to solve.

Let us, then, take first a type one probability statement and state it in a form in which specificatory evidence appears—we have seen that it does not matter either way. Let us ask " Is it probable that rain will fall within 24 hours on the evidence that the glass has fallen one inch within the previous 24 hours? "

Compare with it this question. " Is it probable that all cows are ruminant on the evidence that cows of many ages and many breeds have been examined and found to be ruminant, but no cows have been found which are not ruminant? " How would we set about answering the first question, the one about the weather? Does a drop of one inch in 24 hours more frequently, or more likely presage a gale, or rain, or what? we may ask. In order to answer this question we must ask for evidence, for substantial evidence. And this evidence would naturally take the form of meteorological statistics. In other words, we are answering an empirical question by empirical means. But turn now to the second question : " Is it probable that all cows are ruminant on the evidence that all examined cows have been ruminant? " Is this an empirical question? Surely not! If it is, what kind of empirical evidence would you require to solve it? To examine more cows and perhaps find one that is not ruminant, while it would be relevant to the question "Are all cows ruminant? " is simply irrelevant to the question " Is it probable that all cows are ruminant on the evidence that all examined cows have been ruminant? " Thus we are led to formulate our third difference between type one and type two probability statements. *Type one probability statements*, while it is true that they cannot be conclusively verified or falsified, *are empirical statements* in the sense that it is the records of ordinary experience which lead us to accept or to reject them. *Type two probability statements*, on the other hand, *are not empirical statements* in this sense. This, of course, leads on to the interesting question " If type two probability statements are not synthetic *a posteriori*. what are they? Are they synthetic *a priori*? Are they analytic? Or are they something quite different again? "

I now come to the fourth and final difference between the two types which I wish to notice. *Type one probability statements*, though the probability may only be given roughly, *can always be given with a precise numerical value without change of character*.

It may not always be practicable to give a reliable figure—our evidence may only be sufficient either to warrant or to verify an approximation. But the procedure of discovery and verification is not in principle altered by giving a numerical value. For example, my statement that the probability of living to be a hundred years old is very low is of the same type and based on the same kind of evidence, though less elaborate evidence, as the precise numerical value which an actuary would be prepared to give. *But type two probability statements are not naturally given a numerical value.* Supposing that I say that the corpuscular theory of light is probably correct. Well, is the probability nine-tenths or ten-elevenths, or, shall we say, are the odds 9—1 or 10—1? And if I give the odds 10—1, who is to prove, and how is he to prove, that the odds should have been 9—1? I suppose one can bet about almost anything, including the truth of theories. But if bets are made not on the truth, but on the probability, of theories, I, for one, would not care to arbitrate either as to what would be fair odds or as to who is the winner if odds are assigned. Keynes and many others have noticed this fact that some probabilities can reasonably be given a precise numerical value, and others not. That is not a new point. The point I wish to make is that type one statements fall into the numerical class, type two into the non-numerical. The difference has a clear explanation and should not be left, as Keynes left it, as a strange but ultimate fact.

To sum up, I have pointed out four differences between two types of probability statement.

1. Favourable evidence confirms the numerical value of probabilities in the case of type one probability statements, unfavourable evidence decreases or increases or destroys such alleged probabilities. For type two statements favourable evidence increases, unfavourable evidence decreases the probability.

2. Type one probability statements are only relative to evidence if the evidence is specificatory evidence. Type two statements are relative to evidence of the substantial non-specificatory type.

3. Type one probability statements are empirical statements, to be tested by experience. Type two statements are not.

4. Type one probability statements may always be given a numerical value without change of character. Type two statements are not naturally given a numerical value.

To avoid misunderstanding let me add that

(a) I have not offered an " analysis " of any kind of probability statement.

(b) I have not denied that there are sub-types within the two types of statement which I have distinguished.

(c) I have not suggested that there is any ready-made criterion for judging from the verbal form of a probability statement to which type it belongs.

(d) I have not suggested that all probability statements fall within one or other of my two types.

## MORE ABOUT PROBABILITY

### By C. H. WHITELEY

MR. J. O. Urmson argues that the word ' probable ' has at least two different senses. Some statements about probability (his " type one ") are empirical statements; e.g. " The probability of a man of 80 living 10 more years is low "; " The probability of suicide is higher in peace than in war ". Other statements about probability (his " type two ") are not empirical and cannot be modified by any further evidence ; e.g. " In the light of available data it is probable that the probability of suicide is higher in peace than in war"; " Given that all examined cows have been ruminant, it is probable that all cows are ruminant ". I wish to examine this distinction further.

What sort of empirical fact is stated by " type one " probability statements? The most plausible answer to this question is that they state a statistical fact, a ratio between positive and negative instances. If I say " The probability of suicide is higher in peace than in war ", I am stating, or at the least implying, " Proportionately more people commit suicide in peace than in war ", which is an empirical fact. I cannot see any other empirical fact, beyond this kind of fact about the proportionate number of instances, in which the " probability " might consist. Probabilities of this kind can, as Urmson says, be given a numerical value without change of character, because they are relations between numbers of cases. Seeing that this is so, many philosophers have straightforwardly defined ' probability ' in terms of ratios or " frequencies ". If such a definition is accepted, then " I see that most houses in Birmingham cost more than £2,000; so if I want to buy a house there I shall probably have to pay more than £2,000 for it ", would be a tautology. But it looks like an inference ; and those who speak of probability as a " relation between propositions " appear to assimilate the probability-relation to implication. Yet, if this is an inference, what is its conclusion? There seems to be no assertion appearing in the conclusion over and above the statement about the frequency of houses in Birmingham costing over £2,000 which formed the premise. It seems to me that what is reached in arguments of this kind is not a conclusion but a decision. ' Probably ' is a cue for action ; probability statements have the function of giving us advice. (Hence " Probably you should do so-and-so" is a normal manner of speech.) If I am interested in history or economics, I say " Very few houses in Birmingham can be bought for less than £2,000 ". But if I am concerned about changing my residence I say " I shall probably have to pay more than £2,000 if I want to buy a house ". So one talks rarely of the probability of a kind of event in general (of rain after a fall of the barometer, say) but often of the probability of a particular case (rain this afternoon), concerning which one has to take decisions and form expectations. So there is a use of the word ' probable ' in which its function is to recommend a course of action. What this course of action is cannot be stated precisely apart from the context. It is usually, though not always, to act as though what is said to be probable were actually the case. The probable happening is the one which we are to expect and be prepared for ; the highly improbable happening is one for which we need make no preparations. So I venture to expand " The probability of an adult Englishman understanding the word ' waistcoat ' is very high " into two components : (1) " Most adult Englishmen understand the word ' waistcoat ' ", and (2) " When we are talking to an Englishman we should assume that he will understand the word ' waistcoat ' ". The word ' probability ' has now disappeared. Its function in the original statement was to effect the transition from (1) to (2). It will be seen that (1) is an empirical statement and (2) is not—it is not even a statement. So, if this analysis is correct, it has disclosed, not two senses of ' probable ', but two factors in the meaning of some probability-statements. One of these factors seems to be identical with Urmson's " type one ". The other resembles his " type two " at least in not being an empirical statement. In cases of this kind, then, "An A is probably B " asserts that there are more As which are B than As which are not B, and asserts nothing else ; but it adds a recommendation that one should be prepared for a A to be B rather than for it to be not B. There is an analogy here with the analysis of some ethical statements : the difference between " X is the action which will have the best possible results in this situation " and " X is your duty " is that the latter makes a demand upon you which the former does not. And in both the ethical case and the probability case, we may ask, as Hume did, How is the transition from an empirical fact to a decision effected? In making this transition, we assume a principle which can be roughly stated, " Do not expect the unusual. If most As are B, assume that this A will be B ". And the analysis of " probability " would be incomplete if I did not point out that in reasoning about probabilities I do not merely accept and work on this principle, but I expect and require that other men will do so too, and regard it as " reasonable " to do so and " unreasonable " to do other- wise. We therefore appear to accept it as a maxim of right conduct in the treatment of hypotheses, not to assume or expect an event to happen which, if it did happen, would be very rare or unusual of its kind. This principle is not " constitutive" (as the principle of the Uniformity of Nature is), but " regu- lative ". It recommends a procedure, but does not assert a fact. Nor does it in any way follow from the principle of the Uniform- ity of Nature, being indeed a rule for dealing with classes which are not uniform. Nor does it follow from any principle of deductive logic. We find ourselves accepting it as an independent principle.

It would be generally agreed that this is *a* principle of probable reasoning ; that " Most As are B " is one kind of good reason for asserting " a given A is probably B " and for forming an expecta- tion that A given A will turn out to be B of a degree of confidence proportionate to the proportion of As which are B. But it would not be generally agreed that it is the only principle of probable reasoning, and that all valid probable arguments make use of it. I shall maintain that this is in fact the case. As regards the probability of single cases, there is not much difficulty in seeing that my principle applies always, if we bear in mind three complications.

1. The information on which a probability-judgment is based may be either vague or precise ; more often it is vague. If I have to meet an Italian stranger at the station, I think it reasonable to look for a dark man, for I know that most Italians are dark ; but I do not know the exact proportion of blondes in the Italian population, and therefore cannot give a numerical value to my probability. If I now ascertain this proportion, I can give the probability a numerical value. If we choose to say that this is fresh information, which provides me with a fresh probability, then it will not be the case that all probabilities have a numerical value. If we choose to say that it is not fresh information, but the same information given with greater precision, we can conclude that all probabilities, at least of this kind, have a numerical value. I do not think it matters much which way of putting the matter we adopt (though I prefer the second), so long as we recognise that whenever a vague probability-judgement is made, the possibility of a corresponding precise probability-judgement is implied ; just as, if I say that Smith is taller than Jones, I imply that he is taller by a specific number of inches, though I may not know that number.

2. When we are dealing with the probability of a particular case, we seldom treat it as an instance of only one generalisation, a member of only one class of cases. It will be a member of many classes, and thus subject to a number of different calculations of its probability. To take Keynes' example, when the barometer is high fine weather is probable ; when the clouds are black, rain is probable : what is the probability of rain when the barometer is high and the clouds are black? It seems to me that if we are able to estimate probabilities at all in such cases, we can still do it only by comparing numbers of instances. If the proportion of rainy days with a high barometer is smaller than the proportion of fine days with black clouds, we can decide to trust the barometer (this is all that can be meant by saying that the barometer is a

more reliable indication of the weather). If we have no information of this kind, we cannot form a rational judgement. Most
practical problems are more complex than this, and involve the
interlocking of many probability-generalisations ; but I cannot
find that probability ever rests in the end on anything other than
a greater number of favourable cases.

3. Besides unusual single events, there are unusual combinations of events, *i.e.* selections from the main class. While a
single Italian will probably be dark (*i.e.* most Italians are so), a
collection of 1,000 Italians will probably contain a few fair
individuals (*i.e.* most such collections do). The mathematics of
probability is largely concerned with working out how unlikely
particular combinations of cases are.

But this interpretation of the ground of probabilities seems
to fail when we come to Urmson's " type two " probabilities,
viz. the probability of generalisations. We say " Given that all
observed cows have ruminated, probably all cows ruminate " ;
and " The corpuscular theory of light is probably true ". We
also say that such generalisations become more probable as
evidence accumulates. Now we cannot say that the probability
of the generalisation is measured by the ratio between observed
favourable cases and observed unfavourable cases. That would
mean that if I have observed 5 sheep, of which 4 are white, it is
4 to 1 that the same proportion holds universally, and if I have
observed 5 sheep which are all white, it is certain that all sheep
are white ; which is absurd. But until we have established our
right to transfer to unobserved cases proportions which are
known to hold in observed cases, we can make little use of any
kind of probability-argument. How is such an extension justified?
I believe that the probability of an inductive generalisation is
established by the same principle as the probability of a particular case—viz. that the possibility of a very uncommon event is
not to be taken seriously. The difference is that inductive arguments work in the opposite direction. Given that most As are
not B, that we should encounter an A which is B is improbable ;
that we should encounter a long series of As which are all B is
much more improbable, and we cannot reasonably expect to do
so (in the absence of quite special reasons for such an expectation).
But, conversely, given that we *have* encountered a long series of

As which are all B, it is, in the same degree, improbable that most As are not B ; *i.e.* to assume that most As are not B would violate our principle of not believing in highly unusual occurrences if we can help it. And if the sequence of As which are all B is sufficiently extensive, if it is a sequence which would be highly exceptional on the assumption that more than an infinitesimal proportion of As are not B (which is the case with the sequence of observed ruminant cows), then it constitutes good evidence that all As (or a majority practically indistinguishable from all) are B. Of course, an argument of this kind is only a first step in inductive reasoning ; in every actual case the evidence is much more complex than " that there have been a series of As which were all B ". But the mainspring of all induction is the argument from simple enumeration ; and it seems to me that the force of simple enumeration must be interpreted in the above fashion.

To sum up. The function of the *word* ' probable ' and its equivalents is to invite us to hold provisionally a given hypothesis. The *principle* on which we proceed in making these decisions is always that of provisionally accepting the common, and rejecting the uncommon ; and the more uncommon it is, the more confidently do we think that it should be rejected.

## SUBJUNCTIVE CONDITIONALS

### *By* STUART HAMPSHIRE

' IF Hitler had invaded in 1940, he would have captured London.' Statements of this kind have constituted a problem for three overlapping classes of philosophers : (*a*) those who wish to insist that all complex statements must be truth-functions of their constituent statements : (*b*) those who wish to insist that saying that an empirical statement is true is equivalent to saying that it corresponds to a fact : (*c*) those who wish to insist that to understand a sentence as being an empirical statement involves being able to prescribe how it might in principle be, directly or indirectly, verified or falsified.

I shall not discuss the perplexities of the truth-functional or correspondence-theory philosophers, partly because these philosophers seem to me wrong in principle, apart altogether from the special case of conditional sentences in the subjunctive mood. I shall assume that it is one of the characteristics of ordinary languages, distinguishing them from constructed languages, that they are not truth-functional ; and I shall assume that we do not need to invent special categories of facts so that true statements may correspond to them. But it does seem to me that when we are considering whether a sentence can be interpreted as a significant empirical statement, we are always and necessarily asking a question about the possibilities and appropriate procedures of verification and falsification ; that is, ' I understand this sentence as an empirical statement ' is equivalent to ' I know how this might in principle be verified or falsified ' ; and if I cannot answer the question ' What tests would lead the assertor to withdraw this sentence? ' , then it follows logically that I do not know what is being asserted.[1]

Subjunctive conditional sentences present a problem because it looks as if they are often used to make statements which, though intelligible, cannot be said to be in principle either verifiable or falsifiable.

Consider the following dialogue. A : ' If this family had been on either the third or the first floor, they would not have been killed by the bomb.' B : ' You mean that when bombs of this kind hit houses of this kind, the first and third floors are generally safe?' A: 'No, I do not mean that; I do not want to commit myself to any statement about what generally happens in these cases; I do not know what generally happens, but I do feel certain about this particular case.' B : 'But I can show you that you are wrong, by showing you other houses similar to this in which people have not survived on the first or third floors.' A : ' But whatever evidence you produce about the effects of bombs on houses, it is still logically possible that *these particular* people would not have been killed in *this particular* house ; and that is my firm conviction ; it may be irrational, but it may nevertheless be true, as many irrational beliefs are.' B : ' Of course, I agree that you may make irrational statements ; you may gamble and guess ; but my objection is, not that your statement is irrational, but

---

[1] Of course there are degrees of vagueness in understanding. I may know only *roughly* what tests are to be taken as decisive, in which case I know only *roughly* what is meant.

that it is in principle undecidable, and so not a genuine statement, just as a bet which is admitted to be in principle undecidable is not a genuine bet.' A : ' But you cannot deny that I have made a genuine statement : for suppose (what I do not in fact expect) that we later find this family alive somewhere, and find also that they were on the third floor and not (as we had thought that they were) on the second, then you will admit that what I said was true'. B: 'No, I will not: if that is the possibility of verification you had in mind, the form of your statement was misleading, because it suggested that you were making a causal statement. If you were not, you ought not to have used the subjunctive form ! '

Two connected points emerge from this dialogue. The first is that the use of the subjunctive conditional form normally suggests that some causal, and therefore general, proposition is being asserted. It is natural to try to interpret every subjunctive conditional sentence as (at least in part) a disguised general statement. Whenever they can be so interpreted, we can always prescribe a method for establishing their falsity (i.e. we can look for a negative instance) ; and of course sentences of the subjunctive conditional form are often used to express general statements—e.g. ' If you had had no faculty of sight, you would have had no conception of distance ', which can properly be used as equivalent to ' Men without sight have no conception of distance, and you are a man '. This is an ordinary form of causal statement, which can be falsified either by finding a negative instance which upsets the general statement, or by denying the statement of particular conditions. The second point of the dialogue is that it brings out the logical force of the subjunctive as opposed to the indicative mood (at least as these moods are used in English). The difference is that the subjunctive form *explicitly implies* that the condition specified is contrary to fact, the antecedent unfulfilled, while the indicative has no such explicit implication ; it leaves it open. That a singular hypothetical statement should *in fact* be unverifiable or unfalsifiable, because its antecedent is *in fact* unfulfilled, presents no problem for upholders of the verification principle ; and therefore singular hypothetical statements in the indicative mood present no problem. The problem arises when we are presented with putative statements, the grammar of which explicitly suggests that they are intended to be in principle undecidable; and singular subjunctive conditionals, in any context in which they cannot be replaced by a combination of general statements and statements of particular conditions, are of this kind; for the force of the subjunctive is to suggest a statement of the form ' If $p$, then $q$, but not $p$ ', which, unless ( as normally) it is a causal and so a general statement, is explicitly undecidable in principle.

When and why do we use sentences of the subjunctive conditional form, without being willing to replace them by general statements and statements of particular conditions? Suppose we replaced them entirely by statements of the form, 'If anything is a $\phi$, it is always as a matter of fact a $\psi$', and ' this is (or is not) a $\phi$ ', and never used the form, ' If this had been a $\phi$ it would have been a $\psi$ ', what would we lose? Theoretical scientists would lose nothing; they can state their laws without using subjunctive forms. But judges, courts of inquiry, historians, and moralists would certainly be embarrassed, if challenged to replace all their singular conditional sentences—' If he had not acted as he did, the disaster would not have occurred '—by a combination of general statements and singular categorical statements. The judge, court of inquiry or moralist needs to be able to say that if a *particular individual* had not acted in a *particular* way in this *particular* situation, the disaster would not have occurred. Experts supply the falsifiable general statements of the form, 'All arsenic-takers die, and this man took arsenic ', but the court of inquiry's *judgment* must be formulated in the form—' If this man had not taken arsenic, he would not have died'. There is a sense in which the court of inquiry's judgment goes *beyond* the experts' scientific statements; for it is logically possible to accept the scientific statements, and yet to disagree with the court of inquiry's decision.

Similarly the historian is professionally expected to make judgments of the form ' If Hitler had invaded in 1940, he would have captured London'. If challenged to translate this judgment into a set of falsifiable statements in logistics (in the military sense), he would be unable and unwilling; he might justifiably reply ' History is not science ', meaning precisely that the historian is not primarily concerned to establish general statements falsifiable by experiment, but that his conclusions (if any) are judgments about particular persons and particular events, judgments which may be more or less reasonable, but which cannot in principle be verified or falsified.[1] It is to be noticed that, both in referring to the sentences which express a court of inquiry's conclusion and to the sentences which express a historian's conclusion, we are normally inclined to speak of ' judgments ' (reasonable and unreasonable) rather than ' statements ' (true or false) ; the dissenting member of the court would not normally say ' It is not true that if he had not taken this drug, he would not have died ', but rather ' I do not agree with your interpretation of the facts'. Similarly historians admit that their disagreements about hypothetical conditions are disagreements of ' interpretation ' or ' judgment ', using these words to discriminate them from the decidable disagreements of scientists.

Certainly the distinction between a judgment (reasonable or unreasonable) and a statement (true or false), or between an interpretation and a scientific theory, is one of degree and admits a multitude of border-line cases. The language of science (by definition) consists wholly of decidable statements. When we ask ' Is economics a science? ' we are in effect asking whether sentences like ' If the rate of interest had been lowered in January, the level of unemployment would have fallen in March ' are intended to be taken as in principle conclusively refutable by experiment, or whether they are to be taken as judgments or interpretations, justified as plausible by reference to general statements and statements of particular conditions, but not reducible to them. So A in the above dialogue could have defended himself by saying that he was offering only his judgment (plausible or unplausible) in a matter in which no decision by experiment is possible. A rigid application of the verification principle—in so far as it involves a refusal to admit the gradations of difference between practical and historical judgments and decidable statements—amounts to a recommendation that all discourse should be scientific discourse.

The elimination from our language of subjunctive conditional sentences would not only remove the possibility of expressing

---

[1] The problem of historical method, or of the nature of historical judgment, *is*, in logical terms, the problem of subjunctive conditionals.

ordinary practical and historical judgments, but would also compel philosphers to abandon the phenomenalist analysis of ordinary statements about material objects. It is an odd paradox that phenomenalism, which has been generally represented as the logical consequence of strictly applying some form of verification principle, is the doctrine that even the most innocent categorical statements are more clearly expressed by a set of conditional sentences, many of which are contrary-to-fact conditionals expressed in the subjunctive mood. It seems perverse, if one is concerned to maintain that all genuine empirical statements must be in some sense verifiable or falsifiable, to convert them all into singular hypothetical sentences in the subjunctive mood. Phenomenalists are in fact recommending a move away from a language which is logically clear, or which approximates to the language of science.

I am also inclined to think (but I am not certain) that we should have some difficulty in talking about ' dispositions ' (now a favourite word of logical empiricists) in a language which excluded subjunctive conditionals. Do we not want to say that ' he knows' or ' he understands' means more than that whenever the has a certain stimulus, he in fact always or generally responds in the appropriate way? We are certainly inclined to say that, in conditions which cannot in principle be fulfilled, he always *would* ; certainly the subjunctive form suggests itself as part of what we mean by attributing a disposition to someone. Statements about dispositions do not seem replaceable by causal statements (general statements plus statements of particular conditions) ; they have the irreducible indefiniteness and undecidability which is the point of the subjunctive conditional form. When we make statements about people's characters or dispositions we can be said to be *interpreting* their behaviour ; disputes about such statements are naturally described as differences of interpretation, to be distinguished (though only as a matter of degree) from disputes which can be settled by discovery of the negative instance which upsets a general statement.

*Conclusion.* Singular subjunctive conditional sentences are sometimes used in contexts in which they are not intended to be replaceable by falsifiable general statements plus statements of initial conditions ; when so used, they can be described as expressing judgments, or interpretations, of the facts, to distinguish them from their use in strictly scientific discourse, when they are wholly replaceable by falsifiable general statements and statements of initial conditions. It is the distinguishing characteristic of practical and historical judgments (as opposed to statements of fact and scientific statements) that the conditions of their falsification are not exactly prescribed. Certainly we can indicate under what conditions they will be held to have been shown to be so unreasonable as to have been in effect falsified. But, where the subjunctive conditional form is irreplaceable, we cannot in principle prescribe tests which are final and decisive. The verification principle can be, and should be, so stated as to allow for the characteristic indefiniteness of non-scientific interpretations of experience.

# HYPOTHETICALS

## By David Pears

This article treats of hypotheticals which say something about the non-linguistic world, something which does not owe its truth solely to convention. They will be represented by " If this is a raven it is black " ($\eta$), and its parent general hypothetical " If anything is a raven it is black " ($\theta$) : both spoken by someone who was prepared to face a counter-example. These two hypotheticals are simple and stark : but in this investigation bones must be shown on an X-ray film before flesh is shown in technicolour.

Treated first as truth-functional statements they will present difficulties. One of these difficulties will be shown to be largely illusory : another to be inevitable from any human point of view ; and the rest to be the inevitable result of the logician's professional neglect of descriptive words. In the second part of this paper it will be shown that none of these difficulties can be evaded by calling hypotheticals ' rules ' ; though this name is in some ways more appropriate. Thirdly and finally something will be said about the way hypotheticals are embedded in different locutions.

First, then, taken as truth-functional statements they present five connected difficulties. General hypotheticals (open ones)

are not completely verifiable (*a*). What verification they do get
is sometimes peculiar (*b*). The verification of singular counterfactual hypotheticals is always peculiar (*c*). '⊃' involves two
symmetrical paradoxes (*d*). And singular connterfactual hypotheticals do not seem to be deducible from their parent general
hypotheticals (*e*). *a* is at least the inevitable result of human
myopia. It will be shown that *b, c,* and *d* are inevitable if a constant
meaning is sought for ' If—then ' : so that their remedy is not
to seek a stronger constant meaning than '⊃', but to recognize
the factors which logicians' blinkers hide from view, factors
which vary too widely to permit any single criterion of reasonable
hypotheticals. And finally that *e* is largely illusory.

If hypotheticals are taken as truth-functional statements, the
full fourfold matrix must be used. For, as will appear later, the
view that a hypothetical is applicable only where its antecedent
is true, though it emphasizes what is important, entirely omits
what is not unimportant. What then does ' ⊃ ' do? It can
hardly be said to state a connection : since often there is nothing
to be connected ; and, even where there are two things to be
connected, there is never any third thing to connect them.
Nor will the more cautious view, that it connects statements,
quite do : since ' unasserted statement ' contains a contradictio
in adjecto.[1] But this question can be temporarily shelved. For
meanwhile the more fully the relations between hypotheticals
and the non-linguistic world are described, the less will semiotic
labels matter.

Interpreted truth-functionally a general hypothetical is true
or false in a very peculiar way, This peculiarity can be brought
out by asking what a general hypothetical is about. If it is
expandible into an endless conjunction of singular hypotheticals,
clearly it is about what these are about. But these, like their
parents, do not specify the situations to which they apply. $\eta$ is
related to the non-linguistic world in three alternative ways : it
might be taken to apply either to this if it is a raven, or to this if
it is not black, or to this tout court.[2]

[1] I owe this point to an unpublished paper by Professor G. Ryle.
[2] See C. G. Hempel " Studies in the Logic of Confirmation " I, *Mind,* January,
1945, particularly the footnote on p. 21 : II, *Mind,* April 1945 : C. H. Whiteley's
reply to I, *Mind,* April 1945 : C. G. Hempel's rejoinder, *Mind,* January 1946 ; and
Janina Hosiasson-Lindenbaum " On Confirmation ", *Journal of Symbolic Logic,* 1940,
particularly pp. 136–141.

Now it seems most natural to say that $\eta$ and $\theta$ apply only where their antecedents are true (type 1 cases). Why? For it is at least an inevitable result of human myopia that $\theta$ cannot be completely verified, but only falsified (a). Why then is it unnatural to say that all situations which fail to falsify it confirm it equally ; and so that it applies both to things which are not black (type 2 cases), and to anything at all (type 3 cases)?

First consider type 2 cases. Since $\eta$ and its brothers can be contraposed, $\theta$ is equivalent to " If anything is not black it is not a raven." And, put like this, it applies to situations where the consequents of $\eta$ and $\eta$'s brothers are false. Why then do type 2 cases seem queer? Because people are too myopic to verify general hypotheticals, and so want to make the fullest use of the limited evidence which they do get. They therefore consider that a general hypothetical does not merely escape falsification ; but is confirmed to the extent that it ran the risk of being falsified.[1] But it runs less risk of being falsified in a type 2 case than in a type 1 case. For, if there were a counter-example, it would be more likely to occur in a type 1 case than in a type 2 case : since the class of things which are ravens is smaller than the class of things which are not black (assumption A). This is an assumption about the classes picked out by descriptive words, and so is beyond the purview of the logician. But the fact that people do make it explains why type 2 cases are thought to provide less confirmation than type 1 cases.

Next consider type 3 cases. Since $\eta$ and its brothers can be transformed into disjunctions, $\theta$ is equivalent to "Anything is either not a raven or black ". And, put like this, it applies to any situation whatsoever, whether the antecedents or consequents of $\eta$ and $\eta$'s brothers are true or false. Why then do type 3 cases seem queer, queerer even than type 2 cases? Again because people, being myopic, want graded confirmation. But $\theta$ runs less risk of being falsified in a type 3 case than it runs in a type 1 case, and even than it runs in a type 2 case. For, if there were a counter-example, it would be more likely to occur in a type 1 case than in a type 3 case, and more likely to occur even in a type 2 case than in a type 3 case : since the universe class is larger than the class of things which are ravens (assumption B),

---

[1] See Janina Hosiasson-Lindenbaum, *loc. cit.*, p. 134 footnote.

and larger even than the class of things which are not black
(assumption C). These two assumptions too are about the
classes picked out by descriptive words, and so are beyond the
purview of the logician. But the fact that people do make them
explains why type 3 cases are thought to provide less confirmation
than type 1 cases and even than type 2 cases.

This shows why it is unnatural to attach the same importance
to all three types of cases : and that the logician is professionally
debarred from recognizing the greater importance of type 1
cases. And, since the oddities of ' $\supset$ ' are the result of neglecting
descriptive words, it is foolish to try to avoid them by seeking a
stronger constant interpretation of ' If—then '. Anyway no
other constant interpretation could be as closely related to the
non-linguistic world as ' $\supset$ '. For instance, there could be no
better evidence for the application of a binary logical predicate
to two statements than there is for the use of the truth-functional
connective ' $\supset$ '.[1]

It might now appear that type 2 cases and type 3 cases are
utterly unimportant. For, if those three assumptions are made
at all, it is natural to make them in such a strong form that type
2 cases and type 3 cases would provide a contemptible amount of
confirmation. But, if the field of investigation were restricted
to birds, an investigator would be safe if he tested $\theta$ by testing
" (x) (bird x $\supset$ (raven x $\supset$ black x)) " ($\gamma$). For, since " (x) (raven
x $\supset$ bird x) " ($\delta$) is analytic, he would be sure that no counter-
example of $\theta$ could fall outside this restricted field. Now type
2 cases and type 3 cases of $\theta$ would be thus parasitical on type 1
cases of $\gamma$. But still, within such limits, people do confirm general
hypotheticals by examining type 2 cases and type 3 cases. Such
experiments are rare, since even with this restrictions it is obvious
that type 2 cases usually,[2] and type 3 cases always provide less
confirmation than type 1 cases. And, just because they are rare,
the additional specification given by $\gamma$ (which is not needed for
type 1 cases of $\theta$, since $\delta$ is analytic) is not usually expressed. But

[1] W. V. Quine, " Mathematical Logic " 1947, p. 29, suggests that an appropriate
binary logical predicate might be found to replace ' $\supset$ ' in the interpretation of
' subjunctive ' conditionals. Cf. R. Carnap " Logical Syntax of Language ", pp.
254–5. I hope to show later that the problem of ' subjunctive ' conditionals is part
of the general problem of confirmation.

[2] Perhaps always. But see Janina Hosiasson-Lindenbaum, loc. cit., p. 140 footnote.

they do occur. Therefore type 2 cases and type 3 cases are not unimportant, and the notion that hypotheticals apply only where their antecedents are true is an error.

But all this still gives no criterion of reasonable general hypotheticals. For giving the highest common factor of the meaning of ' If—then ' in general hypotheticals does not tell us when it is reasonable to utter them. For instance $\eta$ and $\eta$'s brothers are each said to mean negatively one thing, but positively any one of three things. And the reasonableness of $\theta$ might depend on how many of them mean which of these three things.

Now giving a criterion of reasonable general hypotheticals might be described as " giving the contextually varying extra meaning of ' If—then ' in general hypotheticals ".[1] But whether this description is correct or not is a question which can be permanently shelved. For here too the relations between general hypotheticals and the non-linguistic world are more important than semiotic labels.

Certainly vacuous truth and copious truth are the two most obvious ways in which a general hypothetical might be (unfalsified but) unreasonable. And these two ways can be blocked by adding two more assumptions about the classes picked out by descriptive words : that there is at least one thing which is a raven (assumption D), and that there is at least one thing which is not black (assumption E). All five assumptions can now be compressed into the formula " $1 > \sim B > R > 0$ ". Now the importance of A, B and C is that they allow discrimination between the amounts of confirmation provided by cases of type 1, 2 and 3. But D and E play a more recessive role. For, if the speaker knew that D was false, he would knew that $\theta$ could never encounter a type 1 case, and so that it would always be vacuously true. And, if he knew that E was false, he would know that $\theta$ could never encounter a type 2 case, and so that it would always be copiously true. But the only point of his making assumption D is that, if he makes it, he assumes that $\theta$ has a chance of encountering a type 1 case. But, even if he does not make it, $\theta$ might still encounter a type 1 case for all he knows. And the only point of his making assumption E is that, if he makes it, he

---

[1] See H. Reichenbach, *Elements of Symbolic Logic*, p. 379, on a closely related question.

assumes that $\theta$ has a chance of encountering a type 2 case. But, even if he does not make it, $\theta$ might still encounter a type 2 case for all he knows.

General hypotheticals, taken as truth-functional statements, are like trawls which the speaker lets down into the non-linguistic world in order to catch a counter-example, a peculiar kind of fish. Now all the fish in the sea might be too long to fit into the trawl (perpetual copious truth : no type 2 cases). Or all the fish might be too thin to be caught by its mesh (perpetual vacuous truth : no type 1 cases). Or all the fish might be too long and too thin (perpetual copious and vacuous truth : no type 2 cases or type 1 cases, but only type 3 cases). But, unless the fisherman knew that all the fish were either too long (contradictory of E), or too thin (contradictory of D), or both, he could not know either that his trawl could never encounter a type 2 case, or that it could never encounter a type 1 case, or that it could never encounter either (respectively). Nor would he know that he could never catch a fish, and so that even type 3 cases would provide confirmation which simply was not needed : not needed, because, if he knew that fish were like that, trawling would be a work of supererogation. But since he does not know this, he might catch a fish for all he knows. And, if he makes assumption A, he thinks that his trawl has more chance of catching when it approaches a fish which he knows is not too thin (type 1 case) than when it approaches a fish which he knows is not too long (type 2 case). And, if he makes assumption B, he thinks that his trawl has more chance of catching when it approaches a fish which he knows is not too thin (type 1 case) than when it approaches a fish which for all he knows might be too thin and too long (type 3 case). And, if he makes assumption C, he thinks that his trawl has more chance of catching when it approaches a fish which he knows is not too long (type 2 case) than when it approaches a fish which for all he knows might be too long and too thin (type 3 case).

But unfortunately vacuous and copious truth are not the only ways in which a general hypothetical can be unreasonable. For nearly always D and E are not enough ; and the reasonableness of a general hypothetical depends on how many type 1 cases and how many type 2 cases it encounters. And sometimes

D and E are too much; and the reasonableness of a general hypothetical depends instead on its deducibility from another general hypothetical, or from other general hypotheticals, which themselves . . . etc. In fact the necessary condition of their reasonableness seems to be a complex disjunction which can be discovered only by careful investigation.[1] And, if this is true, the same careful investigation should discover the necessary condition of the reasonableness of singular counterfactual hypotheticals.[2] Anyway the notion that the necessary condition of reasonableness is single and simple, that the extra meaning of ' If—then ' is constant, is an example of a common error in philosophy, which might be called the ' Monistic Fallacy '. Here ends the discussion of $b$.

Before treating singular hypotheticals as statements it will be worth while to elaborate the close connection between the confirmation of general hypotheticals and their choice by elimination. The connection is that speed of elimination, like strength of confirmation, is a function of the likelihood of finding a counter-example. Now $\theta$ may be taken to say that $B$ is a necessary condition of $R$, or that $R$ is a sufficient condition of $B$, or both (however successful the elimination, ' necessary ' and ' sufficient ' remain always partly bluff).[3] And, if it were taken in the first way, it might be chosen by eliminating rivals which apply to the same type 1 cases. If so, situations where $R$ was present would be examined, and a short list of strong candidates for the post of necessary condition of $R$ would be chosen from among other properties which present say $B$, $C$ and $D$. Then other situations where $R$ was present would be examined, and in these other situations some of the three properties $B$, $C$ and $D$, and some of their disjunctions $[B \lor C]$, $[B \lor D]$, $[C \lor D]$ and $[B \lor C \lor D]$ might be absent (conjunctive necessary conditions need not be considered)[4]. Thus this process of elimination might eventually

[1] See H. Reichenbach, loc. cit., c. viii, for such an investigation of the reasonableness of general hypotheticals.

[2] See H. Reichenbach, loc. cit., c. viii also for such an investigation of the reasonableness, of singular counterfactual hypotheticals: also R. M. Chisholm. " The Contrary-to-fact Conditional ", *Mind*, October 1946, and F. L. Will, " The Contrary-to-fact Conditional " *Mind*, July 1947.

[3] See C. S. Peirce, " Collected Papers ", Vol. II, p. 456 footnote : G. H. Von Wright, " The Logical Problem of Induction ", c. iv ; and C. D. Broad, " Hr. Von Wright on the Logic of Induction ", I, *Mind*, January 1944.

[4] See G. H. Von Wright, loc. cit., p. 73.

leave $B$ in the field. But, if it left $B$ in the field, it would also leave all the disjunctions which included $B$, namely $[B \vee C]$, $[B \vee D]$ and $[B \vee C \vee D]$. And elimination could not enable us to choose between them. For, if any of these disjunctions were eliminated, $B$ too would be eliminated. Therefore, it would be possible to choose between them only on other grounds. And elimination could leave a single candidate in the field only if that single candidate were the disjunction of the whole initial group $[B \vee C \vee D]$.

Symmetrically, if $\theta$ were taken in the second way, it might be chosen by eliminating rivals which apply to the same type 2 cases. If so, situations where $B$ was absent would be examined, and a short list of strong candidates for the post of sufficient condition of $B$ would be picked from other properties which were absent, say $R$, $S$ and $T$. Then other situations where $B$ was absent would be examined, and in these other situations some of the three properties $R$, $S$ and $T$, and some of their conjunctions $[R.S]$, $[R.T]$, $[S.T]$ and $[R.S.T]$ might be present (disjunctive sufficient conditions need not be considered).[1] Thus this process of elimination might eventually leave $R$ in the field. But, if it left $R$ in the field, it would also leave all the conjunctions which included $R$, namely $[R.S]$, $[R.T]$ and $[R.S.T]$. And elimination could not enable us to choose between them. Therefore, it would be possible to choose between them only on other grounds. And elimination could leave a single candidate in the field only if that single candidate were the conjunction of the whole initial group $[R.S.T]$.

Of course either method might have failed to leave $\theta$ in the field. For $B$ or $R$ might have been eliminated. And $[B \vee C \vee D]$ or $[R.S.T]$ might have been eliminated. And $B$ or $R$ might not have been included in the initial short lists of strong candidates which are produced by a judgment of relevance (ravens croak too, and ebony too is black). But, if $\theta$ were eventually left in the field, then logically there is no reason to prefer the method which uses type 1 cases to the method which uses type 2 cases. For, only if assumption $A$ is made, is there any reason to think that the method which uses type 1 cases will forward elimination more rapidly than the method which uses type 2 cases.

[1] See G. H. Von Wright, loc. cit, p. 73.

Finally, if $\theta$ is taken in the third way, it might be chosen by eliminating rivals which apply to the same type 3 cases. This method would treat all general hypotheticals as rivals, because they are all about the Whole of Reality. And, only if assumptions $B$ and $C$ are made, is there any reason to think that it will forward elimination less rapidly than the method which uses type 1 cases or the method which uses type 2 cases.

We must approach Nature not as pupils, but as masters ; and as masters who pose questions which are likely to be answered quickly. And, when we choose general hypotheticals by elimination, we pose a disjunctive question " Is this one true, or that one, or . . . ? " and we pose it by observation and experiment. Now Nature never gives the answer ' Yes ' to any limb of the disjunction, but only the answer ' No ' to some or all of its limbs. But Nature is unlikely to give a quick answer ' No ' to any limb of the disjunction unless the question is posed by a searching investigation. But, on assumption $A$, the investigation will not be sufficiently searching if it scrutinizes only situations where the consequents are false. And, on assumptions $B$ and $C$, it will be even less searching if it relies merely on an indiscriminate rummaging of the whole universe.

This parenthesis may be closed with the observation that $\gamma$ plays the same role in $\theta$'s choice by elimination that it played in $\theta$'s confirmation.[1]

The next three difficulties, $c$, $d$ and $e$, are presented by singular hypotheticals taken as truth-functional statements.

$c$ was that the verification of singular counterfactual hypotheticals is always peculiar (not ' subjunctive hypotheticals ' since the falsehood of the antecedent in modern English is usually conveyed not by mood but by tense and auxiliaries). For disagreement about the truth-value of a singular counter-factual hypothetical is compatible with agreement about the truth-values of its components. Its verification does not exhaust the speaker's full meaning : he also means that this *would have been* black if it *had been* a raven. Yet this extra meaning, if support-

---

[1] Professor G. H. Von Wright, " Confirmation ", *Xth International Congress of Philosophy*, Fasc. II, p. 794, seems to argue against all that I have said about the queer ways of confirming and eliminating general hypotheticals. But this is only because he does not there consider type 3 cases at all, or type 2 cases in relation to sufficient conditions.

able, is borrowed from the parent general hypothetical, and so the evidence is truant from the single situation. Nor is this truancy surprising. For the singular counterfactual hypothetical would hardly have been uttered unless it had been deduced from its well confirmed parent general hypothetical. And again there is little point in debating whether the semiotic label ' meaning ' is to be restricted to the highest common factor of meaning supported by the evidence in the single situation ; or is to be extended so as to include the varying extra meaning supported by the truant evidence. It is more important to see exactly how singular counterfactual hypotheticals are related to the non-linguistic world ; that their extra meaning, if it is concentrated on the single situation, cannot be evidential, but only ' picture preference '.[1] For we may prefer to picture a connection indicated by each singular hypothetical (an idle connection if the singular hypothetical is counterfactual) ; but the evidential support of this extra meaning can only be truant.

For instance, this peculiarity in the way singular counter-factual hypotheticals are related to the non-linguistic world might be described by saying that they are interpretations.[2] (Another reason for saying this will be given later). Or it might be described in more detail by saying that their verifica-tion does not exhaust their full meaning : that complete evidence for them would include the (unattainable) complete evidence for their parent general hypotheticals ; and that their verification yields little confirmation for their parent general hypotheticals, because it is not got from type 1 cases, and so, by reflection, little support for their own extra meaning. But it must not be described by saying that they are really about hypothetical facts. For this description looks like an answer to the question " How are they related to the non-linguistic world ? " but what it actually says is that they are related to a world which is neither linguistic nor non-linguistic. And an alleged close link with a logically inaccessible world is no substitute or consolation for a familiar loose link with the sublunary world. $c$ is true but inevitable.

Now the second, more detailed, description has the advan-

[1] See John Wisdom, " Other Minds .', I, particularly p. 381, *Mind*, October 1940.
[2] See Stuart Hampshire, " Subjunctive Conditionals ', this volume pp. 204-210.

tage of revealing that $c$ is only a special case of the general difficulty $b$. For a singular counterfactual hypothetical yields little confirmation for its parent general hypothetical only because it cannot apply to a type 1 case. It can be verified only either in a situation which endorses its components as false-false or in a situation which endorses its components as false-true (in an $FF$ situation or in an $FT$ situation). But an $FT$ situation yields even less confirmation than an $FF$ situation. For a type 1 case is a situation which could develop into $TF$ : and, whereas an $FF$ situation could develop out of a type 2 case, an $FT$ situation could develop only out of a type 3 case. In fact an $FT$ situation is unique in this respect. For an $FF$ situation could develop out of either a type 3 case or a type 2 case or both : and a $TT$ situation could develop out of either a type 3 case or a type 1 case or both. Nor is it surprising that there is an option about the way situations $FF$ and $TT$ can be taken. For amount of confirmation depends on probability of falsification, which is relative to evidence contained in a case. So, both when a singular hypothetical is verified in an $FF$ situation and when it is verified in a $TT$ situation, there are two alternative possible claims to the amount of confirmation which it yields for its parent general hypothetical. But $c$ was described by saying that singular counterfactual hypotheticals yield little confirmation for their parent general hypotheticals. Therefore $c$ is only a special case of the general difficulty $b$, which has already been discussed. Therefore it is partly an error to say that singular counterfactual hypotheticals present a peculiar difficulty (only partly an error for reasons which will be given in the third part of this paper).

It is now possible to show that $d$ too is only another aspect of the general difficulty $b$ which has already been discussed, that the paradoxes are not really paradoxical. For an $FF$ situation is associated with the paradox of trivial truth : a $TT$ situation with the paradox of ponderous truth ; and an $FT$ situation with both paradoxes. Thus trivial truth is incompatible with a type 1 case : ponderous truth with a type 2 case ; and both with either a type 1 case or a type 2 case. But, if we concentrate on the situation in which a singular hypothetical is verified and refrain from stealing surreptitious glances at the truant evidence, then these paradoxes cease to be paradoxical. For, when there is no type 1 case, the property mentioned in the antecedent is absent : and any property, present or absent, might be the necessary condition of an absent property. And, when there is no type 2 case, the property mentioned in the consequent is present : and any property, present or absent, might be the sufficient condition of a property present. And, when there is no type 1 case or type 2 case, both these difficulties are combined. Now it is true that we do not use ' follows from ' like this. But that is not because the situations in which singular hypotheticals are verified exhibit some connection : but only because we do not utter singular hypotheticals unless they have been deduced from parent general hypotheticals which have been confirmed already to some extent.

But singular counterfactual hypotheticals do not appear to be deducible from their parent general hypotheticals[1] (difficulty *e*). However this appearance is partly illusory and partly presents no difficulty. For it is true that a singular counterfactual hypothetical implies that its antecedent is false, and that the falsehood of its antecedent cannot be deduced from its parent general hypothetical. But this presents no difficulty. On the other hand the impossibility of deducing its purely hypothetical element (interpreted truth-functionally) from its parent general hypothetical, which would have been a real difficulty, is in fact an illusion. It is an illusion produced by concealing the universal reference of the parent general hypothetical.[2] The truth is rather that the parent general hypothetical is not completely verifiable : that, if its confirmation had already involved the verification of the singular counterfactual hypothetical, the deduction would be otiose ; and that a singular counterfactual hypothetical often has more than one parent. This last complication is an additional reason for calling singular counterfactual hypotheticals ' interpretations '.[3] For, if a singular counterfactual hypothetical stands at the point of intersection of several general hypotheticals, judgment is needed in order to assess what would have been the outcome (particularly in history). But then each aspect of the

[1] See William Kneale, " Probability and Induction ", p. 75 : and *Proceedings of the Aristotelian Society*, Supplementary Volume XXII, pp. 163–5.
[2] See K. R. Popper, "A Note on Natural Laws and so-called ' Contrary-to-fact ' Conditionals ", *Mind*, January, 1949.
[3] See Stuart Hampshire, loc. cit.

singular counterfactual hypothetical is still deducible from its
own parent general hypothetical, and judgment is needed only
in order to conflate the results of the separate deductions.

It might still be objected that it is impossible to deduce
what *would have been* the case from what *is* (timelessly) the case.[1]
But this is tantamount to the old objection that singular counter
factual hypotheticals cannot be interpreted truth-functionally:
about which enough has been said. After all, from what other
confirmable sentence could a singular counterfactual hypothetical be deduced? From a sentence indicating a connection?
But such a sentence expresses only ' picture preference '. Or
from a sentence describing hypothetical facts? But, if, because
the actual world houses the situation FF, a shadow-world is
postulated in order to house the situation TT, parity of reasoning
demands two more shadow-worlds, one for the situation FT
(since singular counterfactual hypotheticals do not present a
peculiar difficulty), and one for the situation TF (for ' negative
facts '). And, even if we dropped ' negative facts ', each singular
hypothetical (of whatever kind) would still require three worlds,
one actual and two possible ; and so each general hypothetical
would require an infinite number of worlds, produced by combining in various ways the three worlds of each member of its
infinite family ; only one of which would be actual. Hypothetical facts are the objects of an insatiable craving. From what
other confirmable sentence then could a singular counterfactual
hypothetical be deduced?

Here, at the end of the first part of this paper, it might seem
appropriate to reopen the shelved question " If hypotheticals are
statements, exactly what sort of statements are they? "[2] But,
since the reasons for affixing semiotic labels are more important
than the labels themselves, it is no longer imperative to answer it.

But nothing has yet been said about the reasons for calling
hypotheticals ' rules '. And this second part of this paper is the
place to give them. However, it is beyond its scope to give them
fully.[3] Briefly, they may be called rules in so far as they guide
the user in inferring the unknown from the known (strictly

[1] See William Kneale, *loc. cit.*
[2] See Lewis Carroll, "A Logical Paradox ", *Mind*, July 1894.
[3] See F. P. Ramsay, " General Propositions and Causality " in *The Foundations of Mathematics*, p. 237.

nothing is known in a type 3 case) : and they may be called rules because they are not only applied, but also learnt, possessed and taught. And a general hypothetical, which is an inexhaustible sheaf of singular hypotheticals, may be regarded as a rule which can be applied many times, just because it has many clauses, each of which can be applied only once.

But this way of looking at hypotheticals does not evade the difficulties *a—e*. For, when a singular hypothetical is taken as a truth-functional statement, it is shown to be true by the same situation which shows it to be correct (and so of no further use) when it is taken as an applied rule. And, when a general hypothetical is taken as a truth-functional statement, its truth is confirmed by the same situations which confirm its correctness (and so its uselessness henceforward in these situations) when it is taken as an applied rule. In fact the only effect of regarding hypotheticals as applied rules rather than as truth-functional statements is to substitute 'correct' for 'true' in the meta-language.[1]

However, if hypotheticals are regarded as rules, the difficulties *a—e* do become less urgent. There is of course a sense in which the speaker (or hearer or silent possessor) always has his eye open for a possible counter-example to a general hypothetical, whether taken as a statement or as a rule—or anyway not closed to a possible counter-example : and in which he eventually applies a singular hypothetical, whether taken as a statement or as a rule, even when the situation is *FT*. And in this sense general and singular hypotheticals apply not only to type 1 cases and type 2 cases (after contraposition), but also to type 3 cases ("~R v B "). But the speaker teaches, the hearer learns and the silent knower possesses a rule which is, in another sense, in abeyance, usually until a type 2 case or, better still, a type 1 case appears. And these two senses can be marked by distinguishing rules in application from rules in abeyance. And, because rules often are in abeyance, the difficulties *a—e* become less urgent when hypotheticals are taken as rules.

Finally, there is a complication, neglect of which leads to error. Hypotheticals, when applied, can always be regarded as state-

[1] See I. Berlin, *Proceedings of the Aristotelian Society*, Supplementary Volume XVI p. 66, for a closely related argument.

ments, but not always as rules. For an applied rule is used in order to guide an inference from the known to the unknown. But, for instance, a singular counterfactual hypothetical cannot be used in order to guide an inference from the known to the unknown. And this is not only because, since the antecedent is known to be false, it cannot be applied to a type 1 case : but also because, although the consequent is known to be false, it cannot be used in a type 2 case, since the truth-value of the antecedent is known too ; and also because, since the truth-values of both antecedent and consequent are known, it cannot be used in a type 3 case either. Hence singular counterfactual hypotheticals cannot be regarded as applied rules. They are obsolete clauses of rules, obsolete even at the moment of their origin. But hypotheticals expressed by " If—then " cry out for application to a type 1 case : type 1 cases are more important ; and their greater importance is reflected by the alternative locutions which put the antecedent as a question or as a command. And this strong suggestion produces the erroneous notion that either there is a shadow-world of hypothetical facts in which singular counterfactual hypotheticals will be able to apply to type 1 cases ; or else, since there is no actual situation to which they apply as rules, therefore there is no actual situation to which they apply as statements.

I have gradually slipped into talking about ' general hypotheticals ' instead of about ' general hypotheticals like $\theta$ ', and about ' singular hypotheticals ' instead of abou'. ' singular hypotheticals like $\eta$'. But are all general hypotheticals like $\theta$, and all singular hypotheticals like $\eta$ or $\eta$'s counterfactual brothers? Clearly not. For instance " If he was surprised he didn't show it " is unlike $\eta$ for three reasons. Its components are not both of the subject-predicate form : ' If ' is v ed concessively ; and, if ' it ' means genuine surprise, the class of situations which endorse the consequents of its brother singular hypotheticals as false cannot be larger than the class of situations which endorse their antecedents as true. But what, in full detail, makes hypotheticals too unlike $\eta$ and $\theta$ to be treated like them?

To answer this question is beyond the scope of this paper. Instead this third part of it will be devoted to showing how singular hypotheticals can be embedded in different locutions.

This will not be done for general hypotheticals : partly because the locutions in which they are embedded do not vary in such an interesting way, and partly because a comparison of the different locutions in which the purely hypothetical element of singular hypotheticals can be embedded will throw some light on the position of singular counterfactual hypotheticals. These locutions are set out in the following table (in which LO=leaves the truth-value open : IT=implies that the truth-value is ' true ' ; and IF=implies that the truth-value is ' false ').

| | Antecedent | Consequent | Locution |
|---|---|---|---|
| i | I T | I F | (None used by sane people). |
| ii | I T | I T | " This is black because it is a raven." |
| iii | I F | I F | " If this had been a raven it would have been black." |
| iv | I F | I T | " If this had been a raven it would have been a reason for the fact that it is black." |
| v | I T | L O | " Since this is a raven, it must be black." (Here ' must ', though strong, is bluff, and leaves the truth-value of the consequent open). |
| vi | I F | L O | " If this had been a raven it would have been a reason for its being black." |
| vii | L O | I T | " If this is a raven, it is a reason for the fact that it is black." |
| viii | L O | I F | " If this had been black its being a raven would have been a reason." |
| ix | L O | L O | " If this is a raven it is black." " If this is not black it is not a raven." " Either this is not a raven or it is black." (These are the three ways of expressing a pure hypothetical). |

Now this table is not complete on its right-hand side. Nor does it say all that might be said about the locutions which it does list on its right-hand side : it merely classifies them according to the exhaustive division given on its left-hand side. But it does throw some light on the position of singular counterfactual hypotheticals (iii). For iii, like all the other locutions except ix, is not a pure hypothetical, but contains a purely hypothetical element. Also it shares inapplicability to type i cases only with iv and vi. And type i cases are the most important. And iv and vi are far rarer than iii. Hence iii holds a unique position. But ii, iv and vii are alone inapplicable to type 2 cases. And, since iv and vii are far rarer than ii, ii also holds a unique position, complementary to the unique position held by iii. And iv too holds a unique position which combines the disadvantages of the other two, being the only locution—and a rare one—which is not applicable either to type i or type 2 cases. Now ii, iii and iv present the same difficulty in different forms. ii and iii present it more insistently than iv, because they are common while it is rare. And iii presents it more strikingly than ii, because, unlike ii, it is expressed by 'If—then'. But, when it is seen that no locution can apply to more than two types of cases, and that for all three locutions the difficulty arises from the relative importance of the three types of cases, it is clear that it is the inevitable result of the logician's professional neglect of descriptive words. And, when the three assumptions which discriminate the amounts of confirmation provided by the three types of cases are made explicit, the difficulty is largely dissolved. There still remains the residual difficulty that, for instance, locutions which logically cannot apply to type i cases causally (or logically, given A and B) cannot yield as much confirmation as those which can. But this is inevitable from any point of view. One can only explain and acquiesce.

# NATURAL LAWS AND CONTRARY-TO-FACT CONDITIONALS

## By WILLIAM KNEALE

In his article Mr. Pears argues against the view that the possibility of deriving contrary-to-fact conditionals from statements of natural law shows the latter to be something different from universal material implications of the form :

$$(x) \cdot \phi(x) \supset \psi(x).$$

It is true, he says, that a singular contrary-to-fact conditional cannot be deduced from a universal material implication, but that is only because the former implies that its antecedent is false, whereas the latter says nothing either way about that antecedent considered in itself : on the contrary, " the impossibility of deducing its purely hypothetical element (interpreted truth-functionally) from its parent general hypothetical . . . is in fact an illusion . . . produced by concealing the universal reference of the parent general hypothetical ". In support of this assertion he cites a note by Professor Popper in *Mind* LVIII (January 1949).

If contrary-to-fact conditionals were of the form :

$$\sim \phi(a) \cdot \phi(a) \supset \psi(a),$$

what Mr. Pears says would obviously be correct. But one of the concerns of those who have recently raised the problem of contrary-to-fact conditionals is precisely to deny the sufficiency of the analysis which Mr. Pears seems to accept in his parenthetical remark. And in order to see the queerness of that analysis we need only reflect that the formula given above follows from '$\sim \phi(a)$' as sole premiss. Surely a man who says " If this bird were a raven, it would be black " thinks, and thinks rightly, that he is saying more than " This bird is not a raven ". If we want to use the notion of material implication in explaining what he means, we must suppose that his remark contains an implicit reference to a *universal* material implication. That is to say, we must offer some such analysis as :

$$\sim \phi(a) \cdot (x) \cdot \phi(x) \supset \psi(x).$$

If this interpretation were correct, a contrary-to-fact conditional would indeed follow from the negation of its antecedent taken together with a universal material implication of the appropriate kind ; for it would be just a conjunction of those two premisses. But the second interpretation seems to me no better than the first. I do not want to dwell here on the falsity of the suggestion that a precisely formulated universal material implication can be derived from every contrary-to-fact conditional ; for this difficulty might perhaps be removed by putting the reference in a vaguer form. My main reason for dissatisfaction is that I cannot see the relevance of any material implication to the proposition we are trying to analyse. In order to explain my point I shall consider Professor Popper's account of the matter.

In the note mentioned by Mr. Pears Professor Popper says that the difficulties of persons like myself arise from failure to notice the difference between terms which can be defined extensionally and those which cannot be so defined. It is true, he says, that "All my friends speak French " does not entail " If Confucius were one of my friends he would speak French ", but that is because anyone who utters the first statement is thinking of the class of his friends as closed, whereas anyone who utters the second statement is thinking of the class of his friends as open. In other words, the expression ' my friends ' is not used in quite he same way in the two sentences. When, however, it is said that sentences which purport to state natural laws are equivalent to universal material implications, it is to be understood that the terms involved are not mere substitutes for lists of proper names but unrestricted descriptions. And once this distinction has been made clear, there cannot, he maintains, be any serious objection to saying that statements of natural law are equivalent to universal material implications. For a universal material implication in which the terms are unrestricted descriptions does indeed allow inference to contrary-to-fact conditionals.

In this argument Professor Popper seems to assume, like Mr. Pears, that a contrary-to-fact conditional is of the form :

$$\sim \phi(a) \: . \: \phi(a) \supset \psi(a).$$

But I am not concerned now with that difficulty. My present purpose is to point out that universal material implications have no relevance to contrary-to-fact conditionals. In order to make this clear it is important to consider a suitable example phrased in ordinary speech.

When we see the formula :

$$(x) \: . \: \text{raven} \: (x) \supset \text{black} \: (x),$$

we commonly read it to ourselves as though it were an abbreviation of the statement :

Anything, if it is raven, is black.

Now the second expression has indeed the logical form of a suggestion of law ; for the word ' if ' and the timeless present are well-known devices for the formulation of laws. But to get an accurate rendering of the original formula into ordinary English we should first transform it into the equivalent formula :

$$\sim (\exists x) . \text{raven} (x) . \sim \text{black} (x),$$

and then read this as an abbreviation for :

> There has never been a raven that was not black,
> and there will never be a raven that is not black.

This rendering, with its explicit distinction of times, has the merit of not containing any expressions which beg the question at issue, and I think it will be agreed that it does not look very like a statement of law. But let us examine it in more detail.

Clearly the second part, which refers to the future, has no special interest for a man who wonders whether in certain conditions which did not in fact obtain there would have been ravens that were not black. Is the first part any more useful to him? Surely not. For there is no incompatibility between this and the suggestion that if ravens had been tempted to live in a very snowy region they would have produced descendants that were white although still recognizably ravens. The fact, if it is a fact, that no ravens have lived in very snowy regions may be only an accident of history, and so too the fact, if it is a fact, that there has never been a raven that was not black. But to say that is just to say that, even if (*per impossible*) we could know the second fact, we should still not be entitled to assert such a contrary to-fact conditional as " If some inhabitants of snowy regions were ravens, they would be black ".

Philosophers who treat suggestions of law as universal material implications say in effect that there is no sense in talking of historical accidents on the cosmic scale. According to their account of the matter there are only two possibilities to be considered : either (i) it is a law of nature that all ravens are black, or (ii) there has been or will be somewhere at some time a raven that was not or is not black. For if they are right, the first of these is just the contradictory of the second, and any one who tries to deny both at once abandons the principle of the excluded middle. Perhaps Professor Popper has this in mind when he says at the end of his note : " It may be useful and, for some purposes, necessary to assume a general principle stating that every kind of event that is compatible with the accepted natural laws does in fact occur in some (finite) space-time region ". But if so, he does not go far enough. The principle to which he refers cannot be for him a mere assumption which we may find it useful or necessary to adopt for certain purposes. It is a direct consequence of his thesis that statements of law are universal material implications ; and if it is unplausible, so too is that thesis. I shall offer two examples from different fields to show that the principle is inconsistent with our ordinary view of natural laws.

It is at least conceivable that there has never been a chain reaction of plutonium within a strong steel shell containing heavy hydrogen, and it is also conceivable that there never will be. But in order to accept these two suggestions we need not suppose that there is a law of nature excluding such events. The fact, if it is fact that none has occurred in the past may be explained satisfactorily by the extreme improbability of the occurrence of suitable conditions without human planning ; and the fact, if it is fact, that none will occur in the future may be explained by the prevalence of a belief that such an event would have disastrous consequences.

Again, let us suppose that a musician composes an intricate tune in his imagination while he is lying on his death bed too feeble to speak or write, and that he says to himself in his last moments " No human being has ever heard or will ever hear this tune ", meaning by ' this tune ' a certain complex pattern of sounds which could be described in general terms. Obviously he does not think of his remark as a suggestion of natural law. It is, of course, irrelevant to my argument whether any musician has ever made or will ever make such a remark correctly. For my purpose it is sufficient that we can conceive an unrestrictedly universal material implication without regarding it as a statement of law. In short, we do not ordinarily believe that every natural possibility must be realized somewhere at some time.

What I have said about universal material implications of the kind Professor Popper considers has an obvious bearing on the problem of confirmation. Let us return once more to the formula :

$$(x) \cdot \text{raven}(x) \supset \text{black}(x).$$

Clearly this is equivalent to a conjunction of the three sentences :

(1) There has never been an observed raven that was not black.

(2) There has never been an unobserved raven that was not black.

(3) There will never be a raven that is not black.

For to obtain these three sentences we need only subdivide the first of the two assertions discussed in an earlier paragraph. Now statement (1) above is very well confirmed by the evidence at our disposal. And so this evidence may perhaps be said to provide confirmation for the conjunction of (1), (2) and (3), but only in the sense in which the fact that it is raining provides some confirmation for the conjunctive statement that it is raining and the moon is made of green cheese. When we wish to make inferences to the unobserved, (2) and (3) are the only parts of our triple assertion that can be of any use to us as premisses. But neither of these is more reliable merely because it belongs to a conjunction which has been confirmed in the Pickwickian sense just mentioned. We do, of course, think that suggestions of law may be confirmed in a useful way by observed facts, but that is only because our notion of confirmation is bound up with a policy of trying to find laws which are not merely universal material implications.

# CHAPTER IX.  THE PROBLEM OF TRUTH.

## FACTS AND PROPOSITIONS

### *By* MORITZ SCHLICK

WHEN in the spring of last year I wrote my short paper on " Das Fundament der Erkenntnis ", sitting leisurely on a balcony over-looking the blue bay of Salerno, it did not occur to me that I was arousing a violent discussion of the " logical positivists' theory of truth ". I regarded my little article as nothing but a gentle warning of a true empiricist against certain tendencies towards what seemed to me a rather dogmatic or rationalistic formulation of positivistic principles. I was, therefore, a little surprised when, on account of that paper, I was accused of being a metaphysician and a poet. Finding it impossible, however, to take this indict-ment seriously, I was neither shocked by the one nor flattered by the other and did not intend to take up the discussion. I hoped my article would speak for itself in spite of the objections raised.

The appearance of Dr. Hempel's clever article in "Analysis " (vol. 2, no. 4) has changed my mind. He has shaped his arguments clearly and nicely, and I feel it my duty to point out once more, as simply as possible, why I cannot be satisfied with some of the views professed by some of my friends. I shall restrict myself to what seems to me to be the most critical point, i.e. the relation-ship of " propositions " to " reality ".

I have been accused of maintaining that statements can be compared with facts. I plead guilty. I have maintained this. But I protest against my punishment : I refuse to sit in the seat of the metaphysicians. I have often compared propositions to facts ; so I had no reason to say that it couldn't be done. I found, for instance, in my Baedeker the statement : " This cathedral has two spires," I was able to compare it with " reality " by looking at the cathedral, and this comparison convinced me that Baedeker's assertion was true. Surely you cannot tell me that such a process is impossible and that there is a detestable metaphysics involved in it. You say you did not mean it that way ? But I assure you that I meant nothing but a process of this kind when I spoke of testing propositions by comparing them with facts. No one who is familiar with my recent writings can suppose that I used the term " reality " for anything but empirical objects like churches, trees, clouds, etc.[1] not for any " metaphysical " entities. A cathedral is not a proposition or a set of propositions, therefore I felt justified in maintaining that a proposition could be compared with reality.

Perhaps you say : " But if we analyse the process of verification of Baedeker's assertion we shall find that it amounts to a comparison of propositions." I answer : I don't know ; it will depend on what you mean by ' analysis '. But whatever the result of your analysis may be, at any rate we can distinguish between cases in which a written, printed or spoken sentence is compared with some other written, printed or spoken sentence, and cases like our example, where a sentence is compared with the thing of which it speaks. And it is this latter case which I took the liberty of describing as a " comparison of a proposition with a fact ". If you don't like to use this expression for the case described it will merely be a difference of terminology.

You insist that a statement cannot or must not be compared to anything but statements. But why? It is my humble opinion that we can compare anything to anything if we choose. Do you believe that propositions and facts are too far removed from each other? Too different? Is it a mysterious property of propositions that they cannot be compared with anything else? That would seem to be a rather mystical view. We are assured that the " cleavage " between statements and facts " is nothing but the result of a redoubling metaphysics ".[2] That may be true. But who believes in such a cleavage? Those who say that the one cannot be compared to the other, or the humble empiricist like myself, for whom propositions are facts among other facts and who sees no difficulty, no " embarrassing consequences " in comparing them?

What is a proposition, after all? In my opinion it is a series of sounds or other symbols (a ' sentence ') *together with the logical rules belonging to them*, i.e. certain prescriptions as to how the sentence is to be *used*. These rules, culminating in ' deictic ' definitions, constitute the ' meaning ' of the proposition. In

---

[1] See e.g. *Les énoncés scientifiques*, chap. IV, Paris 1934.  [2] *Ibid.* p. 51.

order to verify the proposition I have to ascertain whether those rules have actually been obeyed—why should that be impossible? In our example it is done by looking at the cathedral and at the sentence in the book and by stating that the symbol ' two ' is used in connection with the symbol ' spires ', and that I arrive at the same symbol when I apply the rules of counting to the towers of the cathedral.

You will reproach me for using again the " material mode of speech ", instead of the " formal mode ". I fully acknowledge the importance of the distinction between these two, and I have admitted that in epistemological analysis we should endeavour to use the formal mode. But I think it is wrong to say that the use of this mode is " much more correct ". I am convinced, with Carnap, that the material mode as such is not faulty, only it is apt to engender pseudo-problems *if it is employed without sufficient precaution.* Dr. Hempel says : " Saying that empirical statements ' express facts ' . . . is a typical form of the material mode of speech." Perhaps so ; but what harm is there in it? This particular phrase is an innocent tautology—for what on earth could statements express except facts? On the other hand : saying that certain black marks in my Baedeker express the fact that a certain cathedral has two spires is a perfectly legitimate empirical assertion. By the way, it is easy to express in a purely " formal " way my opinion that facts and propositions can be compared : words denoting symbols and words denoting other things may occur in the same sentence.

Sometimes we are told that it is in " a logical respect " that propositions cannot be compared to anything but propositions. This may be true, but I don't know whether it is true or not, because I don't know what is meant by a comparison in a " logical respect ".

Is it true that we are unable " to give a precise account of how a comparison between statements and facts may possibly be accomplished, and how we may possibly ascertain the structure of facts "?[1] I think it is not true. Or was the description faulty which I gave of such a comparison a little while ago? It consisted of the simplest empirical prescriptions of a kind which we carry out many times almost every day. You can easily make

[1] *loc. cit.* p. 51.

the description more precise by adding details, but that is not even necessary, because it would not change the principle of the matter.

If you assert, as you seem to do, that we cannot " possibly ascertain the structure of facts, " I must confess that such a statement reminds me a little of the metaphysics of " things in themselves " which, it is alleged, must for ever remain unknown to us. Since you do not deny the existence of facts[1] why should you deny that we can know their structure? I should say, for instance, that by counting the spires of a cathedral I get acquainted with the structure of a certain fact. Perhaps you merely want to say that it is nonsense to speak of " structures of facts " at all? I answer: that may be so if you adopt certain rules for the use of your words, but it is not so if the words are employed in the way in which I used them. It must be remembered that no sentence is meaningful or meaningless *per se*, but only in regard to the definitions and rules which have been stipulated for the use of words occurring in it.

This applies to the whole issue in discussion. If it is true that " facts " and " propositions " cannot be compared, then those words are used in a way which differs from the way I used them. They have a different meaning, and the dispute is merely verbal.

The simplest way of maintaining the impossibility of the comparision in question would be to say *that there are no " facts "* (in the formal mode ; the rule for the word ' fact ' is simply that it shall not be employed at all). But I see no reason why this convenient word should be banished and, if I understand rightly, you do not actually want to go so far.

Perhaps you mean to say that although the facts which we call propositions *may* be compared with other facts, it is actually *never done in science*? I think that this is true for the purely theoretical work of science, e.g. for the mathematical physicist whose business consists in formulating and comparing natural laws and also " protocol statements, " uniting them into a coherent system and computing the consequences. His work is done by means of pencil and paper. But I assert most emphatically that it is *not* true for the experimenting scientist whose work consists in making observations and comparing the predictions

[1] *Ibid.* p. 54.

of the mathematician with—I do beg your pardon—the observed facts.

It is at this point, I believe, that the psychological source of the criticised view reveals itself : its advocates are theoretically minded men who take their stand *within* science. Science is a system of propositions ; and—without being aware of it—these thinkers substitute science for reality ; for them facts are not acknowledged before they are formulated in propositions and taken down in their notebooks. But Science is not the World. The universe of discourse is not the whole universe. It is a typical rationalistic attitude which shows itself here under the guise of the most subtle distinctions. It is as old as metaphysics itself, as we may learn from a saying of old Parmenides, which runs : ταὐτὸν δ' ἐστὶ νοεῖν τε καὶ οὕνεκεν ἐστι νόημα. . . . .

Our good friends and opponents think of the system of truths as the mathematician thinks of theoretical physics : for him it is quite true that his only task is to make all scientific statements *coherent* among each other ; and it is also true that if there are several coherent systems his choice of the " true " one is solely determined by " the scientists of his culture circle "[1]; he has no other canon because they furnish the " protocol statements " which he uses as his material without submitting them to an experimental test. It is true, therefore, that the system of protocol statements which he calls " true " is " the system which is actually adopted by mankind ".

But the matter is different for the experimenting observer and for unrelenting empiricists like myself. It is one thing to ask how the system of science has been built up and why it is generally believed to be true, and another thing to ask why I myself (the individual observer) accept it as true. You may regard my article on " Das Fundament der Erkenntnis " as an attempt to answer the last question. It is a psychological question. If anyone should tell me that I believe in the truth of science ultimately because it has been adopted " by the scientists of my culture circle ", I should—smile at him. I do have trust in those good fellows, but that is only because I always found them to be trustworthy wherever I was able to test their enunciations. I assure you most emphatically that I should *not* call the system of

[1] *Ibid.* p. 57.

science true if I found its consequences incompatible with my own observations of nature, and the fact that it is adopted by the whole of mankind and taught in all the universities would make no impression on me. If all the scientists in the world told me that under certain experimental conditions I must see three black spots, and if under those conditions I saw only one spot, no power in the universe could induce me to think that the statement " there is now only one black spot in the field of vision " is false.

In other words : the *only ultimate* reason why I accept any proposition as true is to be found in those simple experiences which may be regarded as the final steps of a comparison between a statement and a fact and which I have spoken of as " Konstatie-rungen "—without attaching any importance to the word. One can perhaps give a better description of them than I have done, but no one can convince me that they are not the only ultimate basis of all my beliefs.

## THE CRITERION OF TRUTH

### By A. J. AYER

IN opposition to the physicalists, Professor Schlick maintains that the truth of a system of synthetic propositions does not consist merely in the freedom of the system from self-contra-diction, but rather in its agreement with reality. Is there any sense in which we can accept this? I propose in this article to show that there is. And if we do accept this, have we then any ground for asserting, as Schlick does, that there is a class of synthetic propositions which are absolutely indubitable and thereby form the completely solid basis of all our empirical knowledge? I propose to show that we have not.

The first point that I want to establish is one that Ramsey expressed by saying that " there is really no separate problem of truth but merely a linguistic muddle ".[1] For if we consider any sentence in which there is a reference to truth, we invariably find either that it is itself of the form "*p* is true ", or else that it

[1] *Foundations of Mathematics* : ' Facts and Propositions ', pp. 142–3.

contains a sub-sentence of the form "$p$ is true", and that when it is translated in such a way as to make this sub-sentence explicit it contains no other mention of truth. Thus the sentences "all the propositions in Ramsey's article are true" and "he has discovered a new truth", to take two examples at random, are equivalent respectively to "for all $p$, if $p$ occurs in Ramsey's article, then $p$ is true" and "there is a $p$ such that he was the first to discover $p$ and $p$ is true". This indicates that to ask What is truth? is tantamount to asking What is the analysis of the sentence "$p$ is true"? where the values of $p$ are propositions. But it is evident that in a sentence of the form "$p$ is true" or "It is true that $p$" the reference to truth never adds anything to the sense. If I say that it is true that Shakespeare wrote *Hamlet*, or that the proposition "Shakespeare wrote *Hamlet*" is true, I am saying no more than that Shakespeare wrote *Hamlet*. Similarly, if I say that it is false that Shakespeare wrote the *Iliad*, I am saying no more than that Shakespeare did not write the *Iliad*. And this shows that the words 'true' and 'false' are not used to stand for anything, but function in the sentence merely as assertion and negation signs. That is to say, *truth* and *falsehood* are not genuine concepts. Consequently, there can be no logical problem concerning the nature of truth.[1]

Must we then regard all 'theories of truth' as attempts to answer a fictitious question, and so as nonsense? No, we may regard them as attempts to answer the genuine empirical question How are propositions actually validated? So that when Professor Schlick says that the truth of a synthetic proposition consists in its agreement with reality, and not merely in its logical compatibility with other propositions, we may assume that he is attempting to show what is the criterion that people actually apply to their beliefs. In this view, what he is saying is that, as a matter of fact, we are not prepared to accept a system of synthetic propositions as valid merely on the ground of its logical self-consistency, but require also that it should agree with reality. Can we accept this as a correct account of our procedure? I think we can, if we give a suitable interpretation to the objectionably vague expression 'agreement with reality'.

---

[1] This argument is set forth at greater length in ch. 5 of my 'Language, Truth, and Logic,' [1st. edition, London 1936.]

To begin with, we must make it clear that when we say that people test the validity of synthetic propositions by seeing if they agree with reality, we do not mean that they test their validity by comparing them, as physical objects, with other physical objects. I do not say that such a comparison is not legitimate, though I myself should distinguish propositions from the sentences which express them, and speak only of the sentences as physical objects ; but it is surely irrelevant to the subject under discussion. The fact that it is significant to say, for example, that there are more words in a given sentence than there are chairs in a given room, has no connection that I can see with the question How are propositions validated? Yet it is only in this sense that propositions can be said to be literally comparable with reality. Accordingly, if we are to say that the condition which we expect synthetic propositions to satisfy is that of agreement with reality, we must make it clear that by 'agreement' we do not mean 'resemblance'.

The word 'reality' is also misleading. We may concede to Dr. Hempel that it is often used in a metaphysical way, and had therefore better be avoided. But in the usage with which we are now concerned, it is not metaphysical. For it refers to nothing more than our own sensations. And when we say of a proposition that it 'agrees with reality' all that we mean, in this usage, is that our sensations are what the proposition in question said they would be. For every synthetic proposition may be regarded as asserting that certain sensations would occur in a given set of circumstances. And if, in a given case, the relevant conditions are fulfilled, and the sensations do occur, then, in Professor Schlick's terminology, the proposition is found to agree with reality. And we are taking it to be his contention that the criterion by which we all actually test the validity of synthetic propositions is their agreement with reality, in this sense.

As thus interpreted, Professor Schlick's view is surely intelligible, and I should say that it was correct. That is, I agree with him that people will accept a synthetic proposition as valid only if it conforms to their experience, in the sense just indicated, or they have reason to believe that it would do so. And I do not dispute what he says about our readiness to uphold the verdict of our own observations against the statements of other people, and about the feelings of pleasure which attend the verification of a hypothesis. But I think it should be emphasised that all these are contingent facts. There might very well be people who suffered great pain whenever their observations substantiated one of their hypotheses, and immediately abandoned it; and conversely there might be people who became extremely elated whenever their observations confuted one of their hypotheses, and immediately assumed it to have been substantiated. I do not say that such people exist; but I do say that their existence is not unthinkable. And therefore, while we may accept what Professor Schlick says as an accurate account of the procedure which we actually employ in connection with the validation of synthetic propositions, we must not assume that no other procedure is possible.

Unhappily, Professor Schlick in his defence of empiricism is not content with showing that the criterion by which we test the validity of empirical propositions is their accordance with our observations. He adds that the propositions which describe our immediate observations are absolutely indubitable. And here I am unable to follow him. For one thing, I find it very difficult to see what Professor Schlick and his followers really mean to assert when they say that propositions which record direct observations are ' certain ' or ' indubitable ' or ' unalterable '. Presumably, they are not referring to our subjective attitude towards these propositions. They are not merely saying that we are absolutely confident of the truth of these propositions, directly they are formulated, and never bring ourselves to doubt them. At least if they do intend to assert this, it is not all that they intend to assert when they say that propositions recording direct observations are indubitable. They apparently mean also to assert that these propositions are *objectively* certain. But the only sense which I can attach to the statement that a given proposition is objectively certain is that it is such that its contradictory is self-contradictory. Yet if we consider propositions such as " this is green " or " I feel pain " which are given us as examples of propositions recording direct observations, we do not find that they are objectively certain in this sense. " This is not green " is not self-contradictory. What does seem to me self-contradictory is to maintain that a synthetic proposition can be valid in virtue of its form alone. For this is surely the characteristic mark of an analytic proposition.

To this I suppose that Professor Schlick would reply that he never suggested that a proposition such as " I am in pain " or " this is green " was valid in virtue of its form alone, or that it could not legitimately be contradicted. All that he maintained, he would say, was that *at the moment at which I was actually having a sensation of pain, or of green*, the proposition " this is green " or " I am in pain ", which I might use to describe my immediate sensations would be absolutely, ' objectively,' certain. But here we must distinguish between two propositions one of which is false and the other true, but trivial. It is true to say that it is ' objectively ' certain that when I am feeling pain then I am indeed feeling pain. For this is to say no more than that it is objectively certain that $p$ implies $p$. But it is false to say that when I am feeling pain, then the proposition that I am feeling pain is objectively certain. For this is a special case of the proposition '$p$ implies that ($p$ is objectively certain).' And this proposition is false when, as is the case here, $p$ is a synthetic proposition. I can not help thinking that Professor Schlick and his followers have been guilty of confusing these two propositions, and have come to believe the second only because they mistook it for the first.

That Professor Schlick is himself uneasy about his own view is indicated by his vagueness concerning the nature of his ' Konstatierungen ', which he supposes to be absolutely indubitable. He speak of them as propositions, yet he says that they are not to be identified with anything that can be expressed, which suggests that he is thinking of the actual sensations, as opposed to the propositions which describe them. But here we may present him with a dilemma. If by ' Konstatierungen ' he means actual sensations, then it is nonsensical to say that they either are or are not indubitable. For a sensation is not the sort of thing that can be doubtful, or not doubtful. It simply occurs. If on the other hand he means by ' Konstatierungen ' the propositions which we use to describe our sensations, then we have shown that these propositions are not ' objectively certain ', in the only sense which we are able to attach to this expression.

# TRUTH AND SIGNIFICANCE

## By C. LEWY

I WANT to discuss in this paper an alleged paradox involving the word ' true ', which has recently been suggested by Professor W. V. Quine. In the course of a review of E. J. Nelson's article in *Mind* on " Contradiction and the Presupposition of Existence ", Quine says,[1] "At the beginning of the discussion I showed that there is no need to allow inference of ' *a* exists ' from ' *fa* ' and from ' ~*fa* '. Now there is a curious line of thought, tangent at that point, which merits passing mention in conclusion. Viz. : Even if ' *a* exists ' cannot be inferred from ' *fa* ' and from ' ~*fa* ', still ' ' *a* ' is meaningful ' can, and doesn't this revive the original problem in another form? " (The original problem, which I shall not discuss here, was briefly whether the singular propositions *fa* and ~*fa* are contradictories. Langford has argued that they are not ; for both of them entail ($\exists x$). *fx* $\lor$ ~*fx* and " *a* exists ", which are not logically necessary). Quine goes on, " One possible rejoinder is that ' ' *a* ' is meaningful ', if true, is analytic, so that ' *fa* ' and ' ~*fa* ' can still be contradictories ; but before resting content with this rejoinder I should like to see a satisfactory analysis of meaningfulness. Another possible rejoinder is that ' ' *a* ' is meaningful ' cannot be inferred from ' *fa* ', but only from ' ' *fa* ' is meaningful '. But then there is the counter-rejoinder that ' ' *fa* ' is meaningful ' follows from ' ' *fa* ' is true ', and ' ' *fa* ' is true ' follows from ' *fa* '. Paradoxes involving the word ' true ', however, are no novelty." I think it will be agreed that we should not rest content with another paradox involving the word ' true ', however common such paradoxes may be. And I want to show that in fact, if certain important distinctions are not overlooked, no " paradox " will arise.

In order to avoid a number of points which would unnecessarily complicate the main issue, let us consider the suggested paradox in a somewhat modified form. Take the proposition (1) " Vienna is large ". I think Quine might suggest that (1) entails (2) " The word ' ' large' is meaningful ", and that (2) is also entailed by (1A) " It is not the case that Vienna is large ".

[1] *The Journal of Symbolic Logic*, Vol. 12, No. 2, (June 1947), p. 55.

But since (1) and (1A) seem to be contradictories, we should have to suppose that (2) is analytic. I think, however, that it is quite certain that neither (1) nor (1A) does entail (2). For the sake of brevity, let us leave out (1A), and consider (1) and (2) only. The suggestion then is that (1) entails (2). But now (1) is the same proposition as the proposition (1') " Wien ist gross " ; hence (1) cannot entail (2), unless (1') entails (2). It is quite obvious, however, that (1') does not entail (2) : it is quite obvious that (1') entails nothing whatever about the English word ' large '. It follows that (1) does not entail (2) either. And of course, since (1) entails nothing whatever about the German word ' gross ', neither does (1')). I think this is one way of showing, quite conclusively, that (1) does not entail (2) ; I believe this can also be shown in other ways, which are equally conclusive ; but it would be superfluous to attempt to do so here. Further, it is also quite obvious that (2) is not analytic, or, as Quine sometimes says, " logically true ". For in order to find out whether (2) is true or false, one would obviously have to conduct some sort of empirical enquiry (*e.g.*, one might look up an English dictionary) : one could not possibly find this out by logical considerations alone. This again is only *one* way of showing that (2) is contingent, but I think there is no need to mention others. (It may be worth while, however, to ask simply whether the denial of (2) is self-contradictory. I see no way of deducing a contradiction from the proposition " The word ' large ' is not meaningful "). I think, therefore, that we can say, quite safely, that any analysis of meaningfulness on which (2) was analytic could be immediately dismissed as incorrect.

I have been trying to show that (**1**) does not entail (2). And this leads naturally to what Quine would regard as " another possible rejoinder ", namely, that (2) is not entailed by (1), but only by (3) " The sentence ' Vienna is large ' is meaningful ". And to this we must, I think, agree : the proposition, " The sentence ' Vienna is large ' is meaningful, but the word ' large ' is meaningless ", does seem to me to be self-contradictory. But now the next rejoinder would be that (3) is entailed by (4) " ' Vienna is large ' is true " ; and since (4) is entailed by (1), it follows that (2) is entailed by (1). And this is precisely what I have claimed to be certainly false. Is it true, however, that (3) is entailed by (4)? And is it true that (4) is entailed by (1)? It seems to me that we can so use the *sentence* (a) " ' Vienna is large ' is true ", that the proposition expressed by it *is* entailed by (1). But if we do so use it, then the proposition expressed by it does *not* entail (3). On the other hand, we can use the sentence (a), and use it just as correctly, in such a way that the proposition expressed by it does entail (3) ; but then the proposition expressed by it is not entailed by (1). This seems to me to be a point of some importance in other connexions as well, and I should like to explain it more fully. One way of using the sentence (a), and using it correctly, is such that the proposition expressed by it, when it is used in this way, can also be correctly expressed by using the sentence (b) " The proposition that Vienna is large is true ", or the sentence (c) " It is true that Vienna is large ". But if (a) is used in this way, then the proposition expressed by it does not entail (3) : for the proposition expressed by (b) or by (c) certainly does not entail (3). If we were to translate (b) or (c) into German, we should have to translate the words " Vienna is large " as well as the remaining words : and since the proposition expressed by the German sentence which we should thus get clearly does not entail (3), neither does the proposition expressed by (a), when (a) is so used that it expresses the same proposition as that which is expressed by (b) or (c).

It is, I think, worth while to point out that the fact that (a) can correctly be used in this way has an important consequence. It shows that it is simply false to maintain that whenever we use the expression " ' Vienna is large ' ", we are always saying something about the sentence " Vienna is large " : for in (a) we do use the expression " ' Vienna is large ' ", and yet we can so use (a) that the proposition expressed by it entails nothing whatever about the sentence " Vienna is large ".

But now (a) can also be used, equally correctly, in another way: it can be so used that the proposition expressed by it does entail (3). For (a) can be so used that the proposition expressed by it, when it is used in this way, can also be expressed, just as correctly, by the sentence (d) " The proposition expressed by the sentence ' Vienna is large ' is true ". And the proposition expressed by (d) does entail that the sentence " Vienna is large " is meaningful. But if (a) is used in *this* way, then the proposition expressed by it is not entailed by (1). What does entail the proposition expressed by (a), when (a) is used in this way, is not (1) alone, but the conjunction of (1) and (1B) " The proposition expressed by the sentence ' Vienna is large ' is the proposition that Vienna is large ". And (1B) is a *contingent* proposition : for the sentence " Vienna is large " might have expressed the proposition that Vienna is ugly. Whether it does or not can only be established by an empirical inquiry. But if the sentence " Vienna is large " did express the proposition that Vienna is ugly, and hence if (1B) were false, then the proposition (1) would have been true, and yet the proposition expressed by (a), when (a) is used in the way in question, would have been false.

Now it may be said that the sentence (d) can also be used in such a way that the proposition expressed by it entails (1B). And hence it may be said that the sentence (a) can be used in this way too. But in this case the proposition expressed by (a) would still not be entailed by (1), though it would, of course, entail (1). Similarly, if there is a use of the sentence (b) in which the proposition expressed by it entails (1B), then the proposition expressed by (b), when (b) is used in this way, does entail (3) ; but then it is not entailed by (1). The crucial point is, however, that there is *no* correct use of (a) in which the proposition expressed by it both entails (3) and is entailed by (1). Hence, the suggested paradox does not arise.

## THE SEMANTIC DEFINITION OF TRUTH

### By Max Black

### 1. Introduction

I was led to write this paper by a suspicion that others, too, had found it hard to understand the significance of the so-called " semantic " definition of truth constructed by Professor Alfred Tarski.[1] Part of the trouble is due to the fact that Tarski defines the term ' true in *L* ', where *L* is one of a number of *artificial* languages of relatively simple structure. His definition is complex.

[1] The basic source is Tarski's famous essay, " Der Wahrheitsbegriff in den formalisierten Sprachen ", *Studia Philosophica*, vol. 1, 261–405 (Lwów, 1935). This is a German translation of a Polish work published in 1933. A more popular outline, containing replies to criticism, is the same author's " The semantic conception of truth ", *Philosophy and Phenomenological Research*, vol. 4 (1944), 341–375. I shall refer to these works as *WFS* and *SCT*, respectively.

But when its technicalities have been mastered, one is left wondering how far the definition could be adapted to "ordinary" English or any other "natural" language. And one may wonder how far the results illuminate the "*philosophical* problem of truth".[1]

I shall try to describe, as simply as possible, the distinctive features of Tarski's procedure. Then I shall consider what modifications are needed if a similar definition of truth is to be framed for a *natural* language ("ordinary English") and I will end with some critical remarks about the philosophical significance of the semantic definition.

## 2.  THE NEED FOR SEMANTICAL TYPES

One feature of Tarski's procedure which we must be careful to imitate is a rigorous observance of the distinction between an "object-" and a "meta-" language. The need for this, or an equivalent, is easily shown by an argument making use of the following figure :

> The statement printed within a rectangle on
> this page is false.

To save tiresome verbiage, let ' *c* ' be agreed to be an abbreviation for the words, ' The statement printed within a rectangle on this page '. If the reader will consider the meaning of ' *c* ' and then *examine this page*, he should be led to accept :

(1) *c* is identical with the statement ' *c* is false '.

On the other hand, it seems hardly possible to deny :

(2) ' *c* is false' is true if and only if *c* is false.

From (1) and (2) there follows[2] :

(3) *c* is true if and only if *c* is false.

---

[1] Tarski himself claims *philosophical* significance for his work : " Its central problem—construction of a definition of a true statement (*Aussage*) and establishment of the scientific foundations of the theory of truth—belongs to the domain of theory of knowledge, and is even reckoned as one of the main problems of this branch of philosophy. So I hope that this work will interest epistemologists (*Erkenntnistheoretiker*) and that they will be in a position to analyze critically the results contained therein, and use them for further research in this field . . . " ((*WFS*, 392, translated).

[2] (2) has the form $k$ is true $\equiv l$ ; (1) has the form $m = k$ ; substitution of $m$ for $k$ in (2) yields (3).

which is a self-contradiction. From an empirical truth, (1), and a statement apparently true by definition, (2), a contradiction has been deduced.[1]

This paradox arises through ambiguous use of the term ' statement ' and may be resolved by introducing an appropriate distinction. If statements containing the term ' true ' or ' false ' are systematically labelled " secondary ", to distinguish them from the " *primary* " statements, from which those terms are absent, no paradox will arise. For the rectangle on this page must now be supposed to contain the words, ' The *primary* statement printed within a rectangle on this page is false ', which themselves constitute a *secondary* statement, say *s*. Since no primary statement is in fact printed within the rectangle, it is easily seen that *s* is false,[2] but not self-contradictory.

Similar puzzles can be constructed by using such " semantic " terms as ' designates ' or ' name of '. A general distinction between object- and meta-language will prevent any of them from occurring. A further precaution is an injunction against the admission of such semantic words as primitive or undefined terms ; it is a major task of semantics, in Tarski's programme, to provide clear *definitions* of these suspects.

How this is to be done in the case of ' truth ', I shall soon illustrate by means of an example (section 4 below).

## 3. THE CENTRAL IDEA OF TARSKI'S METHOD

The ideas which guide Tarski's search for a semantic definition of truth are deceptively simple : (i) He decides to interpret ' true ' as a predicate of object-language *sentences* (so that a sentence of the form ' *s* is true ' belongs to the *meta*-language). (ii) He tries to construct a definition of ' true ' of which the following will be consequences :

| | | |
|---|---|---|
| ' Today is Monday ' is true | $\equiv$ | Today is Monday,[3] |
| ' London is a city ' is true | $\equiv$ | London is a city, |
| ' Tom loves Mary ' is true | $\equiv$ | Tom loves Mary, |

and so on

[1] This version of the Epimenides paradox is attributed to J. Lukasiewicz (cf. *WFS*, 270).

[2] Assuming Russell's analysis of the definite description, " *the* so-and-so ".

[3] Here ' $\equiv$ ' is the sign of logical equivalence, synonymous with ' if and only if '.

The enumeration of instances is deliberate ; for it is impossible to give an adequate formal translation of the words ' and so on '. In order to see the point of Tarski's work, it is essential to understand why this is so.

The natural way to generalise the condition (ii) above would be to say :

($\Theta$) For all $x$, if $x$ is a sentence, then ' $x$ ' is true $\equiv x$.

But this formula is easily seen to be nonsensical. According to the usual conventions for quotation marks, the symbol occurring immediately after the word ' then ' (in $\Theta$) refers to *a constant*, *not a variable*. In fact, ' $x$ ' is the twenty-fourth *letter* of the alphabet, and not even a sentence. Thus to say " ' $x$ ' is true " is as non-sensical as to say " Tom is true ".[1]

We might try to replace $\Theta$ by some such formula as :

For all $x$ and $y$, if $x$ is a sentence and $y$ uniquely designates $x$, then $y$ is true $\equiv x$.

But this does not belong to the *meta*-language, in which we wish the definition of ' true ' to be formulated : it is a sentence of the *meta-meta*-language.[2] And the undefined semantic term, ' uniquely designates', is no less problematic than the term ' true ' which is to be defined.

In default of a *simple* definition expressing the intent of condition (ii) above, the best we can do is to write a *schema* :

(S)                    $s$ is true $\equiv x$.

We may say, informally and inexactly, that an acceptable definition of ' true ' must be such that every sentence obtained from **S** by replacing ' $x$ ' by an object-sentence and ' $s$ ' by a name or definite description of that object-sentence shall be true. But we must remember that to talk in this way is equivalent to paraphrasing the unacceptable formula $\Theta$. At all events, **S** is *not* a definition of truth, but at best a criterion to guide us in the search for a definition.[3]

---

[1] For reasons against interpreting ' ' $x$ ' ' as the name of a variable sentence, see *WFS*, 274–6.

[2] It refers to " primary " and " secondary " terms, and must itself, therefore contain *tertiary* terms.

[3] This point, made emphatically in both *WFS* and *SCT*, has been overlooked by many critics. Wrongly assuming **S** or some equivalent to be the proposed definition, they remain understandably puzzled by the pointlessness of the further manoeuvres

As the simplified language now to be described will illustrate, Tarski's definition of truth has quite a different form from that of the schema, **S**.

## 4. AN ILLUSTRATIVE MODEL[1]

We suppose our object-language, **L**, to contain the following vocabulary :

$$\text{' a ' ' b '} \qquad \text{' r ' ' s '} \qquad \text{' } p \text{ ' ' } n \text{ '}$$

The first four of these symbols are to be understood as respectively synonymous with ' the Amazon ', ' the Baltic ', ' is a river ', and ' is a sea '; ' $p$ ' is the sign of a logical product, ' $n$ ' the sign of negation.

As illustrations of *sentences* of **L** we take ' ra ', ' $n$sb ', and ' $n$prasb '. These mean the same as ' the Amazon is a river ', ' the Baltic is not a sea ', and ' it is not the case that the Amazon is a river and also the Baltic is a sea '.

The meta-language, **M**, in which we talk about signs belonging to **L**, includes (i) all signs belonging to **L**, (ii) the signs 'A' ' B ', ' R ', ' S ', ' $P$ ', ' $N$ ', which are names for ' a ', ' b ', ' r ', ' s ', ' $p$ ', ' $n$ ', respectively, (iii) a convention stipulating that ' RA ' shall be a name for ' ra ', ' NRA ' a name for ' $n$ra ', and so on,[2] (iv) the usual symbols of the logical operations, ' $\sim$ ', ' $\vee$ ', ' $(x)$ ', ' $=$ ', etc.

The definition of ' true in **L** ' proceeds in two stages. First we define ' sentence in **L** ' or, as we shall say for short—' Sentence ' (a term belonging to **M**, of course).

Using English, rather than **M**, as our meta-language, we can say informally that a sign, u, (belonging to **L**) is a Sentence if and only if one of the following three conditions is satisfied :

(i) u is ' ra ' or ' rb ' or ' sa ' or ' sb ',

(ii) u is a sign composed of a Sentence preceded by ' $n$ ',

(iii) u is a sign composed of a Sentence preceded by a Sentence preceded by ' $p$ '.

---

[1] Another helpful model may be found on p. 154 of M. Kokoszynká's illuminating paper, " Uber den absoluten Wahrheitsbegriff und einige andere semantische Begriffe ", *Erkenntnis*, vol. 6 (1936), 143–165.

[2] In a formal presentation, this vague description would have to be replaced by formal rules for the " concatenation " of symbols belonging to **M**.

The formal definition, expressed in **M**, will be :

u $\epsilon$ Sentence = $_{Df}$

$\{[(u = RA) \lor (u = RB) \lor (u' = SA) \lor (u = SB)]$
$\lor [(\exists v)(v \ \epsilon \ \text{Sentence} \ . \ u = Nv)]$
$\lor [(\exists v)(\exists w)(v \ \epsilon \ \text{Sentence} \ . \ w \ \epsilon \ \text{Sentence} \ . \ u = Pvw)]\}.$

This is a " recursive " definition : it supplies us with a means of deciding in a finite number of steps whether any given formula belonging to **L** is or is not a sentence.[1]

Now we supply a definition of ' true in **L** '. Informally, using English again as a meta-language, we may say that a sign, u, (belonging to **L**) is True provided that u is a Sentence (as previously defined) and, in addition, one of the following three conditions is satisfied :

(i) (u is ' ra ' and ra is the case) or (u is ' rb ' and rb is the case) or (u is ' sa ' and sa is the case) or (u is ' sb ' and sb is the case),

(ii) u has the form ' *nv* ' and v is *not* True,

(iii) u has the form '*pvw* ' and both v and w are True.

The formal definition, expressed in **M**, is :

u $\epsilon$ True = $_{Df}$

(u $\epsilon$ Sentence) &
$\{[u = RA \ . \ ra) \lor (u = RB \ . \ rb) \lor (u = SA \ . \ sa) \lor (u = SB \ . \ sb)$
$\lor [(\exists v)(u = Nv \ . \ \sim(v \ \epsilon \ \text{True}))$
$\lor [(\exists v)(\exists w)(u = Pvw \ . \ v \ \epsilon \ \text{True} \ . \ w \ \epsilon \ \text{True})]\}.$

Even in this highly simplified model, the definition of ' True ' has a formidable appearance. Yet its central notion is easy enough to grasp. Our object-language, **L**, has an infinity of sentences belonging to it, all of which, however, are constructed in a particularly simple fashion out of the four simplest sentences, RA, RB, SA, and SB, either by prefixing $N$ to a given sentence, or by prefixing $P$ to the combination of two given sentences. In the case of the simplest sentences, ' RA $\epsilon$ True ' is defined to be equivalent to ' ra ' (' The Amazon is a river ' is true if and

---

[1] Thus suppose the formula is PRANRB. Clause (iii), or its formal equivalent, reduces the question whether this is a Sentence to the question whether both RA and NRB are Sentences. Clause (i) shows RA to be a Sentence, while clause (ii) shows NRB to be a Sentence if RB is one, which clause (i) again guarantees. Thns PRANRB *is* a Sentence.

only if the Amazon is a river) and similarly for the other three simplest cases ; while the more complex cases are reducible to the simpler ones, by means of the recursive definition provided.

An example may help to make this clearer. We wish to determine whether $PRANRB$ is true. We already know $PRANRB$ to be a sentence (see footnote above). The third clause of the definition requires us to determine whether *both* RA and $NRB$ are true. According to the first clause, RA is true if and only if ra ; and according to the second and first clauses, $NRB$ is true if and only if $\sim$rb. Now our *geographical knowledge* entitles us to affirm both ' ra ' and ' $n$rb ' (the Amazon *is* a river and the Baltic is *not* a river). Thus we may affirm that $PRANRB$ is true.

In all cases the procedure will be similar. A given complex sentence of L will either have the form '$n$ (. . .)' or the form '$p$ (. . .) (- - -)'. If the first, we shall need to inquire whether '(. . .)' is *not* true ; if the second, whether *both* '(. . .)' and '(- - -)' are true. In either case the problem has been reduced to that of the truth of simpler sentences.

It will be noticed that ' $PRANRB$ ' is the name of the sentence, '$pranrb$' ; and that the criterion of the truth of $PRANRB$ is explicitly expressed by '$pranrb$'. A similar situation will arise in general, *though we are not allowed to say so*. We can " see " that the test of the assertion " $NRB$ is true " is expressed by ' $n$rb ' ; the test of " $PSASB$ is true " is expressed by ' $p$sasb ' ; and so on.[1] But every attempt to *say* this leads back to the illegitimate formula, $\Theta$, rejected in section 3 above.

It is not hard to see the relation between our definition of ' true in **L** ', and the schema (**S**) of page 248 above. The *technical* interest of the definition arises from its success in, as it were, generalizing the particular instances of this schema. And we can now see how this was done. In place of the futile attempt to treat ' ' $x$ ' ' in

$$' x ' \text{ is true} \equiv x$$

as a variable, we achieved the desired end by *enumerating* the

[1] In our special case, we might even formulate a maximum of procedure : To test a statement of the form ' . . . is true ' where ' . . . ' is wholly composed of capital letters, test the statement ' - - - ', derived from ' . . . ' by substituting the corresponding small letters. This maxim, however, is subject to the criticisms explained in section 3. If we formulate the maxim explicitly, we get a statement similar to $\Theta$ or S.

criteria in the simplest cases, to which all the more complex cases were made reducible.

## 5. TECHNICAL APPLICATIONS OF TARSKI'S DEFINITION

The model I have used differs from the simplest case discussed by Tarski in the following respects. His simplest object-language contains an infinite number of variables (where **L** contains none), no individual constants (where **L** contains ' a ' and ' b '), no predicates with a single argument (while **L** contains ' r ' and ' s '), a single two-termed relation of inclusion (none in **L**) and a universal quantifier (none in **L**). Where **L** consists only of trivial combinations of four trivial statements, Tarski's first object-language is already sufficiently " rich " to express a general theory of class relationships.[1]

To those interested in the formal aspect of such studies, the most interesting of Tarski's results concern the conditions in which a definition of truth of the type he desires (*i.e.* conforming to schema **S** above) is possible. It appears that the meta-language used must be " essentially richer " than the object language (*i.e.* roughly speaking, must contain variables of higher logical types). And if this condition cannot be fulfilled (as in the common cases where the object language contains an infinity of logical types), an *explicit* definition of truth in the meta-language becomes impossible.[2]

An important by-product of Tarski's work is a method for demonstrating the undecidability of certain propositions in " sufficiently rich " deductive systems.[3]

The technical interest of Tarski's work, however, is independent of its philosophical significance. Indeed it seems to me that if he had replaced ' true ', throughout his formal studies, by ' T ', ' X ', or another arbitrarily chosen symbol, his important

---

[1] This higher complexity of the object-language calls for the use of ingenious special devices in order to formulate a recursive definition of truth. Thus Tarski first defines the notion of " satisfaction " of a sentential *function*, reaching the definition of truth of a sentence only indirectly. For the definition, see *WFS*, 303–16 ; for an explanation of the need of the detour, see *SCT*, 363.

[2] The best we can then do is to introduce ' true ' as an undefined term by means of axioms.

[3] This provides a method of investigating the " completeness " of deductive systems, alternative to the well known methods used in proving Gödel's Theorem. Cf. A. Tarski, " On undecidable statements in enlarged systems of logic and the concepts of truth ", *The Journal of Symbolic Logic*, vol. 4 (1939), 105–112.

results regarding the consistency and completeness of deductive systems would have followed just as well. The question of the adequacy of his work as " philosophical reconstruction " of the pre-analytical notion of truth is quite distinct from that of the value of his contributions to the exact study of formal deductive systems.

## 6. Can Tarski's procedure be applied to " ordinary language "?

Tarski's definitions of truth are formulated in connection with " artificial languages ", *i.e.* generalized deductive systems of varying degrees of formal complexity. The philosophical relevance of his work will depend upon the extent to which something similar can be done for colloquial English (E say).

Bearing in mind the presence in E of the semantic paradoxes discussed in section 2 above, we must expect certain modifications to be made in E. The most important of these will be the rigorous enforcement of the object-language/meta-language distinction and the introduction of suitable typographic devices to distinguish terms belonging to the object-language ($L_E$, say) from those belonging to the meta-language ($M_E$, say). Equally obvious, in the light of our earlier discussion, will be the demand that the formation and transformation rules of $L_E$ (rules of syntax and logical deduction) be completely formalized ; and that all semantic terms such as ' true ', ' false ', ' expressing ', ' name ', and their cognates be deleted from $M_E$ (though they may be re-introduced *by definitions*). More important for our purpose are the following requirements :

(i) All the terms defined in E must be supposed replaced by their definitions, and *a complete inventory of the undefined terms of* $L_E$ *must be available.*

(ii) Every undefined term in $L_E$ must have a distinctive name in $M_E$[1] and *a complete inventory of such names must be available.*

---

[1] This could be done in various ways : We might arrange for each undefined term in $L_E$ to have a number correlated with it ; or ' catcat ' might be the name of ' cat ', ' manman ' of ' man ', and so on ; or the familiar device of quotation marks might be used. But although the names might be regularly formed in some such fashion, $M_E$ could not contain a rule to determine that they *be* so formed. It must, for instance, be a kind of logical accident that the name of a word in $L^E$ is obtained by inserting it between commas. No official notice could be taken of the structural relations between a word of $L_E$ and its name in $M_E$.

With the exception of those I have called (i) and (ii), the above conditions express obvious modifications required in *any* exact treatment of an admittedly inexact vernacular. If *all* of them could be satisfied (which there is no reason to doubt except in the case of (i) and (ii)), there would be no difficulty in principle[1] in applying Tarski's procedure, appropriately modified. As in the case of our simplified model (section 4) we should first need to *enumerate* defining conditions for *every* sentence of the form ' (...) is true ', where (' ...) ' is replaced by the name of a *primitive sentence* in $L_E$ (*i.e.* one containing no logical signs). And then we would have to formulate a recursive definition of ' true in $L_E$ ' of a kind reducing the test of '(- - -) is true ', where ' (- - -) ' is replaced by the name of a *complex* sentence of $L_E$, to the test of simpler cases.

The technical difficulties in completing this programme are of no importance here. It is the first steps—the exhaustive enumeration and designation of the primitive signs of $L_E$ (conditions (i) and (ii) above) that need careful scrutiny. For the consequences are highly paradoxical. If a single proper name, say ' Calvin Coolidge ', were omitted from our inventory, the notion of truth would not have been defined for sentences in which that name occurred. Of the sentence ' Calvin Coolidge was a president of the United States ' we could neither say that it was true, nor that it was untrue  The proper comment would be that since no reference to the name ' Calvin Coolidge ' occurred in our definition, the term ' true in $L_E$ ' had no application to the case in point. (Or we might say that ' Calvin Coolidge ' did not belong to $L_E$, as $L_E$ was defined by us.)

It might be said that the omission of a proper name already in use by speakers of the English language would merely be a symptom of carelessness in the framing of our definition. And no doubt it would. But no matter what meticulous care were taken to obtain a " complete " inventory of primitive terms in the English language, *the resulting list would become obsolete every time a new name came into use.* Every time an infant was christened, or a manuscript received a title, the inventory and, consequently, the definition of truth depending upon that inventory, would

---

[1] Except in so far as $L_E$ proved too " rich " for a definition of ' true in $L_E$ ' to be possible. Cf. section 5 above.

become inaccurate. The " open " character of a natural language, as shown in the fluctuating composition of its vocabulary, defeats the attempt to apply a definition of truth based upon enumeration of simple instances. The attempt is as hopeless as would be that of setting out to define the notion of ' name ' by listing all the names that have ever been used.[1]

## 7. FURTHER CRITICISM OF THE SEMANTIC DEFINITION

Let us waive for the present the objections stated in the last section. The relativity to which I have drawn attention might, after all, prove unavoidable, so that ' truth ' would be a predicate whose definition would vary with the varying fortunes of the English language. And let it be supposed that a semantic definition of the proposed type had been offered of say ' true in the English language *as of January* 1, 1940 '.

To what extent could a competent reader of such a definition *understand* the term ' truth ' thereby defined? If he could follow the technicalities of the recursive definition supplied, he would certainly be in a position to eliminate the term ' true ' from any context in which it occurred. To this extent, then, he would be able to *use* the term correctly as intended, making the correct inferences from all asserted sentences in which it could occur. But he would surely be strongly inclined to say also something like " I understand the *principle* of the definition ". And we ourselves, to come closer home, seem to *understand* Tarski's procedure (in the fashion in which one may grasp the " point " of a mathematical proof without attending to all its details). We seem to see quite clearly that what Tarski is doing is so to define truth that *to assert that a sentence is true is logically equivalent to asserting that sentence.* And in so doing, we feel that we *understand* the definition, besides being able to apply it. But if we try

---

[1] The reader may find it a useful exercise to show in detail why the use of general linguistic predicates in $M_E$, such as ' name ', merely leads back to the formulae $\Theta$ and S of section 3 above. It seems, indeed, that the extensional or enumerative character of the proposed definition is essential to it. And if this is so, we must either resign ourselves to the transitory and fluctuating nature of the " concept " of truth offered or look for some other way to define it. Since the paradoxical consequences result from the attempt to interpret ' truth ' as a property of linguistic objects (sentences), it might be worth while, after all, to try to formulate a " realist " alternative.

to *say* what we think we understand, we sin at once against the canons of syntactical propriety. The phrase " to assert that a sentence is true is logically equivalent to asserting that sentence ", which is intuitively so clear, is in fact, a crude formulation in colloquial English of the inacceptable formula Θ of section 3.

Anybody who is offered a definition of ' true in the English language as of January 1, 1940 ' must, therefore, resolutely abstain from supposing that he " understands " the principle of the definition, in the sense of being able to give an explicit definition[1] of the concept defined. If he tries to give such a formulation, he will succeed only in talking nonsense (uttering a sentence which breaks the syntactic rules of the language to which it belongs).

It might be said, in answer to this, that too much is being demanded, by implication, of a recursive definition. After all, the operation of multiplication (of integers) is defined *recursively* in arithmetic, yet nobody could reasonably complain, *on this account*, that " the concept of multiplication " is not " understood ". If we can use the multiplication sign correctly in all the contexts in which it occurs, so that we make no mistakes in calculation, we " understand " multiplication as well as it can be understood. The rest is psychology. Whether a mathematician has a subjective feeling of " grasp " or " insight " or " understanding " has nothing to do with the question of the logical adequacy of the mathematical definition.

This is all very well for the case of multiplication (and similar terms recursively defined in mathematics). Here ' multiplication ' is defined, uniquely, *once and for all*,[2] and it is sufficient that we shall be able to *use* the sign of multiplication correctly in all its possible occurrences. But the case is different for ' truth '.

If we were to insist rigorously upon the absurdity of any attempt to generalise the definition of ' true in English as of Jan. 1, 1940 ', we should have to insist also that the recursive definition had exclusive *application to the " language " in question.*

---

[1] It is possible to give an *explicit* definition of semantic terms as of other terms introduced by recursive definition. But this involves the use of variables of higher types than those occurring in the original recursive definition and does not resolve our difficulty. On this point see *WFS*, 292 (f.n. 24).

[2] When the operation of multiplication is generalised to apply to an indefinite variety of number systems the case is altered.

To the request to find *another* definition of 'true in French' or even 'true in English as of Jan. 1, 1950', the response would have to be that we had not the least notion of how to begin.

It is as if I were to " define " the term 'telephone number in New York' for a child by enumerating the telephone numbers of all those persons in New York who have telephone numbers. A moderately intelligent child would soon " spot " what I was doing. He might say " I understand : you always give the number which has been assigned by the telephone company ". But if I am to retort : " No, that has *nothing* to do with the case —attend to the definition ! " he would be helpless to extend the definition to other cases. If my admonition were intended seriously, no principle would have been given to determine the extension of the original definition : a " telephone number *in London* " might be a man's height, or his waist measurement, or *any* number associated with him.

Similarly, if we are to take the semantic definitions at their face value, we must suppose 'truth' to have been defined *only* for the cases actually discussed, with no indication at all for extension to other languages. But to pretend that this is the case is self-deception. No account of the semantic approach to the definition of truth can be regarded as satisfactory which prevents us from saying what we undoubtedly understand from the exposition of the theory.[1]

It is worth noting that the formulation of a general criterion of truth is indispensable for a direct[2] solution of the " philosophical problem of truth ". For the philosopher who is puzzled by the nature of truth wants a satisfactory *general* description of usage. To be told that such and such are *instances* of truth will not serve to assuage his thirst for generality. A philosopher who is investigating " the nature " or " the essential nature " of man, will find little assistance in the information that all American citizens are men.

---

[1] A general criterion of truth might perhaps be formulated in a meta-metalanguage (cf. *WFS* 306, f.n. 38) but it remains to be shown that this can be done without reinstating the semantic paradoxes. There is a constant temptation in the formal study of semantics to relegate important questions to a " language " whose structure has not been studied.

[2] I mean an answer *to* the question asked by the philosopher—rather than an attempt to show that the question is illegitimate and should not be asked.

## 8. THE SEMANTIC DEFINITION CONTRIBUTES NOTHING TO THE "PHILOSOPHICAL PROBLEM OF TRUTH".

The clinching argument for this conclusion is that adherents of the correspondence, the coherence, or the pragmatist, "theories" of truth will all indifferently accept the schema S of section 3 above. They would all be prepared to agree[1] that

' It is snowing to-day ' is true $\equiv$ It is snowing,

' London is a city ' is true $\equiv$ London is a city,

### and so on.

And insofar as the semantic definition of truth has such consequences as these *and no others*, the philosophical dispute stays unsettled.[2] The philosophical disputants are concerned about what *in general* entitles us to say " It is snowing " or " London is a city " *and so on*. In other words, they are searching for a general property of the designata of true object-sentences. To this inquiry, the semantic definition of truth makes no contribution.

Nevertheless, the semantic definition does suggest another *philosophical* theory of truth (though one which few philosophers would find attractive). The central idea of this adaptation consists in introducing the term ' true ' into *the object language*, by means of recursive definitions paralleling those of Tarski.[3]

We might indeed stipulate :

(1) $(s)(\text{that } s \text{ is true} = {}_{\text{Df}} s)$,[4]

(2) $(s)[\text{that} \sim s \text{ is true} = {}_{\text{Df}} \sim (\text{that } s \text{ is true})]$,

(3) $(s)\ (t)\ [\text{that } (s \ \& \ t) \text{ is true}] = {}_{\text{Df}} [(\text{that } s \text{ is true}) \ \& \ (\text{that } t \text{ is true})]$.

Further clauses of the recursive type might be added, as needed.

---

[1] Subject to certain possible qualifications, however. On certain " realist " theories of truth, it might be held that the truth of a proposition does not presuppose the existence of a sentence expressing that proposition. On this view, the sign of logical equivalence should be replaced by that of one-way entailment.

[2] I cannot accept Tarski's claim that his definition favours the " classical Aristotelian conception of truth ". I regard his view as neutral to this and all other *philosophical* theories of truth.

[3] Cf. Carnap's discussion of his " absolute " notion of truth, *Introduction to Semantics*, 90.

[4] Notice that the word ' true ' is here attached to a sentence, not to the name of a sentence. This truth must now be a property of what is designated by a sentence (perhaps a proposition?), not a property of a sentence.

On this view, the locution ' that . . . is true ' would be regarded as a linguistic device for converting an unasserted into an asserted sentence.[1] Truth would then tend to lose some of its present dignity. One might be inclined to call the word ' true ' redundant, and to baptize the theory, in the customary misleading fashion, as a " No Truth " theory. Such consequences ought not to abash us, however. For *any* defined term can be viewed as redundant, if we are prepared to suffer the practical inconvenience of dispensing with its use.[2]

We need not be afraid, either, that the proposed notion of truth would allow the reappearance of the semantical paradoxes. For we can continue to " stratify " (separate into semantic types) all terms having linguistic reference in our language. And this is enough to remove the known paradoxes.[3]

More serious is the objection that this proposal would make no provision for such expressions as " *The truth* is hard to discover ", or others in which reference to truth or falsity is made by means of *substantives*. But in this respect the proposed theory is in no worse case than that of Tarski ; and it may claim to be at least as close to common usage.

Yet I am not seriously backing a " No Truth " theory against its more orthodox competitors. My own view is that any search for a *direct* answer to the " philosophical problem of truth " can at best produce a formula that is platitudinous and tautological or arbitrary and paradoxical : and that a more hopeful method for investigating the " problem " is to dispel the confusions of thought which generate it. But this is hardly the place to elaborate upon that theme.

## 9. SUMMARY

I have illustrated the semantic method for defining ' truth ', using for this purpose a simplified, " model ", language. The occurrence in " ordinary language " of semantical paradoxes was seen to make imperative a distinction between " object-

---

[1] So that ' true ' would be an " incomplete symbol " forming a part of the " signpost ", ' ⊦ ', of Frege or Whitehead and Russell?

[2] Cf. Tarski's answer to a similar objection, *SCT*, 358-9.

[3] An unsupported assertion of this sort is not worth much. But I believe it would not be hard to show the consistency of the proposed rules for the use of ' true '.

language " and " meta-language ". This, in turn, suggested a leading notion of Tarski's method, viz. that of treating ' true ' as a predicate of object-*sentences*, definable in an appropriate *meta*-language. Examination of the steps needed to adapt the procedure to " ordinary English " brought paradoxical consequences to light. For the definition would become obsolete whenever new names were introduced into the language ; and the " point " or principle of the definition could be " seen " but apparently not *stated* without inconsistency. The semantic definition can therefore not be regarded as a satisfactory " philosophical reconstruction " of preanalytic usage. Indeed, the neutrality of Tarski's definition with respect to the competing philosophical theories of truth is sufficient to demonstrate its lack of *philosophical* relevance. His exposition does however suggest a " No Truth " theory, which was outlined ; but neither this, nor any formal definition of truth, goes to the heart of the difficulties which are at the root of the so-called philosophical problem of truth.

# TRUTH[1]

## By P. F. STRAWSON

IN the following discussion, I confine myself to the question of the truth of empirical statements. My positive thesis is an elaboration of what was said, a long time ago, by F. P. Ramsey.[2] My negative purpose is the criticism of a current misconception —the Semantic or Meta-linguistic Theory of Truth—which seems to me to repeat, in a new way, some old mistakes. In so far as this theory is simply a contribution to the construction of artificial languages, and is not intended to be regarded as relevant to the use of actual languages, I am not concerned with it. But I think the theory has been claimed by some, and it has certainly been thought by many, to throw light on the actual use of the word ' true ' ; or (which I take to be the same claim)

---

[1] [An extended and in some ways modified version of the views here maintained is to be found in the *Proceedings of the Aristotelian Society*, Supplementary Volume, 1950.]
[2] Ramsey, *Foundations of Mathematics*, pp. 142–143.

on the philosophical problem of truth. I think it *does* throw
some light; but I think it is also seriously misleading. Nothing
that follows, however, is to be taken as implying that the word
'true' is *never* used in the way described by the semantic theory.
It is certainly so used for some technical purposes, and may
sometimes be so used for non-technical purposes as well; though
I know of no such non-technical purposes.

## I

In recent discussions of truth, one or both of two theses are
commonly maintained. These are :

First, any sentence beginning 'It is true that . . .' does not
change its assertive meaning when the phrase 'It is true that'
is omitted. More generally, to say that an assertion is true is not
to make any further assertion at all; it is to make the same
assertion. This I shall call Thesis 1.

Second, to say that a statement is true is to make a statement
about a sentence of a given language, viz., the language in which
the first statement was made. It is (in other and more technical
terms) to make a statement in a meta-language ascribing the
semantic property of truth (or the semantic predicate 'true')
to a sentence in an object-language. The object-sentence concerned should strictly be written in inverted commas to make it
clear that we are talking *about the sentence* ; and the phrase 'is
true' should strictly be followed by some such phrase as 'in L',
where 'L' designates the object-language concerned. This I
shall call Thesis 2.

Of these two theses, the first is true, but inadequate ; the
second is false, but important. The first thesis is right in what
it asserts, and wrong in what it suggests. The second thesis is
wrong in what it asserts, but right in what it implies. The first
thesis is right in asserting that to say that a statement is true is
not to make a further statement ; but wrong in suggesting that
to say that a statement is true is not to do something different
from, or additional to, just making the statement. The second
thesis is right in implying that to say that a statement is true is
to do something different from just making the statement ; but
wrong in asserting that this 'something different' consists in
making a further statement, viz. a statement about a sentence.

Although both theses are sometimes maintained by the same philosopher, it is easy to see that they cannot both be correct. For if it is true that to say (1) " Moths fly by night " is to make the same assertion as to say (2) " It is true that moths fly by night ", then it is false that to say (2) is to say anything about the English sentence " Moths fly by night " ; i.e. false that (2) ought strictly to be written " ' Moths fly by night ' is true in English ". If to say (2) is to make the same assertion as to say (1), then to say (2) cannot be to say anything about an English sentence ; for to say (1) is not to say anything about an English sentence, but is to say something about moths.

Independently of this, one sees how misleading it is to say that the phrase ' . . . is true ' is used to talk *about sentences*, by comparing it with other phrases which certainly are used to talk about sentences (or words, or phrases). For example, someone says, in French, " Il pleuve " ; and someone else corrects him, saying : " ' Il pleuve ' is *incorrect* French. ' Il pleut ' is the right way of saying it ". Or, criticising the style of a passage, someone says : " The sentence ' . . . . ' is *badly expressed*." Similarly, one may ask what a sentence *means*, or say that a sentence is *ungrammatical, misspelt, a poor translation*. In all these cases, it is natural to say that one is talking *about a sentence*. If any statement of this kind were correctly translated into any language at all, the sentence which was being discussed would re-appear, quoted and untranslated, in the translation of the statement as a whole. Otherwise the translation would be incorrect. But it is perfectly obvious that a correct translation of any statement containing the phrase ' is true ' (used as it is ordinarily used) never contains a quoted and untranslated sentence to which the phrase " is true ' was *applied* in the original sentence. The phrase ' is true ' is not *applied to* sentences ; for it is not *applied* to anything.

Truth is not a property of symbols ; for it is not a property.

## II

The habit of calling truth a ' semantic ' concept (' true ' a ' semantical predicate ') does not lessen the confusion involved in saying that ' true ' is a predicate of sentences ; but it helps to

indicate a possible source of the confusion. I shall digress briefly
to explore this source. For light on the use of the word ' semantic '
I quote the following from Carnap's ' Introduction to Semantics '
(p. 22) :

> " By a *semantical system* we understand a system of rules,
> formulated in a meta-language and referring to an object-
> language, of such a kind that the rules determine a *truth-
> condition* for every sentence of the object-language. . . . To
> formulate it in another way : the rules determine the *meaning*
> or *sense* of the sentences."

It will be noticed that the expressions ' truth-condition ' and
' meaning ' are used synonymously. And this suggests that
even if there is no use of the phrase ' is true ' in which that
phrase is correctly applied to (used to talk about) sentences,
there is, or might be, a use of the phrase ' is true if and only if ',
in which *this* phrase is correctly applied to (used to talk about)
sentences ; a use, namely, in which this phrase would be synonymous with the phrase ' means that ' ; which certainly *is* used
to talk about sentences. Suppose, for example, that we wish to
give information about the meaning of the sentence " The
monarch is deceased ". We can do this by making the following
meta-statement :

(i) " The monarch is deceased " means that the king is dead.
Here we put the sentence " The monarch is deceased " in inverted commas to indicate that we are talking about this sentence.
We are making a meta-statement. And the meta-statement is
contingent, for it is a contingent matter that the sentence in
question has this meaning in English, or, indeed, that it has any
meaning at all. To be quite strict, we perhaps ought to write it :

(ia) " The monarch is deceased " in English means that the
king is dead.

If we were to translate this meta-statement into another
language, none of the expressions occurring in it would remain
unchanged except the quoted sentence " The monarch is deceased ". That would remain unchanged ; otherwise the translation would be incorrect. Now the suggestion is that we might,
without unintelligibility, give the same information in exactly
the same way, except that we should replace the phrase ' means

that' with the phrase 'is true if and only if' obtaining the contingent meta-statement :

(ii) " The monarch is deceased " is true if and only if the king is dead
or, more strictly :

(iia) " The monarch is deceased " is true in English if and only if the king is dead.

This seems to be an intelligible procedure. All that I have said of statements (i) and (ia) will apply to statements (ii) and (iia) ; we shall be using the phrase ' is true if and only ', in a contingent statement, to talk about a sentence. Now consider a degenerate case of such meta-statements : the case exemplified in the sentences :

(iii) " The monarch is deceased " means (in English) that the monarch is deceased.

(iv) " The monarch is deceased " is true (in English) if and only if the monarch is deceased.

It is difficult, and, perhaps, for the present purpose, not very important, to decide what status to assign to such sentences as these. Considerations which might tempt us to describe them firmly as true, contingent meta-statements are the following :

(a) Although they are of no use for telling us what the quoted sentence means, they do give us some information about it. They do at any rate indicate that the quoted sentence has some meaning in English.[1] And this is a contingent matter.

(b) These statements could be obtained from the non-degenerate cases by a quite legitimate process of translation, inference and retranslation. (Or, more simply, their correct translation into, say, French would undoubtedly yield a contingent meta-statement).

(c) It is a contingent matter that any sentence means what it does mean, expresses the proposition it does express.[2]

Although these considerations are decisive against calling

---

[1] One can imagine another use for statements (iii) and (iv) ; e.g. if the object-language were written, and the meta-language spoken, English.
[2] Cf. Lewy, " Truth and Significance ", this volume, p. 242.

(iii) and (iv) ' logically necessary ',[1] they are very inadequate grounds for calling them, without qualification, ' true and contingent '. For what contingent matter do they state? If we answer, taking the hint from (*a*), that they state merely that the quoted sentence has some meaning in English, then their form (the use of the expression ' means that ') is utterly misleading. If we demand what contingent matter they state, which falls under the head of (*c*), no answer is possible. One cannot *state* what a sentence means without the help of another sentence.

For these reasons, I propose to continue to refer to statements (or pseudo-statements) like (iii) and (iv) not as necessary, nor as contingent, but simply as ' degenerate cases ' of contingent meta-statements of the type of (i) and (ii). The point is not in itself important; though it is important that no confusion should arise from it.

The next step is to notice the deceptive similarity of the use of the phrase ' if and only if ' in this type of contingent meta-statement to its use in expressions which are not contingent statements, but necessary or defining formulae. An example of such a formula would be :

The monarch is deceased if and only if the king is dead.

Here the phrase ' is true ' does not occur ; and no part of this expression is in inverted commas. The formula itself does not give us information about the meaning of the sentence " The monarch is deceased ", though the statement that it *was* a necessary formula *would* give us such information. Now the similarity of the use of the phrase ' if and only if ' in these necessary formulae to its use as *part* of the phrase ' is true if and only if ' in contingent meta-statements, may have constituted a strong temptation to split the degenerate cases of such meta-statements down the

---

[1] We might be tempted to call (iii) and (iv) " necessary ", because it seems self-contradictory to say :

(iiia) " The monarch is deceased " does not mean in English that the monarch is deceased.

But this would be a mistake. To say that a sentence both has some meaning or other and has no meaning at all would be to say something self-contradictory. To say that a sentence both has and has not some particular, specified meaning would be to say something self-contradictory. But (iiia) does neither of these things. The form of (iii) is appropriate to assigning, and that of (iiia) to withholding, some specific meaning. But since (iii) does not assign, (iiia) does not withhold, any specific meaning. (iiia) is not a selfcontradictory, nor a false, contingent, statement ; but a pseudo-statement.

middle, and to regard what follows the phrase ' if and only if ' as the definiens of what precedes it, i.e. of the phrase " the sentence ' . . . . ' is true (in L) " ; to regard, for example, the whole expression (iii)

" The monarch is deceased " is true if and only if the monarch is deceased

as a specification or consequence or part[1] of a general definition of " . . . . is true " (or of " . . . is true in L "). And this we in fact find ; i.e. we find it said that a satisfactory general definition of truth must have as its consequences such expressions as the following :[2]

(v) " To-day is Monday " is true if and only if to-day is Monday.

(vi) " London is a City " is true if and only if London is a City.

Now we have seen that such statements as (v) and (vi) are degenerate cases of those contingent meta-statements of the type of (ii), which make use of the phrase ' *is true if and only if* ' as a synonym for ' *means that* '. It is only *as a part of the former phrase* that the expression ' *is true* ' is used, in such statements, to talk about sentences. To read the degenerate cases, then, as specification, or parts, of some ideal defining formula for the phrase ' is true ' is to separate the phrase from the context which alone confers this meta-linguistic use upon it, and to regard the result as a model for the general use of ' is true '. It is to be committed to the mistake of supposing that the phrase ' is true ' is normally (or strictly) used as a meta-linguistic predicate. Thus misinterpreted, as defining formulae, such expressions as (v) are both fascinating and misleading. They mislead because, as we have seen, they crystallise the false Thesis 2. They fascinate because they seem to point to the true Thesis 1 ; for part of the expression

---

[1] E.g. Tarski, in *The Semantic Conception of Truth*, ' Philosophy and Phenomenological Research ', Vol. 4, 1943-44, p. 344, says :

" Every equivalence of the form (T) [(T) X is true if and only if p] obtained by replacing ' p ' by a particular sentence and ' X ' by a name of this sentence, may be considered a partial definition of truth, which explains wherein the truth of this one individual sentence consists. The general definition has to be, in a certain sense, a logical conjunction of all these partial definitions."

[2] Cf. M. Black, expounding and criticising Tarski, this volume pp. 245-260.

to be defined (namely, the combination of quotation-marks and the phrase is ' true ') *disappears* in the definiens without being replaced by anything else. (How odd it is, incidentally, to call this definition-by-disappearance ' definition '!). In this way, the view that ' true ' is assertively redundant is represented as somehow combined with, and dependent upon, the view that ' true ' is a meta-linguistic predicate of sentences. We may express, then, the main contention of the semantic theory as follows : to say that a statement is true is not to say something further *about the subject-matter* of the statement, but is to say the same thing about the subject-matter of the statement, *by means of a further statement, namely a statement about a sentence*. Now I said that Thesis 1 is true. A fortiori, a modification of Thesis 1 is true, which I shall call Thesis 1A, and which runs as follows :

To say that a statement is true is not to say something further about the subject-matter of the statement, but, in so far as it is to say anything about that subject-matter, is to say the same thing about it.

Now Thesis 1A, but not Thesis 1, is compatible with Thesis 2. The semantic theory consists in the joint assertion of 1A and 2. I suggest that the semantic theory borrows a lot of its plausibility from the truth of 1A. We swallow 2 for the sake of 1A. I now wish to show that the unmodified thesis 1 is true, and that we therefore can and must assert 1A while rejecting 2 and, therefore, rejecting the semantic theory.

As for the muddle I have described above—the muddle of reading a degenerate case of contingent statements meta-linguistically employing the phrase *is true if and only if*, as a pseudo-defining-formula of which the definiendum consists of a quoted sentence followed by the phrase *is true*—I do not claim that this muddle represents the genesis of the semantic theory ; but I do think that it, too, may have contributed to the plausibility of the theory.

### III

The best way of showing that Thesis 1 is true is to correct its inadequacy. The best way of correcting its inadequacy is to discover the further reasons which have led to Thesis 2. To bring out those features of the situation which lead to the mistake of saying that the word ' true ' is used meta-linguistically (to talk about sentences), I want first to compare the use of ' true ' with that of ' Yes '. If you and I have been sitting together in silence for some time, and I suddenly say ' Yes ', you would, perhaps, look at me with surprise and answer " I didn't say anything ". Of course, a man may say ' Yes ' to himself; and this will be a sign that he has resolved a doubt in his own mind, or come to a decision. But the normal use of ' Yes ' is to answer : and where no question is asked, no answer can be given. Suppose you now ask : " Was Jones there? " and I say ' Yes '; there seems no temptation whatever to say that, in so answering, I am *talking about* the English sentence " Was Jones there? " So, in the case of ' Yes ', we have a word of which the normal use requires some linguistic occasion (a question), without there being any temptation at all to say that it is used to *talk about* the sentence of which the utterance is the occasion for its use. There is indeed a temptation to go further in the opposite direction and say that in answering ' Yes ' I am not talking *about* anything, not making any assertion, at all ; but simply answering. In a way this is correct ; but in a way, it's wrong. For it would be perfectly correct for you, reporting our dialogue, to say of me : " He said Jones was there ". So of the ordinary use of ' Yes ', we may say : first, that it demands a linguistic occasion, namely the asking of a question ; second, that it is not used meta-linguistically, to talk about the question, but to answer it ; third, that in so far as we are making an assertion at all in using it, the content of the assertion is the same as the content of the question. Now imagine a possible, and perhaps vulgarly current, use of the expression ' Ditto '. You make an assertion, and I say ' Ditto '. In so far as I assert anything, talk about anything, I talk about and assert what you talk about and assert. Of course—and this points to the inadequacy of Thesis 1 and the reason for the meta-linguistic error—to say ' Ditto ' is not *the same as* to make the statement in question ; for, whereas I might have made the statement before anyone else had spoken, it would be meaningless for me to say ' Ditto ' before anyone else had spoken. ' Ditto ', like ' Yes ', requires a linguistic occasion. But again, and largely, I think, because the expression ' Ditto ' does not consist of a grammatical subject and gram- matical predicate, there is absolutely no temptation to say that in thus using ' Ditto ', I should be talking *about the sentence* you used, and the utterance of which was the linguistic occasion for my use of this expression. I am not talking about what you said (the noise you made, or the sentence you spoke, or the proposition you expressed). I am agreeing with, endorsing, underwriting what you said ; and, unless you had said something, I couldn't perform *these* activities, though I could *make the assertion* you made. Now the expression ' That's true ' sometimes functions in just the way in which I have suggested the expression ' Ditto ' might function. A says " Jones was there " and B says ' That's true ' ; and C, reporting the conversation, can correctly say : " Both A and B said that Jones was there ". But the point is that B couldn't have said that Jones was there in the way he *did* say it, (i.e. by the use of the expression ' That's true '), unless A had previously uttered the *sentence* " Jones was there ", or some equivalent sentence. It is, perhaps, *this* fact about the use (*this* use) of the word ' true ', together with the old prejudice that any indicative sentence must describe (be ' about ') some-thing, which encourages those who have become chary of saying that truth is a property of propositions to say instead that in using the word ' true ', we are talking about sentences. (What I have said about the use of ' That's true ' applies, of course, with suitable alterations, to the use of ' That's false ').

Now those who assert that ' true ' is a predicate of sentences have not, in general, considered these simple cases of the use of ' true ' (and ' false '), but the more puzzling cases which lead, or seem to lead, to paradoxes : such as the case where someone utters the isolated sentence " What I am saying now is false ", or writes on an otherwise clean blackboard the sentence " Every statement on this blackboard is false ". The solution on meta-lin-guistic lines is to treat these sentences as making statements of the second order to the effect :

(1) that there is some statement of the first order written on the blackboard (or said by me now) ;

and (2) that any first-order statement written on the blackboard (or said by me now) is false.

By means of this distinction of orders, the distinction between meta- and object-language, the puzzling sentences are said no longer to engender contradictions : either they are simply false,

since the existential part of what they assert is false ; or, alternatively, leaving out the existential part of the analysis, and
treating them solely as hypotheticals, they are seen to be vacuously true, since no first-order statements occur. This solution
is formally successful in avoiding the apparent contradictions.
But it seems to me to achieve this success only by repeating the
fundamental mistake from which the contradictions themselves
arise, and also, and consequently, involving the difficulties
mentioned at the beginning of this paper. That is, first, it involves
the view that to say that a statement is true (or false) is to make a
further, second-order, statement (thus contradicting Thesis 1) ;
and, second, it (usually) involves the unplausibility of saying that
this second-order statement is *about* a sentence or sentences. Now
the point of the previous discussion of the actual use of ' Yes ',
the possible use of ' Ditto ' and the actual use of ' That's true ' is
to show that these expedients are unnecessary. When no-one has
spoken, and I say ' Ditto ', I am not making a false statement
to the effect that something true has been said, nor a true statement
to the effect that nothing false has been said. I am not making a
statement at all ; but producing a pointless utterance. When
somebody has made an assertion previously, my saying ' Ditto '
acquires a point, has an occasion : and, if you like, you may say
that I am now making a statement, repeating, in a manner,
what the speaker said. But I am not making an additional
statement, a meta-statement. It would perhaps be better to say
that my utterance is not a statement at all, but a linguistic performance for which in the first case there was not, and in the
second case there was, an occasion : so that in the first case it
was a spurious, and in the second case a genuine, performance.
Similarly, the words ' true ' and ' false ' normally require, as an
occasion for their significant use, that somebody should have
made, be making or be about to make (utter or write), some
statement. (The making of the statement needs not precede the
use of ' true ' : it may follow it as in the case of the expression
" It is true that . . . "—a form of words I shall discuss later).
But in all cases the indicative clause of which the grammatical
predicate is the phrase ' is true ' does not in itself make any kind
of statement at all (not even a meta-statement), and *a fortiori*
cannot make the statement, the making of which is required as

the occasion for the significant use of the words ' true ' or ' false '. This is not, as it stands, quite accurate. For an indicative sentence of which the grammatical predicate is the phrase ' is true ' may sometimes, as I shall shortly show, be used to make an implicit meta-statement. But when this is so, the phrase ' is true ' plays no part in the making of this meta-statement. The phrase ' is true ' *never* has a statement-making role. And when this is seen, the paradoxes vanish without the need for the meta-linguistic machinery ; or at least without the need for regarding the words ' true ' and ' false ' as part of that machinery. The paradoxes arise on the assumption that the words ' true ' and ' false ' can be used to make first-order assertions. They are formally solved by the declaration that these words can be used only to make second-order assertions. Both paradoxes and solution disappear on the more radical assumption that they are not used to make assertions of any order, are not used to make assertions at all.

I said, however, that indicative sentences of which the grammatical predicate is the phrase ' is true ' or the phrase ' is false ' may be used to make an implicit meta-statement, in the making of which these phrases themselves play no part. To elucidate this, consider the following sentences :

(1) What I am saying now is false.

(2) All statements made in English are false.

(3) What the policeman said is true.

It is certainly not incorrect to regard each of these sentences as implicitly making an *existential* meta-statement, which does not involve the words ' true ' or ' false '. The implicit meta-statements in these cases might be written as follows :

(1a) I have just made (am about to make) a statement.

(2a) Some statements are made in English.

(3a) The policeman made a statement.

These are all second-order assertive sentences to the effect that there are some first-order assertive sentences, uttered (*a*) by me, (*b*) in English, (*c*) by the policeman.

These second-order assertive sentences we can regard as part of the analysis of the sentences (1), (2) and (3).[1] Obviously they

---

[1] [I should now say, not that sentences (1a)—(3a) are parts of the analyses of sentences (1)—(3), but that any statements made by the use of sentences (1)—(3) would presuppose the truth of statements which might be made by the use of sentences (1a)—(3a).]

are not the whole of their analysis. The sentence " The policeman made a statement " clearly has not the same use as the sentence " What the policeman said is true ". To utter the second is to do something more than to assert the first. What is this additional performance? Consider the circumstances in which we might use the expression " What the policeman said is true ". Instead of using this expression, I might have *repeated* the policeman's story. In this case, I shall be said to have *confirmed* what the policeman said. I might, however, have made exactly the same set of statements as I made in repeating his story, but have made them *before* the policeman spoke. In this case, though the assertions I have made are no different, I have not done what I did in the other case, namely ' confirmed his story '. So to confirm his story is not to say anything further, *about* his story, or the sentences he used in telling it, though it is to do something that cannot be done unless he has told his story. Now, unlike the confirming narrative which I might have told, the sentence " What the policeman said is true " has no use *except* to confirm the policeman's story[1]; but like the confirming narrative, the sentence does not say anything further *about* the policeman's story or the sentences he used in telling it. It is a device for confirming the story without telling it again. So, in general, in using such expressions, we are confirming, underwriting, admitting, agreeing with, what somebody has said; but (except where we are implicitly making an existential meta-statement, in making which the phrase ' is true ' plays no part), we are not making any assertion additional to theirs; and are *never* using ' is true ' to talk *about* something which is *what they said*, or the sentences they used in saying it. To complete the analysis, then, of the entire sentence (3) " What the policeman said is true ", we have to add, to the existential meta-assertion, a phrase which is not assertive, but (if I may borrow Mr. Austin's word) performatory.[2] We might, e.g., offer, as a complete analysis of one case, the expression : " The policeman made a statement. I confirm it " ; where, in uttering the words " I confirm it ", I am not describing something I do, but

---

[1] This needs qualification. Uttered by a witness, the sentence is a *confirmation* ; wrung from the culprit, it is an *admission*. No doubt there are other cases.

[2] Cf. J. L. Austin, ' Other Minds ', P.S.A. Supp. Vol. XX, pp. 169–175 for an account of some words of this class.

*doing* something.[1] There is, then, a difference between the more complicated cases in which the phrase ' is true ' is preceded by a descriptive phrase, and the simpler sentences (e.g. ' That's true ') in which the phrase ' is true ' is preceded by a demonstrative. The former may be regarded as involving an implicit meta-statement, while the latter are purely confirmatory (or purely ' admissive '). But in neither sort of case has the phrase ' is true ' any assertive (or meta-assertive) function.

There may still be some uneasiness felt at the denial that the phrase ' is true ' has any assertive, or descriptive, function. Partially to allay this uneasiness, I will again say something familiar, that I have said already : that is, that when I say ' That's true ' in response to your statement, I am in a manner making an assertion, namely the assertion you made ; describing something, namely what you described. But pointing this out is quite consistent with saying that ' That's true ' makes no statement in its own right. It makes no meta-statement. If there is any residual uneasiness, it ought not to be allayed. For its source is the ancient prejudice that any indicative sentence is, or makes,[2] a statement. I call it a prejudice : we could, instead, make it a criterion. And there would even be no harm in adopting this criterion for ' statement ', if we could simultaneously divorce the word, in this strictly grammatical use, from its logic in other uses : from that logic which leads us, given a ' statement ', to enquire : What is it about? What does it describe? What property, or what relation, does it assert to belong to, or hold between, what entity or entities? Asking these questions when confronted with such a sentence as " What Pascal said is true ", we are led to look for the entity which is *what Pascal said* ; looking with cautious, contemporary eyes, we find only his words ; and so are induced to say that, in using this expression, we are talking about the French sentences he wrote or spoke. It is, then, the out-of-date desire that the phrase ' is true ' should be some kind of a descriptive phrase, that leads to the up-to-date suggestion that the word ' true ' is a second-level predicate of first-level sentences. More important than simply to reject *this* view is to

---

[1] Cf. also ' I admit it '. To *say* this *is* to make an admission.

[2] Throughout I have used such mild barbarisms as " This sentence makes a statement " as shorthand for such expressions as "Anyone who uttered this sentence would be making a statement ".

have the right reason for rejecting it : the reason, namely, that the phrase ' is true ' is not descriptive at all. If we persist that it describes (is about) something, while denying that it describes (is about) sentences, we shall be left with the old, general questions about the nature of, and tests for, truth, about the nature of the entities related by the truth-relation, and so on. Better than asking " What is the criterion of truth? " is to ask : " What are the grounds for agreement? "—for those we see to be not less various than the subjects on which an agreed opinion can be reached. And this will perhaps also discourage us from seeking to mark the difference between one kind of utterance and another by saying, for example, " Ethical utterances are not true or false ". It is correct to say that utterances of any kind are true or false, if it is correct usage to signify agreement or disagreement with such utterances by means of the *expressions* ' true ' or ' false '.

Of course, the formula that I have adopted in the discussion of one use of ' true ' is not immune from another variant of that argument from grammar which leads to treating ' true ' as a descriptive word. Someone might say : in order for you to *confirm* anything, there must be some *object* of this activity ; a sentence or a proposition : and to perform this activity upon this object is nothing other than to assert that the object has the property, stands in the relation, referred to by the word ' true '. Anyone who says this is misled partly by the fact that the verb ' confirm ' takes a grammatical object ; and partly by the fact that the linguistic performance (of ' confirming ') requires, not an object, but an *occasion*—a fact which I declared to be the misunderstood element of truth in the semantic theory. Even this assertion—that there must be, or be thought to be, some kind of sign-occasion for the significant, or genuine, use of the word ' true '—is not quite correct, if it means that some spoken or written utterance must occur, or be thought to occur. For it would not be incorrect, though it would be unusual, to say : " What you are thinking is true " ; when nothing has been said. (But, then, a conversation *can* be carried on by glances and nods).

## IV

In philosophical discussion of this whole subject, very little attention has been paid to the actual use of ' true '. And I want

to conclude by distinguishing some of its normal uses in a little
more detail. The uses mentioned so far I was tempted to call
' performatory '. But this is a misnomer. A performatory word,
in Austin's sense, I take to be a verb, the use of which, in the
first person present indicative, seems to describe some activity of
the speaker, but in fact *is* that activity. Clearly the use of ' is
true ' does not seem to describe any activity of the speaker ; it
*has seemed* to describe a sentence, a proposition, or statement. The
point of using Austin's word at all is the fact that the phrase ' is
true ' can sometimes be replaced,[1] without any important change
in meaning, by some such phrase as " I confirm it ", which is
performatory in the strict sense. I shall take the substitute
performatory word as a title for each of these cases ; and shall
speak, e.g., of the ' confirmatory ' or ' admissive ' use of ' true '.
What commends the word as, e.g., a confirmatory device is its
economy. By its means we can confirm without repeating.

The word has other, equally non-descriptive, uses. A familiar
one is its use in sentences which begin with the phrase " It's
true that ", followed by a clause, followed by the word ˝ but ',
followed by another clause. The words " It's true that . . . but
. . . " could, in these sentences, be replaced by the word 'Although ' ; or, alternatively, by the words " I concede that . . .
but . . ." This use of the phrase, then, is concessive. The
inappropriateness of the meta-linguistic treatment seems peculiarly
apparent here.

The purely confirmatory use is probably no more common
than other uses which look much the same, but which are, I
think, distinct. A man may make an assertion to you, not wanting
you to confirm it, to remove the doubt of others or his own ;
but wanting to know that you share his belief, or his attitude.
If, in this case, you say ' That's true ', you are not *saying*, but
*indicating*, that you do share his belief. It seems to me natural
to describe this simply as ' agreeing '. Again, it seems to me
that we very often use the phrase ' That's true ' to express, not
only agreement with what is said, but also our sense of its novelty
and force. We register the impact of what is said, much as we
might register it by saying : " I never thought of that ". Contrast
the ironical ' very true ' with which we sometimes rudely greet

[1] Of course, not *simply* replaced. Other verbal changes would be necessary.

the obvious. The use of ' true ' here is effectively ironical just because we normally use it to express agreement when our agreement is in doubt, or to register a sense of revelation. Sometimes, in sentences beginning " Is it true that . . .? " or " So it's true that . . . ", we could preserve the expressive quality of the utterance by substituting the adverb ' really ' for the quoted phrases, at an appropriate point in the sentence ; to convey, as they do, incredulity or surprise.

No doubt, the word has other functions ; but those I have mentioned are probably as common as any. The important point is that the performance of these functions (and, I suspect, of all other non-technical jobs the word may do) does not involve the use of a meta-linguistic predicate ; and that we *could*, with no very great violence to our language, perform them without the need for any expression which *seems* (as ' is true' seems) to make a statement. For instance, the substitution of ' although ' for " It's true that . . . but . . . " is an obvious way of dealing with the concessive use ; an extension of the practice of the inarticulate election-candidate whose speech consisted of " Ditto to Mr. X " might deal with the confirmatory and, partly, with the expressive uses ; and so on. The selection of the substitute-expressions would of course be governed by the propagandist consideration that they should provide the minimum encouragement to anyone anxious to mistake them for statement-making phrases, or descriptive words.

One last point : a suggestion on the reasons why the puzzle about truth has commonly got entangled with the puzzle about certainty. It is above all when a doubt has been raised, when mistakes or deceit seem possible ; when the need for confirmation is felt ; that we tend to make use of those certifying words of which ' true ' is one and of which others are ' certain ', ' know ', ' prove ', ' establish ', ' validate ', ' confirm ', ' evidence ' and so on. So that the question " What is the nature of truth? " leads naturally to the question " What are the tests for truth? ", and this, in its turn, to the question " What are the conditions of certainty? " The historical or judicial search for truth is the search for the evidence which will set doubt at rest. The philosophical endeavour to characterise truth *in general* has tended to become the endeavour to characterise that which *in general* sets doubt at rest ; really and finally at rest. Where you find the indubitable, there you find the true. And this metaphysical road branches into different paths, at the end of one of which you find the Atomic Fact, and, at the end of another, the Absolute.

Finally, I will repeat that in saying that the word ' true ' has not in itself any assertive function, I am not of course saying that a sentence like " His statement is true " is incorrect. Of course the word ' statement ' may be the grammatical subject of a sentence of which the phrase ' is true ' is the grammatical predicate. Nor am I recommending that we drop this usage. But for the usage, there would be no problem.

# CHAPTER X. ANALYSIS AND DIALECTS.

## LENIN'S THEORY OF PERCEPTION

### By G. A. Paul

" Are our sensations *copies* of bodies and things, or are bodies *complexes* of our sensations? " This for Lenin is " the fundamental question of the theory of knowledge " (p. 146), and he makes it the main topic of his book *Materialism and Empirio-Criticism*.[1] because he holds that as people differ in giving an " idealist " or a " materialist " answer to it so they will tend to differ in whether they take a reactionary or a progressive attitude to questions of practical importance. He is particularly concerned with three points :—

(1) It is established by scientists that inanimate matter was in existence before there were any living creatures at all ; and it is inconsistent with this, he holds, to suppose that bodies are complexes of our sensations. Now if people are led by their philosophy to deny a scientific fact so well attested as this one, there will be no end to their tinkering with scientific conclusions in general with a consequent loss of respect for careful examination of things as a way of finding out about them.

(2) This loss of confidence will be most felt in any field where the facts are difficult to muster and where consequently conclusions are difficult to establish. In particular it will be felt about attempts to find laws according to which changes take place in the organisation of human beings in groups—laws of a kind Lenin is anxious to find and use to alter some of the existing ways of organisation.

(3) He wishes to combat metaphysical (and in particular religious) speculation in order that people may turn rather to bettering the world about them—gaining control of it by looking for laws which it obeys, rather than spinning fancies which may persuade themselves and others that it is really other than common knowledge and science take it to be.

[1] English translation from the Russian, Martin Lawrence Ltd. I have freely italicised those parts of quotations to which I wished to draw attention, and hope that I have not in any case altered the sense by doing so.

So he tries to find the theory of knowledge nearest to common sense and giving least ground for speculative building—a theory which by showing how our knowledge is acquired will show about what things we do know and about what things we cannot know. Thus he insists that his theory of knowledge is just that contained in the simple, robust common sense of the ordinary person—the workman, the housewife, the scientist; and that it is a plain, straightforward theory in contrast with the sophisticated, finely spun fantasies of bourgeois professors. " The ' naive ' belief of mankind is consciously taken by materialism as its theory of knowledge " he says (p. 47), and later he speaks of materialism as " an inference, which all of us draw in practical life and which lies at the basis of a ' practical ' theory of knowledge " " Its fundamental belief " he goes on (p. 78) " is that *outside of* us and independently of us there exist objects, things, and bodies : that our perceptions are *images* of the outer world. The converse theorem of Mach (bodies are complexes of sensations) is nothing but sheer idealistic foolishness."

He is taking, we see, a representative theory of perception, and he claims that " in practical life ", this theory is *used* by " all of us ". The chief points of his theory are :—

(1) *Outside us* there are *material things.*
(2) They exist *independently of us.*
(3) We can get to *know* the nature of any material thing, and sometimes we do so.
(4) The *means* by which we get to know the nature of a material thing *outside* us is our having *inside* us a sense-perception which *represents*[1] the material thing.

It is not the aim of this paper to deny that these statements express a theory which gives a correct description of what and how we perceive, nor yet to agree that they do : we shall try, rather, to see whether they do play any part in ordinary life and science, and if so what it is.

Do they play, for example, the part of a simple description of how something works? Do they act as a description of how the human perceiving apparatus works? Let us compare them with

---

[1] His most common expression is that inside us we have an *image* which is a *reflection* of the thing outside.

some such simple description or theory and see how alike or different the two are. We might choose to compare them with a simple theory of how certain areas of Britain come to be so much wetter than others, how lack of sun brings about ill-health, how grain goes into a mill at one end and comes out as flour at the other, and so on; but it will be more useful to compare them with an explanation of an occurrence very similar in important respects to this one which Lenin puts forward of how people manage to see things outside themselves—so similar in fact that the two can be expressed in almost the same words. Just as Lenin asks " How do people see things outside themselves? " so we may ask " How do people see things out of submarines? " People from time to time move about some distance below the surface of the sea in an opaque container : their activities are made possible by a contrivance which enables them to look out while the container is submerged and see what is above the surface of the sea for some distance round. The nature of the contrivance needs some explanation : one may be told that they see out of a submerged submarine " by having in a mirror inside the sub-marine an image which is an accurate reflection of the things outside it ", just as Lenin would explain that we see material things outside us " by having inside us an image which is an accurate reflection of the things outside us ". We often see things by their reflections in mirrors, so we know what this is, and it has now been explained that seeing out of submarines is a case of it : we now understand, for example, that they do not see out by having a window through which they look directly, and that they do not have an electrical arrangement whereby a sensitive instrument floating on the surface is connected only by wires to the submerged submarine and a picture produced on a fluorescent screen, and so on. Further, we could demand a more particular account of the arrangement of the parts of this mechanism, and, if we were at all in doubt of its being as described, we could go and examine the mechanism for ourselves, see whether it did contain a mirror, whether the mirror was so placed that it would in fact reflect the things above to a person below, and any other matter we cared. We could also assure ourselves, quite independently of examining the mechanism by which an accurate view of the things is achieved, that it *is* achieved : we could do this, for example, by looking at the view produced by the instrument and comparing what we see there with what we see on coming immediately to the surface.[1]

Now compare Lenin's account of how we see things outside of us with this account of how people in submarines see things on the surface of the water. We have, he says, inside us an *image* ; compare, " they have inside the submarine an *image in a mirror* " : and this image inside us is a *reflection* of things outside us ; compare, " and this image in the mirror inside the submarine is a *reflection* of things outside it " : and, whether in a given case this reflection (in the mind) is an *accurate* representation of the things outside us, *we can find out*; compare, " and, whether in a given case this reflection (in the submarine) is an *accurate* representation of things outside it, *we can find out* : " that is, we see material things outside us *indirectly*, as distinct from directly ; compare, " that is, people see things outside the submarine *indirectly*, as distinct from seeing them directly (e.g., through a glass port-hole) ".

Let us examine the points of comparison.

Lenin says we have inside us an *image* which represents the object. What kind of image does he mean? He does not mean that it is an *image in a mirror* inside us : for who would wish to say there is a mirror in the mind? and certainly no one has ever found one there. Nor does he mean an image as when we say " Conjure up an image of Jones coming through that door over there ", i.e., a *mental image* : for Lenin does not wish to say that having a mental image of Jones is just the same as seeing Jones ; nor yet that whenever I see Jones I must also be having a mental image of him. He is not claiming to have noticed that my seeing Jones is made possible by another familiar process going on in my mind at the same time, viz., my having a mental image of him, as it is claimed that seeing out of submarines is made possible by there being in the submarine a mirror-image of what is outside. For he does not wish either to say there is no

[1] It is of great importance to notice this point that we can, and commonly do, find out whether a reflection or a picture is an accurate reproduction of a thing without knowing at all the working of the process by which it was produced. For example, we need know nothing of the laws governing the behaviour of light to be able to tell whether a reflection of a given thing in a mirror is a good one or not ; and we can find out that my camera takes distorted pictures and yours good ones without knowing what is wrong with mine but not with yours, and in fact without having any notion at all of the physical and chemical processes involved in photography.

difference between having a mental image of Jones and seeing Jones, or to say that when I see Jones I must also be having a mental image of him.[1] In any ordinary use of the word " image " we know how to tell whether a person has an image in his mind or not ; but Lenin uses it without saying how we are to tell whether when we see a material thing we do have an image in our mind or not : he, who insists that everything be found by investigation, gives us no hint of how by investigation we are to find out *this* simple fact. Thus, so far, by contrast with our explanation of seeing out of submarines, we do not even know how to find out whether it is a true description of how we see, and it is of no *use* to us as the other might be—the other gives us directions for making, and repairing (etc.) contrivances for seeing out of closed bodies, but this gives us no idea at all of what we should have to do to see out of closed minds.

Again, we tell whether what we see is a *reflection* or the thing itself by seeing how it alters in appearance as we move or as it moves, by finding whether on touching it we touch a smooth reflecting surface or an object of the sort we take ourselves to be looking at, and so on. The usefulness of the submarine explanation lies partly in our being able to find the reflecting surface, and see that the image is a reflection as distinct from, say, an image on a fluorescent screen produced electrically. But, again, Lenin's words, though similar in appearance, grammatical form, context, way of being said, etc., to the submarine explanation, differ in that they lack this usefulness. It is not their purpose to direct us, if we wish, to a reflecting surface in the mind.

Now, it may be said, you must not take what Lenin says too literally : the point of his remarks is not to tell one the mechanism by which human beings perceive what is outside them, but to bring out *just one particular likeness* between an entity in the mind which enables us to see outside it, and mental images and reflections, viz., the fact that just as mental images and reflections are *representations* (as it were, *pictures*, *likenesses*) of what is imaged

---

[1] It might be thought that Lenin could be defended in this matter on the grounds that his real point is that both when we have a mental image and when we see a thing we have in the mind an entity—let us call it a sense-datum—which is in itself neither a mental image nor a material thing ; and that whether we are at that moment having a mental image or seeing a thing is dependent not on that sense-datum alone, but also on what comes before and after it. But this view is not expressed by Lenin.

or reflected so the sense-perception is a representation, a likeness of the thing seen. We may, for example, just before meeting Smith, whom we have not seen for some time, have an image of him as we expect to see him ; and on his entrance be able to decide whether it was a good or a bad representation. Similarly with an image in a mirror, or with a painted picture of a thing, or with a photograph, we can compare it for likeness with the original. Now Lenin asserts not only that our sense-perceptions[1] of things are likenesses of them, but, also that we can (if we care to) get to know in which cases the likeness is a good one and in which cases bad : i.e., he asserts that we are able to compare the sense-perception with the thing it purports to represent to us. So let us now consider the notion that in perceiving material things what we are face to face with is not a part of thing or of its surface, but an entity which, *though not part of it*, is *comparable with* it. This gives us chiefly the idea of comparing as in comparing a photograph with the original, a reflection in a mirror with the thing reflected, a portrait with the sitter, a mental image of Jones with Jones, etc., and the idea of holding a picture up beside the thing pictured, i.e., holding the sense-perception up beside the thing pictured, i.e., holding the sense-perception up beside the material thing perceived. Here again, as in the earlier cases of *images* and *reflections*, we cannot press the analogy : we do not hold sense-perceptions up beside things in order to compare them ; but Lenin does not think we do, and it will again be said : You are being too crude ; you have taken only the most obvious way of comparing two things ; there are other ways of comparing than by holding the one thing beside the other (for example there is comparing two things by memory, two heights with a footrule, and so on), and it will be some way not so crudely inapplicable that Lenin is meaning. We can soon see if this is so, for by good fortune we have Lenin's answer to this general objection that we can never, on his theory, get to know what the characteristics of a material thing are because we have no way of comparing it with a sense-perception. It is also Engels' answer, for Lenin quotes from him (p. 83) : " . . . this line of reasoning seems hard to beat by mere argumentation. But before there was argumentation there was action. And

---

[1] This is the word used in the translation of his book.

human action had solved the difficulty before human ingenuity
had invented it. The proof of the pudding is in the eating.
From the moment we turn these objects to our own use, according
to the qualities we perceive in them, *we put to an infallible test
the correctness or otherwise of our sense-perceptions.* If these perceptions have been wrong, then our estimate of the use to which
an object can be turned must also be wrong, and our attempt must
fail. But if we succeed in accomplishing our aim, *if we find that
the object does agree with our idea of it. and* does answer the purpose
we intended it for, then that is positive *proof* that our perceptions
of it and its qualities, so far, *agree with reality outside ourselves."*
Lenin now remarks " The materialist theory then, the *reflection of
objects by our mind,* is here presented with perfect clearness : things
exist outside of us. Our perceptions and representations are
their images. The verification of these images, *the distinction of
true and false images, is given by practice."*[1] He then continues the
quotation from Engels : " . . . whenever we find ourselves face
to face with a failure, then . . . generally . . . we find that the
perception upon which we acted was either incomplete and
superficial, or combined with the results of other perceptions
in a way not warranted by them. . . . So long as we take care to
train and to use our senses properly, and to keep our action within
the limits prescribed by perceptions properly made and properly
used, so long shall we *find that the result of our action* PROVES *the
conformity of our perceptions with the objective nature of the things
perceived.* Not in one single instance, so far, have we been led to
*the conclusion that our sense-perceptions, scientifically controlled, induce
in our minds ideas respecting the outer world that are, by their very nature,
at variance with reality,* or that there is an inherent incompatibility
between the outer world and our sense-perceptions of it." Now
we see what Lenin's method of comparing is : it is, he says, by
getting nearer a thing of whose nature we are uncertain, by
touching it, and trying to use it in various ways that we compare
our original sense-perception with the thing. But will this do?
There is in it something which most of us who disagree with

---

[1] Engels notices no difference between : (1) " the *correctness* of our sense-
perceptions ", on the one hand, and (2) " the *agreement* of the object with our
idea of it ", " the *agreement* of reality outside us with our perceptions of it " on the
other. Lenin in turn marks no difference between (2) and (3) " the *reflection* of
objects by our mind ", " our perceptions are their *images* ".

Lenin would not think of denying, viz., that the way to find out whether one has seen a thing right, if one is in doubt, is to get nearer and try to touch it, pick it up, use it, etc. E.g., there may be a dish of fruit before me : my hosts are known practical jokers : are those real apples or not? I cannot tell by looking only, or even by picking one up, but must try biting one. (I can only find out their nature through practice.) Or again, is that a pen on my desk or just a shadow ; I tell by what I feel on putting out my hand.

i.e., by further activity I tell whether I was right or wrong in taking there to be a pen there, or the apples to be real ones. But this is a very different thing from saying—as Lenin and Engels do —that by this I tell whether my original perception was an accurate or inaccurate " reflection " of the thing, a " true or a false image ". Instead of saying only that by further activity we prove our original perception correct or incorrect, they try to give an explanation of what a perception's being correct or incorrect consists in, viz., in its being an accurate " reflection ", or a " true image " of the thing ; and this theory, they say, though difficult to prove by " mere argumentation ", is in fact *believed* by everyone and constantly *used* by them. Compare it now with the explanation that people see out of submarines by a reflecting mirror : this may be *used* to build a similar instrumen , to enable us to repair our submarine if we cease to be able to see out of it, to know where to damage a submarine to prevent the people seeing out of it, and so on ; but no one can repair any-thing, or build anything, or prevent anything with the help of the assertion that, when practice shows that we are seeing rightly, we do the seeing by having in the mind a reflection of the thing seen.

Again in the submarine case there is both what we shall call a *direct* and an *indirect* method of comparing the reflection with the thing reflected. We can compare it by looking from the one to the other, or, indirectly, by cruising about on the assump-tion that the two would be alike *if* we compared them directly : if this cruise is successful in that we reach our destination having circumvented the things seen by means of the periscope, let us say that they and the image in the mirror have been shown to be *indirectly comparable*. Now Lenin's account of perception allows only of *indirect comparsion* of the reflection and the thing : there is no mention of any direct comparison of them. So what is the use of saying : " Success in practice shows us that in this case our perception was a reflection of the thing " when there is no independent way of finding whether there is a reflection or not? It is as if someone were to say : " So their success in the manœuvres shows that they had a periscope," but were using " had a periscope " in such a way that it was to be true that they had a periscope if they succeeded in the manœuvres, and that they had none if they didn't, and no further investigation was to be relevant to whether they had or not ; i.e., if they were using it in such a way that it would still be true that " they had a periscope " even if on looking we could see that they had none. Lenin's use of the phrase, " he has a reflection in his mind ", is such that, no matter what one suggests (other than the " indirect " test of success in practice), it is not to be accepted as a direct test for whether he has one (cf., there is an image in a mirror in the periscope), or as a direct test for the likeness of the image to the thing (cf., I observe, by looking from one to the other, that the image in the mirror is a good likeness of the things mirrored).

What ordinary people—housewives, workmen, scientists, and even philosophers—need for " success in practice " is to be able to distinguish when there is a material thing in their way from when there isn't, to distinguish a thing of one colour from a thing of another, a hallucination from really seeing a thing, and so on ; but to be told that, when they see something, what is happening is that they have in their minds a reflection of the thing, will help them in no way—it will neither guide them in making this or destroying that, or in finding this or avoiding that, or in any other practical activity. What Lenin requires of philosophy is that it should deny neither established facts of science nor plain facts of common sense ; but there are more ways of avoiding denial of these than he was aware of, and certainly it is not necessary in order to avoid it to utter, as a theory believed by all and necessary to the success of their activities, what is little more than a figure of speech. And in doing so he can hardly claim the merit of not going beyond " the naive realism of any healthy person, who is not an inmate of an insane asylum, or in the school of the idealist philosophers " (p. 47).

# THINGS AND PROCESSES

### By Margaret Macdonald

" The great, basic thought," according to Engels, which dialectical materialism inherited from Hegel, was " that the world is not to be comprehended as a complex of ready-made *things*, but as a complex of *processes*, in which things apparently stable no less than their mind-images in our heads, the concepts, go through an uninterrupted change of coming into being and passing away."[1]

I do not propose either to dispute or deny this statement but only to ask what it means. In the first place, Engels says " the world is not to be *comprehended* as a complex of ready-made things ". This, presumably, means, that it is not to be *understood*, or cannot be *known* as composed of or containing a number of *things*. From this it would seem to follow that it does not contain any such things, or, that there are no things in the world. Unless he means to say that although there are or may be *things* we can never conceivably know them but can only know *something else*, viz. *processes*. But what can it mean to say " There are no things but only processes "? What sort of statement is this?

Engels does not say what he means by ' things ' but I assume from his writings that he means at least physical objects, e.g., tables, machines, aeroplanes, cattle, etc., human beings and perhaps societies. Constituents, i.e. of the physical world. For part of his aim is to vindicate the existence of the external world against idealist philosophers. Then it does seem very peculiar to say there are no houses, trees or people but only processes. For it seems to follow from this that all the propositions which we constantly make in ordinary life such as, " The train leaves Paddington at 10.10 ". " These potatoes are cheaper than those ", " There are more than 5,000 people living in Oxford " are always false. For if there are no trains, stations, potatoes or people then propositions about them, other than those which assert or imply their non-existence, must be false. They must be false just as propositions about centaurs, sea serpents and greek gods are false.

[1] *Ludwig Feuerbach*, Martin Lawrence, London, p. 54. Italics in translation.

LIBRARY
SAINT MARY'S COLLEGE
NOTRE DAME INDIANA

But this, it will be said, is a gross misrepresentation of Engels. Was he not a materialist and has it not already been said that his aim was to vindicate the existence of the external world against idealists? He insisted that the world which we perceive through our senses does exist. What he wanted to say was that although common sense rightly believes that an external world *exists* it believes wrongly that what it perceives to exist are things when they are " really " processes. This is confirmed by another passage.

" The analysis of nature into its individual parts, the grouping of natural processes and natural objects in different classes . . . these were the fundamental conditions of the gigantic strides in our knowledge of nature during the last four hundred years. But this method of investigation has left us . . . the habit of observing natural objects and natural processes in their isolation, detached from the whole vast, inter-connections of things ; and therefore not in their motion but in their repose ; not as essentially changing, but as fixed constants ; not in their life but in their death. And when, as was the case with Bacon and Locke, this way of looking at things was transferred from natural science to philosophy, it produced the specific narrow-mindedness of the last centuries, *the metaphysical mode of thought. . . . At first sight this mode of thought seems to us very plausible because it is the mode of thought of so-called sound common sense* ".[1]

I think, from this passage, Engels might be justifiably interpreted to mean that the common sense belief that there are things is, as it were, a piece of primitive scientific classification which is adopted and extended in the early stages of more sophisticated scientific observation, petrified into metaphysical systems by philosophers, but to be superseded as knowledge advances, especially with the help of Hegelian methodology. At a certain stage in this progressive advance we realize that what we had formerly thought were *things* are " really " complexes of *processes*, that the universe is, in fact, a vast complex process which progresses towards a certain end.

I do not intend to discuss the question of this progress of the universal process or set of processes and its end, but to concentrate simply on the point of the process itself. What Engels

[1] *Anti-Dühring*, Lawrence and Wishart, pp. 27 and 28. My italics.

seems to be saying is that " This is a tree " is (*a*) a common sense statement (*b*) an antiquated, though historically justified scientific hypothesis—a piece of Stone Age science (*c*) a metaphysical proposition. Let us first try to sort this out.

An example of an antiquated, though historically justified, scientific hypothesis would be " Phlogiston is exuded by burning substances ". This was proved by experiment to be false and chemists ceased to use the word ' Phlogiston ' except in statements about the history of chemistry. Does Engels wish to assert that " There are trees " is false in the sense in which " Phlogiston is exuded in combustion " is false? If so, then we should cease to mislead each otherby using the word ' tree ', for however historically justified a hypothesis may be, it is unintelligent to maintain it after it has been proved false.

As the result of Lavoisier's experiments chemists substituted propositions about oxygen for propositions about phlogiston. They discovered that they had been mistaken in supposing that a substance was given out in combustion ; what was " really " happening was the absorption of something, viz. oxygen. But if I point out the Coronation Scot[1] to someone and say " There's a train ", in precisely *what* respects do I mislead him, what is even " partially " false about this proposition and how can the information which I wish to communicate be " more correctly " expressed? Unless Engels, or his followers, can answer these questions it seems impossible to make sense of the contention that ordinary propositions about " things " are antiquated scientific hypotheses. We understand the procedure by which one scientific hypothesis is proved by experiment to be false and another substituted for it which is confirmed by all the known facts. But we do not understand how all propositions about " things " which we ordinarily use have similarly been proved false or by what propositions they are to be superseded. So far as one can see Engels and his followers continue to use language in ordinary life as everyone else does although they must believe themselves to be making assertions which are either false or nonsensical. This is as though modern chemists continued to use the language of the alchemists. All I wish to point out here is that Engels' assertion depends on his attempt to use a certain analogy, viz.

[1] A British railway train so named in the honour of King George VI in 1937.

that between ordinary propositions and scientific hypotheses. This can be accepted only if the criteria for the use of scientific hypotheses is applicable also to ordinary propositions. Unless this is so, the analogy remains inapplicable and senseless. But no attempt is made by Engels to show how and by what experiments propositions about processes are to be substituted for propositions about things so that what he is trying to assert remains completely obscure.

Engels makes one mistake in this connection, I think, which is also made by many other philosophers. He confuses what common sense *knows* with what it *believes*. It is often said, e.g. " Of course common sense (i.e. the sense of ordinary people who are neither scientists nor philosophers) believes that the sun goes round the earth but astronomers have proved that this is false ". Then it seems plausible to go further and say " Of course common sense believes that the Coronation Scot is a train but physicists and dialectical philosophers know that there are " really " only complicated series of processes which are most crudely and inadequately described as ' a train ' ." So that all that we say must be corrected by scientists and philosophers. This seems to be a complete mistake. What everyone who is not blind every day *knows* is that the sun is visible at different places in the sky throughout the day. An observer remaining at the same spot throughout the day could perceive these differences and would, quite rightly, say that the sun had changed its position while he had not. This is one of the facts to be accounted for on any astronomical theory and it can be accounted for in different ways. That the sun goes *round* the earth is not of course perceived by anyone but may be an erroneous deduction from what is perceived. But it does not follow that when the labourer points to the east in the morning and says " There's the sun " and above his head at noon and says " Now it is here ", he is saying something false which astronomers must correct. He is asserting the sort of fact without which there could be no astronomy. Similarly we *know* and do not merely *believe* that there are such things as trains, trees and people for we know that some propositions of the form " This is a tree ", " This is a train ", " This is a person " are true and that the use of these words differs from the use of words for what we should ordinarily call ' processes '. This is a linguistic and not an

empirical distinction. It is therefore not disputable by scientists. It is not disputable for the simple reason that the terms in which any attempt to dispute it was made would themselves need to be understood by translation into ordinary language and would thus involve the truth of the propositions in dispute. In order to understand such a proposition as " This is not a physical object or a physical thing but a process " it would be necessary to understand both what is meant by ' physical thing ' and by ' process ' which would involve that at least one proposition of the form " This is a tree ", " That is a train " was true and would thus contradict the required assertion that there are no physical things.

Another example may help to bring out this point. Compare e.g. the proposition, " Whales are really mammals, they are not fish " with " Whales are really processes, they are not things ". There are empirical tests which determine whether a creature is a mammal or a fish. These have been applied to the whale with the result asserted in the first proposition. They verify the proposition and so give it significance. We know in what circumstances a whale is correctly called mammalian and also what other circumstances would justify a creature's being called not a mammal but a fish. That is to say, it is significant both to assert of something that it is a mammal and to deny this in favour of some other predication. This is an essential characteristic of significant, informative assertion. For we mean by such an assertion that circumstances can be described both in which it would be true and in which it would be false. This merely expresses the accepted fact that all empirical propositions, i.e. all propositions which give information about the sensible world can be significantly denied. Their contradictories are never self-contradictory and might have been true. Verbal expressions which do not fulfil this condition may have other important functions but they do not give empirical information. They are of a different type. Consider then the proposition " Whales are really processes, they are not things ". Is this also an empirical proposition? Engels would presumably say, yes. It is a particularly " advanced " scientific proposition. What then are the tests for its significance? How do we examine the whale to discover whether it is a thing or a process as we examine it to discover whether it is a mammal or a fish? Obviously, no answer of this type can be given. For "A whale is a thing " and "A whale is a process " are not propositions of the same form as "A whale is a mammal " or "A whale is a fish " although they look similar. This is shown by the fact mentioned earlier in this paper that dialectical materialists do not wish to deny that there are trees, animals, human beings, etc. To say that the whale is a process and not a thing is not meant to be equivalent to asserting that there are no whales. It is not therefore intended to deny that the existence of whales is known by sense perception, that whales can be seen, touched, etc., and that it is always *sensible* (though it may not always be true) to say on two different occasions " There is that whale again ". And what is true of whales and ' whale ' is true of all physical objects and the use of all physical object words. All physical objects are perceivable by sense perception, are public to many observers, and exist throughout a certain time during which they remain recognizable and such that the same name is applicable to them in the same sense throughout that period. Such criteria as these are part at least of what we ordinarily mean by such words as ' whale ', ' tree ', ' person ', etc. They are what we mean by saying that whales, trees, etc. are physical objects and not hallucinations, subjective images, or personal feelings. To deny them would not be equivalent to denying that these objects have the characteristics expressed by the criteria ; it would be equivalent to denying that their names have any meaning. This is utterly different from denying that whales are mammals. The result is not false but senseless. For if words like ' whale ' have no meaning we certainly do not know what it means to say that whales are processes.

" There are no things but only processes " and "A whale is not a thing but a process " are not significant, empirical statements nor do they represent any empirical scientific discovery about such objects as whales. What then is the point of such remarks? What did Engels think he was asserting and denying?

We may get some hint from alternative (*c*) on page 289. Engels asserts, or implies, that " There are trees " is a *metaphysical* proposition which we make as the result of the influence of the philosophies of Bacon and Locke. Certainly we don't preface the teaching of the names of common objects to children by a course in English empirical philosophy. Nevertheless, it is alleged that in some sense, we have been misled by this philosophy into using these names wrongly and into erroneous beliefs about what they name. We regard them as " fixed constants " and not as series of changes. The short answer to this, I think, is that when we ordinarily assert " There is a tree " we do not assert " There is a fixed constant " or " There is only a series of changes " ; we assert " There is a tree ". But it is certainly true that philosophers have tried to show that certain other propositions are implied by such ordinary propositions as " This is a tree ". Such assertions may be related to the common sense statement but must not be confused with it. Some philosophers, e.g., including Locke, have maintained that " This is a tree " is a proposition similar in form to " This tree is tall " and just as the second ascribes tallness to a tree so the first ascribes ' treeness ' to something else viz. a substratum which underlies and is the subject of all empirical propositions but is itself unknowable since by definition it is that to which all properties are ascribed and its description would therefore involve the assumption of a further subject or substratum and so *ad inf.* Moreover, since changes are very commonly expressed by the ascription of different qualities at different times and the subject or substratum cannot itself be described by describing its properties then it follows that it cannot be said to change, and is, therefore, permanent. Therefore, since no physical objects are permanent, i.e. all such objects come into existence at a certain time and after a period are destroyed i.e. become some other physical object or set of objects, the ultimate substratum, sometimes called ' matter ' becomes the ultimate subject too of all propositions about the physical world. But this, it will be said triumphantly, is just what Engels denies. There is no such ultimate " stuff " ; the only " stuff " just is the series of changes which objects undergo. Yet here again it is necessary to ask what sort of denial this is and what is being denied. Substratum philosophers do not deny that physical objects change. It is partly because they know this is true and also because they assume that all propositions must " really " ascribe predicates to subjects that they discover a logical difficulty in the fact that we use the same name for an object when it has changed most of its characteristics and sometimes when it has changed them all. Most of us have very little resemblance to ourselves in the cradle, yet we are the same persons. Nor can dialectical materialists deny this without talking nonsense. They must also say that " in some sense " compatible with continuous process we are the same persons and that all physical things remain recognizable for certain periods of time. The quarrel between them and the substratum philosophers, therefore, cannot be resolved by any appeal to empirical facts, all of which both admit. Substratum philosophers assert that there *must* be a permanent subject of all propositions about physical objects. They do not assert that they have empirically observed one. Flux philosophers assert that there *cannot* be such a subject; they do not assert that no physical objects are ever recognizable on two occasions, for this would be absurd. What seems clear, therefore, is that the quarrel is not resolvable by more empirical observation, i.e. by more facts. The question is not factual since we have no means of identifying, i.e. it would be logically impossible, to identify or verify the existence of a permanent material substance as the " basis " of physical properties. Hence the dialectical denial of this and the counter assertion that all that exist are " processes " are themselves equally non-significant. " There are no things but only processes " is as metaphysical a statement as any made by Descartes or Locke. There is no possible means of determining empirically that a cake is not a thing but a process.

It is the fashion now to maintain that philosophical propositions like " There is a permanent material substance " and " There are only processes " for which no empirical verification can be suggested are, in some sense, linguistic propositions. This seems to me acceptable but I am not particularly concerned to maintain it here. What seems to me more important to emphasize is the fundamental difference in logical type between such propositions and those ordinary empirical propositions which can be verified, significantly denied, and used to give us information about the external world. The distinction may at some points become vague. Dialectical materialists seem fond of asserting that because distinctions are vague therefore there are no distinctions. One might as well say that because in a patch continuously varying in shade from red to purple it is impossible to state at which point red ends and purple begins, therefore, there is no distinction between red and purple. Similarly, the distinctions in logical type between propositions do exist and it is important to recognize them. Engels, so far as I can see, has no conception of such distinctions although some of them had already been noted by Locke, Hume and Kant. All statements for Engels seem to be on the same level and equally statements of fact. But "A whale is not a fish but a mammal " is a statement of fact while "A whale is not a thing but a process " is not or, at least, not in the same sense and they ought to be distinguished. Such distinctions are even of practical importance, for unless we do become clear about how different sentences in our language function we shall continue liable to be bemused by pseudo-significant statements used as political slogans.

We must then ask Engels, or his followers, " When you assert ' There are no things but only processes ', what does this remark *mean* and to what precisely are you opposing the word ' process '? " Do you wish to say, e.g., " There are no hearts but only processes of circulating blood through the body? " That seems to be merely false. There are both hearts and processes of circulation. Or do you mean " There are no permanent, unobservable material substrata but only the flux of physical changes." This is unintelligible for either we do not know what metaphysical entity is being denied to exist or the use of the word ' flux ' here entails that we can never sensibly use the same common name for the same object on two different occasions which contradicts the ordinary use of language and cannot, therefore, be understood. Or do you wish to say " We propose a new linguistic convention, viz. instead of ordinary words for physical objects we propose to use a new combination of words involving the word ' process ' or some synonym ". This may be a useful convention but its use will not consist in giving us some surprising new information about physical objects but in giving us a new way of expressing facts about them. Our language will have to be translated in terms of this new use of ' process '. For it must be realized that we already have a perfectly good use or series of uses for the word ' process '. We speak, e.g. of the " processes of dyeing and bleaching " but not of the " process " of being a dress or being a person. It may be convenient, for some reasons, to extend this usage to cover dresses and persons, etc. but when the metaphysical aura of such an expression as " There are no things but only processes " has faded, the change will, I think, seem much less important. When it is realized that by calling a whale a ' process ' we don't dissolve it into a mysterious flux but merely either misuse the word ' process ' and talk nonsense or use it as the result of extensive and rather boring re-definition involving the whole of ordinary language, it may appear that we can say all that we wish to say by ordinary language and the technical extensions of it in the sciences, already at our disposal.